The Future of Doctoral Studies in English

Edited by

Andrea Lunsford, Helene Moglen,

and James F. Slevin

Modern Language Association of America
New York   1989

Library of Congress Cataloging-in-Publication Data

The Future of doctoral studies in English / edited by Andrea Lunsford,
   Helene Moglen, and James F. Slevin.
         p.   cm.
    Proceedings of a conference held in Apr. 1987 in Wayzata, Minn.,
   sponsored by the Commission on Writing and Literature of the Modern
   Language Association of America.
    ISBN 0-87352-184-6   ISBN 0-87352-185-4 (pbk.)
    1. English philology–Study and teaching (Higher)–United States–
   Congresses. 2. Degrees, Academic–United States–Congresses.
   I. Lunsford, Andrea A., 1942-   . II. Moglen, Helene. 1936-   .
   III. Slevin, James F., 1945-   . IV. Modern Language Association of
   America. Commission on Writing and Literature.
   PE68.U5F88 1989
   820.71′173–dc20   89-36166

Published by The Modern Language Association of America
10 Astor Place, New York, New York 10003-6981

Contents

Part 3: Exploring the Future: Proposals for Change

Introduction

For the past ten years, the executive director and Executive Council of the Modern Language Association have encouraged and facilitated an extensive process of self-examination within the profession of English studies. That process was begun early in the decade by the Commission on the Future of the Profession, which conducted its explorations in an environment of anxiety and concern: resources were shrinking, jobs were scarce, literature faculties felt themselves beleaguered and under siege. The self-study was continued by the Commission on Writing and Literature, which was established both to implement some of the recommendations made by its parent group and to conduct its own investigations into the troubled relations between literature and writing programs.

This commission completed its work at the decade's end in what its members described as "a spirit of cautious optimism." In a relatively few years, the environment of English studies had changed dramatically: dire demographic projections had proved excessive, college enrollments were increasing, graduate programs expanding, new jobs proliferating. Further, the commission hoped that improvements in material conditions would be beneficial to the intellectual climate as well. Heterogeneous theoretical positions and methodological practices that had seriously factionalized the profession might now be generously reassessed in ways that identified intersecting interests and common purposes. Indeed, commission members believed that several such reassessments were already taking place: most significantly, teachers of writing and teachers of literature had begun to recognize that the same institutional structures and pedagogical practices that had traditionally separated them had also disguised a similarity of theoretical assumptions that could potentially form the basis of a vital new alliance.

This pivotal change in perspective revealed itself at a conference on the present state and future shape of doctoral studies in English. Sponsored by the commission, with funding from the University of Minnesota and the Ford Foundation, the conference was held at the Spring Hill Center in Wayzata, Minnesota, in April 1987. Invited representatives from eighty PhD-granting departments assembled to consider what it is that can now be said to constitute our discipline: the connections among the subjects we teach and the foci of our scholarly efforts; the nature of the profession for which we train and into which we socialize our graduate students, a profession that they, in turn, will define through their own theoretical interests, institutional assumptions, and pedagogical practices.

While no unanimity on any significant issue emerged during the conference, there was a degree of agreement, surprising to many, on two related organizational principles, assumed in the past to be fundamental to our discipline. The dominant view, reiterated throughout this collection of essays, rejected historical coverage along with canonical unity as the invariable reference points that could guide our conceptualization of curricula. As a consequence, there was little certainty about what our graduate students should know both as developing scholars and as apprentice teachers.

What did become clear is that our subject has been destabilized and that our methodologies are being radically questioned. Foreground and background have disappeared. Towering figures who once marked the focal points of an inherited tradition have been swallowed up by the crowds that surround them, barely noticed before. The coronation parade has been lost in the shifting but disciplined realignments of marching bands at half-time ceremonies. Feminists, Marxists, new historians, colonial-discourse analysts, and many other schools or orientations in current literary theory call the tune.

The text is no longer bound and self-contained, a discrete object of painstaking and definitive analysis. It is transformed, rather, by the discourse in which it is situated – cultural, historical, deconstructive, psychoanalytic, phenomenological – its meanings determined by the context that defines its reading and writing. Neither we nor our students can claim expertise on major authors, literary periods, genres, or traditions when all these categories are the sites of heated contestations. To many it seemed that we could only familiarize ourselves with the variety of theoretical approaches, making these theoretical constructs themselves the center of our disciplinary education.

For these reasons an alternative way of conceptualizing what we do seemed an urgent matter to many attending the conference. Participants appeared to be searching for a conception of the discipline that would enable us, first, to investigate a wider range of texts, including not only the "canonical" (however broadly or narrowly conceived) but also, as individual scholars and teachers choose, marginal discursive forms and forms of signifying that are not even discursive. Second, they were seeking a conception that would enable us to raise a wider range of questions about texts: questions that examine meaning and the ways meaning is made possible, that probe the processes of textual production and the nature and consequences of textual reception, that address the ideologies of both writers and critics, and that consider the institutional structures within which, and occasionally in the interests of which, discourse is constructed and construed.

This is not to say that participants at the conference were looking for a single unifying principle for so heterogeneous a field as English studies; the impossibility of such an attempt was certainly recognized. And yet, there was a serious concern to inquire about the intellectual bases for our questions and conversations and about ways to make the PhD program coherent to our students. Perhaps this search represents a quest for nothing more than a useful fiction, but the fiction *is* useful insofar as it permits us to entertain questions about which aims we share and which we don't.

A complex array of perspectives was offered in response to these concerns. Not surprisingly, given the conference's origin in the work of the Commission on Writing and Literature, many of the invited speakers explored conceptions of the discipline that focused on connections between the two "worlds" of literary studies and rhetoric-composition studies. Because composition instruction constitutes so much of the profession's work (MLA statistics show that 60–70% of all college English courses are identified as writing courses) and because rhetoric and composition research is increasingly an important part of the profession's scholarly production, such connections seem well worth exploring and emphasizing. We could not ignore the historical discontinuity between these two fields or fail to appreciate the desire of those in a marginalized area of the profession –"comp"– to locate their projects within the larger, legitimating structure of more privileged groups. While the papers collected here might seem, from the perspective of some graduate programs, to exaggerate the special claims of rhetoric and composition for inclusion in a redefinition of the discipline, it would be derelict to ignore these legitimate demands for consideration, and most participants welcomed the inclusion.

This welcoming was all the more powerful because the immediate institutional circumstances of our current debates about literature and composition have a special urgency. In the last two decades, our departments have come increasingly to rely on faculty members who are poorly paid, ill-treated, marginal, and temporary; more than one-fourth the English faculties in four-year colleges, and as many as half the English faculties in two-year colleges, teach only part-time. Nearly all of them teach composition, an institutional circumstance that among its other consequences compromises the quality of composition instruction and ultimately the status of composition research. Our desire to reconceptualize who we are and what we do derives in part from a more basic desire to challenge these institutional practices and to make possible a mutual respect for all areas of our instruction and scholarship.

The question is not, What will, finally, or even provisionally, give "unity" to English studies? The question is rather, Where can we look for guidance in constructing a way of relating our diverse projects and bringing coherence to our programs? At the doctoral conference, a point of departure for discussions that might reconstitute the discipline was Jonathan Culler's notion of "an expanded rhetoric: a study of discursive structures and strategies, in their relation to systems of signification and human subjects." The general response to such a proposal – evident from comments at the conference and in many of the papers included in this volume – suggests that Culler is not alone in wishing to explore this possibility.

The advantages and contributions of rhetoric are many, and despite potential difficulties that might attach themselves to this or any other conception, it was felt that we should explore seriously the valuable connections it can make possible. Rhetoric, as Culler defines it, provides a model for investigations of discourse broadly conceived – beyond the narrower concerns with canonical texts and forms that seem unnecessarily limiting to contemporary scholarship and criticism. A more significant contribution, perhaps, derives from the simple fact that rhetoric holds a central, fully articulated position in the intellectual history of our culture's production and scrutiny of texts. As such, the very conception of rhetoric is subject to historical scrutiny, allowing us to examine our construction of its principles and aims against versions from different periods. Thus rhetoric, broadly defined, provides a way of posing and organizing our questions about writing and reading so that they take account of many different cultural contexts, including–ultimately–our own.

The special effort to integrate rhetoric and composition within a reconceptualized English studies, and more specifically within the curriculum and aims of English PhD programs, is often reflected in the essays that follow. Those by Richard Lloyd-Jones, Janice M. Lauer and Andrea Lunsford, and Richard Lanham directly address this issue; those by Helene Moglen, Gary Waller, Robert Scholes, Wayne Booth, and Don Bialostosky, while exploring such matters less directly, still imply or suggest sound theoretical bases for reconceiving English studies around a union of writing and literature, each transformed in valuable ways by the variety of possible connections.

It will be clear that rhetoric, however frequently mentioned, is not the only way that conference participants could envision new principles of disciplinary coherence. Indeed, even some of the papers focusing on rhetoric go on to invite alternative proposals and often explore some of these alternatives. For example, "theory"–modified variously by terms like literary, critical, cultural, textual–is repeatedly mentioned as providing a common language for our general conversation, a basis for our working together that depends on a shared willingness to assert and question our assumptions. But the very diversity of these alternatives raises a larger question about the whole enterprise of finding–or imposing–connections on a profession so varied in its scholarly interests and aims. In these essays the desire for coherence emerges as valuable but also highly problematic.

Proposing rhetoric, or theory, as a means of integrating our diverse projects and programs represents only part of the dialogue that one can trace in the following essays and that occurred throughout the Spring Hill conference. That is, "unity" and "integration" represent only one aspect of a dialectic. While recognizing the value of constantly examining current and alternative principles for shaping graduate programs, some essays suggest that the strength of English studies derives from its diversity and so endorse the principle of pluralism both within and among PhD-granting departments and within the profession as a whole. The emphasis here is on difference, variety, and a willingness to tolerate–or encourage–a certain amount of *in*coherence. In such a view, relating the various parts of our discipline, and achieving coherence within individual programs, is of less importance than how precisely we can conceptualize, how carefully we can discuss, and how generously we can come to understand and value our differences and variety. The effort to construct any inclusive "framework" contributes most as the occasion of its own radical questioning. Indeed, it is this questioning that renders the more lasting service, especially to the extent that it enables greater respect for our diverse undertakings.

A commitment to pluralism, however, though it encourages a healthy mutual respect, risks the danger of perpetuating our mutual isolation. While understanding and tolerance are always desirable, and perhaps as crucial now in English departments as they have ever been, they are not necessarily educational ends in themselves. When mistaken for ends, they have had consequences that undermine our work as teachers and scholars. Gerald Graff's history of the profession (*Professing Literature*) insists that "what academic literary studies have had to work with is not a coherent cultural tradition, but a series of conflicts that have remained unresolved, unacknowledged, and assumed to be outside the proper sphere of literary education" (15). For Graff, our professional history is a story of concealment, of masking, of rendering invisible those conflicts that, however occasionally debilitating, are ultimately the source of our greatest intellectual energy. The simple endorsement of diversity, instead of encouraging us to engage one another, has frequently functioned rather to disengage us from one another, to set us apart in isolated corners of our departments or our profession, thereby discouraging fruitful debate. So we must ask, to what extent does pluralism function as a rationalization for not confronting our differences? Whatever advantages it might retain for us, or however inevitable it might seem, does the coverage model, which pluralism often simply rationalizes, ultimately undermine our need for dialogue and frustrate our desire to establish curricular structures that both express and serve our intellectual interests as scholars and teachers?

In this regard, the conference itself and the essays gathered here seem a model for the ways in which our differences can be both acknowledged and productively debated. The essays approach the value and problem of difference in complementary ways: cultural analyses that contextualize these differences and look to history for possible explanations; ideological critiques that account for differences by connecting them to questions that arise outside the discipline; and practical considerations of the diverse, often conflicting, accounts of what English departments, at all levels, ought to be about. In addressing these issues, the essays seem less concerned with offering a single, comprehensive framework than with articulating more localized and specific connections, of the sort that Paul Armstrong recommends when he notes, "Our enterprise is not a neatly organized structure held together by a center we have lost and need to recover. Rather, it is better conceived of as a disparate set of concurrent, sometimes overlapping conversations."

Where our "conversations," not to be confused with "agreements," most often "overlap"—what marks them as our conversations and not those of other disciplines—is in our recurrent interest in the complex activities of reading and writing and their possible connections. Indeed, many of the essays, like much of the discussion in some of the conference's small group working sessions, do not so much argue for adopting rhetoric as our organizing principle or for endorsing pluralism as they urge that reading and writing be integrated at all levels of theory and practice. But like the other points of convergence we have examined, this one marks a site of deep instability and struggle in our profession.

At first blush, the reintegration of reading and writing seems a consummation devoutly to be wished, on any number of grounds: historical, theoretical, pedagogical, and even technological. We can, after all, trace the path of separation between reading and writing etched in the story of nineteenth-century public education, a story that led inexorably to the professional splintering we now embody: MLA, NCTE, CCCC, SCA, LSA, IRA. Given the ways in which reading and writing have been not only separated but sub- and sub-sub-divided among a number of disciplines, Cicero's lament that it was surely idiotic to send students to one place to learn to think (the philosopher's school) and to yet another to learn to speak or write (the rhetorician's school) sounds almost quaint. Reversing this historical trend toward fragmentation seems plausible and highly desirable.

Various theoretical perspectives also urge reintegration. In particular, artificial-intelligence researchers and cognitive psychologists have begun to build models of reading and writing, models that demand interaction of the two arts. Similarly, theorists of composition and literature are moving toward new alliances, recognizing that the production and reception-interpretation of discourse are always intimately related. The case for reintegration looks even stronger when viewed through the lens of pedagogy. Here the split between reading and writing is inscribed most unprofitably in our students, who tend to view reading as a passive act of simple reception and writing as mere encoding of some externally verifiable, neutral data. Bringing the acts of generation and interpretation together in the classroom could jog loose such simplistic preconceptions by focusing on reading and writing as our major means of constructing and sharing knowledge, of knowing and being known. Even in technological terms, integration of reading and writing seems desirable, even necessary. Working with electronic texts, not to mention with complex hardware and software systems, demands not only a fluency but a certain fluidity among the processes of reading and writing.

While serving as good or warrantable reasons for reintegrating reading and writing, however, such historical, theoretical, pedagogical, and technological pressures also complicate writing and reading in some fairly dramatic ways, leading us to ask, for instance, what we really mean by such terms and, more pointedly, what practices or habits would be threatened by reintegration. What, in short, would be at stake in unifying reading and writing at all levels of theory and practice?

As it turns out, quite a lot. Most obviously, of course, a definition of terms. Our glib use of "reading" and "writing" notwithstanding, the terms are perhaps more at issue than ever before. The construct of writing as a neutral system of signs, produced by individual unique imaginations, is under severe attack from many directions. Reading is a similarly elusive term, applied to referents as different and contradictory as behavioristic-based decoding on the one hand and a hermeneutic-based act of self-inscription on the other. A nostalgic longing to integrate reading and writing thus masks a series of radical disagreements over what it means to read or to write.

Let us suppose, however, for the sake of argument, that such disagreements could be resolved or that the disagreements could themselves constitute the substance of reading and writing in English studies, as Graff proposes. What then would be at stake in integrating these communicative arts? Practically everything. For, as suggested previously, a true integration of writing and reading would challenge curricular and institutional hierarchies at every turn and would demand a basic renegotiation of disciplinary turf. Uniting reading and writing suggests, in the first place, that the curricular sequence from basic composition to upper-division and graduate-level pure literature courses would no longer hold. That is to say, it would no longer be possible to reduce writing (composition) to a grab bag of sterile skills and drills designed to measure syntactic maneuverability or punctuation practice. Nor could reading be treated either as a series of vocabulary recognition exercises (as it is in many "reading" labs and in many public schools) or as a process of communing with and assimilating a list of master works, as E. D. Hirsch, Jr., suggests. But the curricular hierarchies based on a separation of writing and reading are linked inevitably to institutional hierarchies that full integration, even if it only came at the graduate level, would also seriously call into question. We refer, of course, to the situation discussed above, in which part-time or other marginal employees deliver the labor-intensive instruction in writing so that the relatively few prestigious places can be reserved for those who teach the reading of literary texts. Integrating reading and writing would thus raise a series of tough economic questions, ones our universities have not been quick to recognize or take up.

Finally, the history of English studies out of which the separation of reading and writing grows comprises a series of turf battles whose outcome would be questioned or threatened by integration. From the time of Harvard's Francis Child, English faculty members have fought hard to make the reading of literature in English a legitimate "field" in the academy. The struggle was bitter but, as we know, eventually successful. The last twenty years have witnessed a similar intense struggle to make writing a legitimate field of academic study, a struggle that has produced, among other things, a growing number of specialized journals, a number of graduate programs emphasizing composition and rhetoric, and even, at several schools, new departments of writing and composition. Such hard-won ground will not and cannot easily be renegotiated on either side.

And yet such a renegotiation is taking place, in the form of the profession-wide conversation of which this volume is a part, and this renegotiation involves every aspect of English studies – literary history, theory, rhetoric and composition, media studies, language studies. The Spring Hill conference offered a scene or site for such a conversation to proceed intensively, one in which the issues we have surveyed here could be raised, explored, and debated, but certainly not settled. This volume represents a continuation of the "polylogue," to use Gary Waller's provocative term, that took place at Spring Hill.

Although the papers collected here represent the proceedings of the conference, additional papers, which further develop viewpoints presented by several participants at the conference, are integrated into part 3, at the invitation of the editors. In part 1 of this volume, "Intellectual and Curricular Structures of Current Graduate Programs," Wayne Booth, Paul Cantor, Richard Lloyd-Jones, Robert

Scholes, and Patricia Meyer Spacks examine the state of English doctoral programs, focusing on our conceptual frameworks and curricular arrangements and the often unsettled and unsettling relations between them. While some concentrate on individual programs, others offer generalizations that apply to many if not all doctoral programs. However broad or narrow the focus, these essays raise important questions about the social contexts of PhD programs and the intellectual foundations of a united literature and rhetoric. They relate these questions to larger intellectual issues within the discipline and to the curricular structures that often block the possibility of change.

In part 2, "The Transition from Graduate Student to Faculty Member," relatively recent graduates of different PhD programs explore the ways that the graduate curriculum did or did not prepare them for what they faced as new faculty members. Their focus – not a surprising one at this stage of their careers – concerns primarily "what they faced." Nancy Comley from Queens College, Geoffrey Green from San Francisco State University, Jeffrey Spear from New York University, and Susan Wolfson from Rutgers University present a disturbing portrait of the untenured years that followed upon their graduate education. These years of probation are marked by discontinuity from graduate school experience, confusion of commitments, threats to intellectual and professional integrity, and, most of all, mystification. This perspective, as much as anything, seems an indictment of graduate programs: however successfully we prepare our students to contribute to the discipline, we fail to help them understand how to survive the profession. We need to enable them to shape their careers and institutions rather than be shaped by these institutions and "careerism."

The papers in part 3, "Exploring the Future," propose ways to strengthen doctoral study in English, suggesting changes that range from modest to radical. Taken together, these papers illustrate the diverse theoretical origins of a reconceived English studies. Representing poststructuralist literary theory (Jonathan Culler, Richard Lanham, Paul B. Armstrong), current and traditional rhetorical theory (Janice M. Lauer and Andrea Lunsford, Gary Waller, and Don Bialostosky), and feminist theory (Helene Moglen and Janel Mueller), the writers make explicit how a reconceived doctoral program can deal with questions of the canon and of pedagogy and how PhDs trained in such programs will be able, as teachers and scholars, to integrate the study of texts and the composing of texts.

We see this volume, therefore, as providing a sketch of the profession's current views of the relation between writing and reading and a map for future exploration. Furthermore, it is possible to translate this radical intellectual questioning into concrete curricula at this time, when expansion is already evident in many English programs. The essays identify some of the exciting possibilities that faculties in graduate programs not only in literature but across the humanities and social sciences will wish to consider in these next years.

AL, HM, and JFS

Part 1:
Intellectual and Curricular Structures of Current Graduate Programs

Reversing the Downward Spiral:
Or, What Is the Graduate Program For?

Wayne Booth
University of Chicago

Suppose we start this consideration of English doctoral study not with graduate programs but with college education and acknowledge the twin assumptions shared by most of us, though not, of course, by all: first, the subjects we group under the catchall term *English* are the most important in the academy; second, they are the most important precisely because in our culture they are the major heirs and last hope of a once glorious liberal arts tradition. The arts that at their best liberate us from our native provincialisms were once largely served by the systematic and universal study of the languages and monuments of the two civilizations that invented those arts. Students who were required to study Greek and Latin classics inevitably had some sort of encounter, deep or shallow, with mathematics, the physical sciences, law, philology, philosophy (including grammar, logic, rhetoric, dialectic, and ethics), history, and the arts: drama, sculpture, and architecture, a wide variety of poems, epics, and satires. What's more, they were expected to develop, in the company of critics like Aristotle and Longinus, habits of sustained critical inquiry – habits of rigorous argument about quality. (Yes, of course, I exaggerate: there never was a golden age when all serious students mastered all that. But in this limited space what can I do but simplify?)

Once the classics were abandoned as a general requirement, the burden of caring for most of that breadth, and all of that depth, gradually fell almost entirely on English. Though at one time or another colleges and universities have attempted to spread the burden, or opportunity, of liberal education over many fields by establishing core curricula and distribution requirements, the fact is that today the required freshman course – or on some campuses the freshman and sophomore English courses – generally gives American college students their only ensured contact with – well, with what? To call it a liberal education, or the liberal arts, begs more questions than it answers, but whatever we choose to call the cat, we are the mice chosen to bell it.

Though we are thus heirs to a tradition, and though we have sometimes been enthusiastic about the inheritance, many now seem to be extremely uneasy about it. Some of us repudiate it entirely, with talk about the tyranny of the canon or the need for new freedoms. Call us the Mods. Others deplore the loss of past riches and curse the innovators with their new fake nondisciplines. Call us the Ancients. The Mods fight to establish new canons and to show that the defenders of the old canons haven't a theoretical leg to stand on. The Ancients—at least the ones who have not given up and taken early retirement—fight to defend practices that forty years ago were revolutionary, thirty years ago fashionable, and twenty years ago established, if not frozen.

The war between the Ancients and the Mods seems to take most of our energies these days. Last week a friend showed me a copy of a communiqué from a symposium director to those who plan to discuss "Literary Theory and Textual Scholarship." The letter begins with an attack on the standard notion that the goal of textual editing is "to establish [canonized] texts for others to read and criticize," with the editor thus serving the interpretive critic. Such traditional editing, the director goes on to say, seeks always to "recover authorial intention," and thus it always produces the "phallotext"; that is, it recovers an implied author, always phallocentrically determined. The notion of an intention implies a text "centered in a recoverable desire for unity, coherence, textual logic." What editors must do instead, he says, is to combat this patriarchal kind of editing with an editing that respects *"l'écriture féminine,"* not only changing the list of texts to be edited but turning each traditional work into "a series of texts," their meaning, for editors and beneficiaries alike, "endlessly deferred." Now my photocopy of this relatively mild Mod manifesto is marked up with the responses of some anonymous Ancient: "Unbelievable bullshit." "Simple as that, eh!!!" "Since Foucault says it, it must be right?"

While this quarrel goes on—seemingly more intense by the month—both the Ancients and the Mods seem to agree that our graduates, who are implicitly expected to know everything by the time they get the hood, offer in their ignorance simple evidence that we are performing badly: "You mean it's possible to get a PhD from your university without having read a word of Aristotle, Sidney, or Samuel Johnson?" "You mean to say that it's possible to get a PhD from your department without having read Derrida or de Man?" "You mean to say you're producing PhDs who know nothing of linguistics, of rhetorical theory, of composition theory, of film theory, of feminist criticism, of folk literature, of . . . ?" Well, as you know, the list of oversights could go on for some time. About the only boast we might all want to make is that our graduates, regardless of their specialties, probably read and write *somewhat* better than those who dodge our ministrations. But if we are to ask them what they are doctors *of*, what they profess to *know*, we receive answers as miscellaneous as the annual MLA convention program. Most of us think that most graduates from most other institutions are ignorant of most of what they should know.

Of course this threat of multiple and unrealizable goals does not come just from new intellectual movements. The institution of scholarship has produced a situation in which the traditional expectation that candidates "cover" any field no longer makes sense. When I did my dissertation on *Tristram Shandy*, I was expected to read, and did read, just about everything ever written on that book, except for the splendid stuff by the Russian formalists that I didn't even hear about until much later. Today it would be absurd to say to any student, "Read everything you can get your hands on dealing with *Tristram Shandy*." Each decade produces more than had been written when I began. There are now more than 500 bibliographical items on James's *Turn of the Screw*. The Saul Bellow bibliography lists about 3,500 articles and books. One year's entry for Faulkner in the *MLA Bibliography* covers five columns. What kind of "learning" do we expect of students faced with such a flood of stuff? What kind of supervision do we offer, knowing that we ourselves cannot cover, and do not want to cover, the literature on the subject? What is the point of producing doctors of a subject if they cannot be said to have mastered something or other about that subject?

When faced with this new miscellaneity, my friends among the Ancients often cannot resist that cry of "bullshit." If we can just convince ourselves that we are attacked by a band of barbarians, then we know how to fight and what to fight for. But anyone who spends more than a few days breaking through the barrier of new vocabularies soon realizes that the new feminisms, new Marxisms, and new deconstructions cannot all be dismissed as nonsense. Indeed, we might well embrace all this multiplicity, thus parting company with both the Mods and the Ancients, *if* we could be convinced that someone else, in some other department, was minding the liberal education store. But for the most part the basic arts of reading and thinking, writing and speaking, as distinct from the art of accumulating information and know-how, have been turned over to us. And it takes no very wide experience with the first books and unpublished dissertations produced by our doctoral programs to see that something is wrong, and that something is not peculiar to either side of the Mod-Ancient divide. Even in the rare instances when the surface of a dissertation or book is polished in a professional way, that is, when a thesis seems to be presented with some style and the supporting scholarship really bears on that thesis, our students show scant mastery of the art of careful and respectful interpretation of texts or of rigorous construction of argument. They generally show little awareness of how their conclusions relate to any conceivable history of similar conclusions; often enough they are not even aware that the issues they raise have been addressed earlier, at much greater depth, by authors who were once on everyone's reading list. In short, our dissertations are produced by honorable, hard-working people who, lacking a general education, read and take notes for a year or so in some isolated corner of the intellectual universe and then do the best they can with the pitifully inadequate intellectual habits picked up in a miscellaneous list of courses. Those courses have themselves too often been isolated from the influences of ethics, politics, history, logic, dialectic, and even grammar.

You might want to object at this point that I have suddenly shifted around and become an unabashed Ancient, as I lament the loss of these liberal arts. Not at all: take as your standard the liberal learning of the founders of deconstruction or feminism: the philosophical groundedness of de Man or Miller, the care with argument and the respect for texts of Derrida or Hartman, the sensitivity to complex historical influences of Jameson, Gilbert, or Jacobus. My lament is that because many of our programs, whether Mod or Ancient, are unsystematic and essentially uncritical, our graduates for the most part receive a miscellaneous set of indoctrinations, not a liberal education. They have been taught *something*— perhaps by the historicists, old and new, how to assemble a collection of citations in a plausible order; perhaps by surviving Ancients how to do a plausible New Critical analysis, tracing an arbitrary chosen theme through a text; perhaps by one of the Mods how to mimic a deconstructive analysis – but they have not learned how to tackle a serious historical or philosophical problem and to bring to bear on it what the major figures, ancient and modern, applied to *their* problems: namely, the kind of critical thought that can be learned through years of immersion in liberal learning.

The ignorance of our graduates is not to be blamed of course on only our chaotic graduate programs. If we could assume that the BAs who come into our programs had been led by somebody toward a good general education, we could then more happily concentrate on whatever we now ask our candidates to concentrate on. We could then be sure that our candidates could build on a broad educational base and therefore become qualified to teach undergraduates in subjects other than the narrowest literary inquiry.

But of course we cannot count on anything of the kind. We can't assume that BAs will come to graduate study knowing any history, any language well enough to read works in the original, any criticism or philosophy well enough to respond to complex arguments without reducing them to easily embraced or rejected polarities.

What do we then do to them? We tell them in effect: "Just take a miscellaneous range of courses, with some distribution to fill in the gaps in your reading, then quickly choose an author or period or type or current school of criticism, dig into the topic for a year or two, say something about it that is more or less intelligible and preferably novel, and we'll give you the badge that just might get you a teaching job." While saying that, we also say – at most of our institutions – "Oh, by the way, you will also begin teaching freshmen, right now, and with no further training for doing so: a required writing course, a *service* course that you will be asked to go on teaching until you earn the blessed right to abandon it, as those of us fortunate ones who hire you have long since done." We reward some of the more highly qualified ones by asking them to teach literature courses as well, just as we bribe the seemingly best new PhDs by telling them that they will teach only courses in what they call their fields: no freshmen! But the introductory literature courses they teach will include no historical, rhetorical, or philosophical works – only novels, plays, poems, except in those places where the latest critical theories have penetrated, where perhaps some recent theory may be added. They are thus likely, throughout their four to ten years with us, to read no philosophy, no history, no rhetorical theory (unless they happen to elect the rhetoric option, which may be intellectually thin indeed). If they are gifted, they may in spite of all this do worthwhile work in their chosen areas – interesting feminist criticism, interesting Marxist criticism, interesting neo-historical revisions, even interesting editing. If they are not gifted – and we must remember that most of them cannot be especially gifted – they will remain un-educated: unable to apply original critical thought either to the world of letters or to any other part of the world. If they do any serious work after turning their dissertations into books, as most new PhDs will not, they will continue to work in the shoddy style that produced their theses. Most of us know this problem from painful experience: we have suffered from shockingly inept reviews and readers' reports, all of them written by people we ourselves must have trained at one time. How – one asks oneself again and again – how could anyone go through sixteen or more years of schooling and still read and think as badly as that? And then one realizes the explanation: these writers have been taught by their kind, our kind; nobody is minding the liberal arts store, all along the line. Ignorant high school graduates enter college and are taught by ignorant new BAs, graduate assistants working for slave wages in appallingly unprofessional conditions. Those BAs find themselves in graduate programs that leave them ignorant. When they teach, they teach courses that do not require them to make up for lost time – either service composition courses, with no depth of rhetorical theory behind them, or literature courses that simply perpetuate the downward spiral.

Having devoted most of these remarks to exaggerating my anxiety of non-influence, I have room now only to raise the questions that come most pressingly to mind as we observe our decline.

The first question may not seem to be our main business, but it comes first because it concerns the institutional driving power behind the downward spiral. How can we reverse the trend toward downgrading the professional status of English teachers, particularly teachers at the beginning levels, where liberal education for the teacher might occur, however belatedly? During the time the reader has spent so far on this paper, intuition tells us, administrators around the country have freshly cut 257 tenure-track lines from their English budgets, replacing them with 752 part-timers and fresh BAs. How can we alert the nation about what that means to our culture?

Putting the point that way, however, may disguise a deeper question, because it seems to put the blame on our various publics. We must remind ourselves that we who are established in the profession profit from the very conditions that we ought to deplore. We have increasingly divorced the teaching of literature from the teaching of writing. We have turned writing instruction into a merely technical matter, not a road to liberal education through the serious study of rhetoric. We have thus given our publics every reason to believe that we ourselves think teaching freshman to read and write is child's play, while teaching this or that fashionable bit of literary theory to advanced graduates is really where the action is. My second question then is: How can we get together with ourselves to recognize that we are painting ourselves into a corner? The best reason our publics have for supporting the vast machinery of what we call "English" is their belief that we are, after all, the final guardians of what I have called liberal education. They have no discernible reason to support us in producing more books asserting why language does or does not refer to reality, or why critical theory is or is not grounded, or even why the canon should be revised. They have every reason to support us if we can claim to educate those who come to us. Though they may put their demands on us in silly language like "back to the basics," they have a right to insist that we do our best to *educate*, not just to give professional training in some specialized literary field. Though we must be free to pursue whatever scholarship interests us, it is absurd to expect any society to continue to pay those best who do least in furthering liberal education. We must persuade ourselves that our own interests require a visible commitment to liberal education.

My third question springs out of the first two and is a bit more precise: How can we reverse the increasing divorce of graduate and undergraduate education, in order to ensure that when BA converts come to us they already have something like a liberal education? Putting the question this way implies that we cannot take our subject here as an invitation to solve our problems by simply reorganizing graduate requirements, though new coherent curricula are desperately needed. (I do hope that we will regain our confidence and require some coherence in our programs.) But whatever curricula we design will not do the job I have in mind unless we at the same time design better combinations of graduate courses and supervised, collegial experience in undergraduate teaching. Every graduate student should have the experience of joining older teachers as they teach not just how to read novels, plays, and poems but how to think critically about the interrelations of historical, philosophical, rhetorical, and literary experience. If all our PhD candidates were asked to join a staff teaching college courses that included philosophy, history, literature, and rhetoric, what a difference that would make, both to their future teaching and to the quality of their dissertations.

The English department that convinces its university to develop and support a PhD program that educates real doctors of philosophy, in this sense, will not thereby gain an immediate national reputation. It would be hard to think of a jazzy title for such a program that would attract as much attention as some titles now dominating our scene. But in the long run, such a department of English, such a department of liberal education, such a department of serious rhetorical theory and practice, could well become known as the precursor of the most important educational revolution of the century.

The Graduate Curriculum
and the Job Market:
Toward a Unified Field Theory

Paul Cantor

University of Virginia

I would like to speak about the forgotten part of the graduate curriculum: the dissertation-writing years. The typical graduate student in English spends at least as many years working on the dissertation as he or she does taking classes. And yet, when a department worries about its graduate curriculum, most of the attention tends to be focused on matters involving course work and examinations. Since writing a dissertation is an individual enterprise, it is of course difficult to lay down rules or even to suggest procedures for the project. Most departments content themselves with setting up a mechanism for approving topics, turning the dissertation writer over to a director or two, and hoping for the best. It would be wrong to fault this laissez-faire attitude. Writing a dissertation is after all the moment when a graduate student proclaims intellectual independence. The dissertation is supposed to be an original piece of scholarship, and it is impossible to regulate originality.

Nevertheless, I see one aspect of the dissertation-writing process that calls for greater guidance: the connection between the dissertation and the job market. Departments have been understandably reluctant to introduce the job market into curricular considerations. For years the prevailing attitude has, I believe, been something like this: "Since so few of our students are going to get positions anyway, why remake our program with the job market in mind? Let's concentrate on giving our students the best intellectual training we can, and let the chips fall where they may." Even when the job market was at its worst, this attitude was ill-advised, since some awareness of the realities of employment can at least increase a student's chances of finding work. But now that the market shows signs of improving and perhaps even turning around into something resembling a seller's market, it is even more incumbent on us to help our students keep the job market in mind throughout their graduate careers.

What I have to say is based primarily on anecdotal evidence accumulated during my two years as placement director for the English department of the University of Virginia. Since our graduate program is very large, my sampling may be fairly representative. After closely monitoring the job searches of some thirty to thirty-five students over the past two years, I have found that the first fact I have to impress on them is the importance, indeed the centrality, of the dissertation. It is remarkable how ill-informed some of them remain about the realities of the job market, how many myths persist. Some still think that the key to getting a good job is having the dissertation director get on the phone and order one up. Some spend an extra year studying for their oral examinations, thinking that a grade of distinction is the passport to fame, fortune, and tenure. Others look to getting articles published in scholarly journals; some expect to rely on the variety of their teaching experience; some even put their faith in their service on departmental committees.

All these factors can of course play a role in a successful job search. But, paraphrasing an old television commercial, I begin by telling students, "You ain't goin' nowhere without that dissertation." I wonder how many of us fully appreciate how central we have allowed the dissertation to become in the hiring process. This is in fact one of the great changes that came about during the transformation of the job market in the 1970s. Many of my older colleagues tell me that they did most of the work on their dissertations *after* they got their first jobs. How they performed on their oral examinations or, more basically, what their professors had to say about them was often the only evidence a potential employer had to go on. For a variety of reasons, some valid, some adventitious, that is now all changed. From what I can tell, the dissertation has become the primary factor in screening candidates and in hiring them.

In choosing likely candidates from the hundreds of applications for a position, departments ask two questions: Is the dissertation topic suited to the position? Does the applicant's description of the dissertation indicate scholarly potential? Pursuing a candidate almost always means first sending for a writing sample, which usually consists of a dissertation chapter. If the writing sample is impressive enough, the candidate is granted an interview at the MLA convention, but that does not mean the dissertation can be left behind. The interview generally begins with the dissertation, tends to concentrate on it, and sometimes hardly gets beyond it. I will never forget the look on the face of one of our more sought-after candidates this year who, after surviving sixteen interviews at the MLA, was innocently asked by one of my colleagues on the plane home, "What *is* your dissertation about, anyway?" And of course candidates invited to make a campus visit are often asked to do a presentation based on the dissertation and once again grilled on it in a series of interviews. By the time a candidate is through, the dissertation may have been scrutinized by more people than will ever read it in book form.

I do not wish to challenge this emphasis on the dissertation in the hiring process, a development that has been the cornerstone of the effort to make the process fairer and more objective. Letters of recommendation inevitably give us the uncomfortable feeling that in between us and the truth stands an observer biased in the candidate's favor, an observer armed, moreover, with a seemingly inexhaustible supply of adjectives. With the sample dissertation chapter, we finally feel we are in the presence of an unmediated vision of the candidate: here is the thing itself, the unaccommodated graduate student. This impression is to some extent an illusion, perhaps the last bastion of the myth of presence in our profession. There is a certain irony in the fact that we seem to have collectively forsworn access to an author's mind in all texts except the writing samples submitted to our hiring committees. And I sometimes wonder if we are not being presumptuous in seeking – on the basis of a thirty-five-page chapter and a forty-minute interview – to outguess the judgment of people who have worked intimately with a candidate for several years, have seen him or her teach in a classroom, and have genuine grounds on which to judge character.

No matter what my misgivings may be, the dissertation will continue to play a central role, especially as long as my colleagues feel that inflated levels of praise have made placement dossiers indistinguishable from one another. The dissertation does offer a substantial basis for judging candidates: it is after all their one major piece of sustained intellectual endeavor and is likely to provide the jumping-off point for a scholarly career. But we should make the importance of the dissertation crystal clear to our graduate students and help them plan their graduate careers accordingly. Above all, we should help them adjust their priorities to the realities of the job market. When, for example, they are trying to apportion their time between studying for orals and getting to work on the dissertation, they should be aware that their performance on their orals is likely to have been forgotten by the time they seek employment and, compared to the impact of the dissertation, will play a minor role in their success. For this reason I always advise my graduate students to get their orals over with as soon as possible and get started on their dissertations immediately thereafter.

Similar considerations prevail in the later years of a graduate career when students are trying to divide their time between teaching and work on the dissertation. Here the situation can become complicated, because frequently a department's self-interest conflicts with the self-interest of its graduate students. We often overburden our best graduate students with teaching assignments and even administrative duties, impeding their progress on their dissertations. I do not see an easy way out of this dilemma, but we should at least be clear about the consequences of what we are doing. In the past few years at the University of Virginia, we have been trying to expedite students' rate of progress on their dissertations. Our major accomplishment has been to obtain funding for between five and ten annual fellowships that allow students to work full-time on their dissertations for a whole academic year. We have also been experimenting with teaching loads, allowing students, for example, to teach twice as much one semester so that they can have the other semester free. Such programs have already begun to accelerate our students' progress toward their degrees. Moreover, our placement percentage has increased significantly since we began several years ago to emphasize the importance of the dissertation. We now try to discourage students from even testing the waters of the job market until they have completed a substantial portion of the dissertation, if not a whole first draft.

We should continue to explore avenues for allowing students to devote themselves more fully to the dissertations we make count for so much in the hiring process. One specific problem is the way search committees tend to pigeon-hole job candidates according to dissertation topic. I find this particularly troublesome because the way the job market divides up the fields of literary scholarship is not always the way our graduate programs do. For example, as in most departments, graduate students at Virginia may specialize in the twentieth century. We happen to ask those who do to prepare both British and American literature and to cover all genres within the period. Turning now to the job market, at first we seem to find a harmony between supply and demand. We turn out specialists in twentieth-century literature and departments seek to hire them. A common entry in the *MLA Job List* is twentieth-century literature, or modern literature, or simply modernism. But because the modern period is popular, the job listings tend to splinter. The field of a job may be defined as modern drama or modern fiction or modern poetry. Or a job will be defined as modern British as opposed to modern American, or as post-1945 rather than pre-1945. So balkanized has the modern period become that a listing like "post-1945 American fiction" is not unusual. It is surely an oddity of the job market that a medievalist may be expected to cover all genres in three or four languages over six or seven centuries, while a modernist may be confined to one generation's output of novels in a single country.

There are of course many reasons why the pie gets sliced so thin in the twentieth century, and I would not object if the dissertation did not turn out to be the knife that makes the cut. It seems that in the job market, "You are your dissertation." One of the lessons I have learned in supervising job candidates is, Don't even bother to apply for a modern fiction job if your dissertation is on Stevens or for a modern poetry job if your dissertation is on Conrad. On the face of it, this situation is irrational. Most departments set up curricula so that a student who learns pre–World War I British fiction will also learn post–World War II American poetry. But the job market will hear none of this. At first I thought it was just a matter of selling oneself and instructed candidates to clarify their qualifications in their letters of application: for example, "Though my dissertation concentrates on Yeats, I have taken two courses on modern American fiction, did my orals on the whole modern period, and taught Pynchon, Hawkes, and Barth in an undergraduate seminar." But even this strategy seems to be of no avail. If the dissertation does not fall into the area specified in a job listing, the candidate seems to stand little chance of getting so much as a writing-sample request.

Having participated in my department's hiring process as well for the past two years, I can appreciate the reason for these rejections. Faced with as many as four hundred applicants for a single position, one searches desperately for seemingly legitimate ways to make choices. One way is to use the dissertation topic. It is easy to resort to such a procedure, but we ought to remember that eliminating candidates solely on the basis of dissertation topics can drastically reduce the pool of talent we have to draw on. Hiring by field at all may be questionable at the junior level. Given the kind of teaching we generally expect from assistant professors, the field of specialization seems far less important than intelligence and teaching ability. But if we are going to hire by field, we should at least be wary of defining the fields too narrowly and above all of defining the suitability of candidates for those fields exclusively on the grounds of dissertation topics. We are after all hiring not dissertations but human beings, whose interests include, but are not coextensive with, the subjects of their dissertations.

One of my greatest frustrations as a placement director is that I reach job candidates too late. Once they have been working on their dissertations for two or three years, they are in no position to make adjustments. It is sad to see a candidate who has been preparing to teach modern fiction but who is also writing a dissertation on Yeats find that he has backed himself into a corner and is now stereotyped for life as a specialist in modern poetry. The fact is that we are currently sending mixed signals to our graduate students. The standards we invoke as dissertation directors are often diametrically opposed to those we invoke when we hire junior faculty members. One has only to consider the mythology that has grown up around the dissertation. If asked how a person should choose a dissertation topic, graduate students will often say, "You should pick as obscure a topic as possible, something no one has worked on before." This is precisely the wrong advice to give someone who wishes to become a viable job candidate. The more obscure the topic of the dissertation, the less likely that it will fit the teaching needs of potential employers.

It may make us uncomfortable, but we ought to come to terms with the increasing divergence between the scholarly needs and the teaching needs of our profession. I have no ready solution to this problem. I cannot see having our graduate students make all their decisions about their scholarly careers with a view to the demands of the job market. This approach would not only prove self-defeating but would also undermine the integrity of literary scholarship. On the other hand, graduate students cannot be kept in the dark about the effect of the dissertation topic on their job prospects. As a dissertation adviser, I would never approve a topic that I would turn around and reject as a member of a hiring committee.

Perhaps the problems I have described are already familiar to a majority of the profession, and I am merely belaboring the obvious. But the reactions I get when I try to explain the facts as I see them to graduate students make speaking out on this issue worthwhile. In particular, I hope to start people thinking about how we might do a better job of bringing the fields in which we hire candidates into line with the fields in which we prepare them as graduate students, or, if need be, vice versa. Though I have facetiously dubbed this the quest for a Unified Field Theory, I hope that we will have greater success in solving this problem than our colleagues in physics have had in solving theirs.

Doctoral Programs: Composition

Richard Lloyd-Jones
University of Iowa

Although professors of English first entered the academy as "rhetoricians," to improve the writing of their students, for most of the later years of this century their descendants have evaded the task as much as possible. Usually the faculties from other fields seemed not to mind, for as their enrollments grew, they espoused multiple-choice examinations and required few pieces of writing from their students. Albert R. Kitzhaber demonstrates that by 1960 American colleges offered little useful instruction in written composition.

In that light the present ADE-MLA job list with its frequent ads for "composition specialists" and the concomitant growth of graduate programs in writing seems peculiar, even a cause for skepticism. Most of us senior citizens grew up in departments emphasizing literature but sometimes tolerating composition, especially if the work could be assigned to graduate teaching assistants. Still, Bettina Huber's report of the MLA survey (see app.) is revealing, for if one-third of the departments want to claim to have doctoral programs in rhetoric, writing, and composition, we can infer there is some recommitment to studying how texts are generated as well as how they should be interpreted.

Increased departmental concern for training PhD candidates to teach composition surfaced in the late sixties (as the dates in Chapman and Tate's survey in *Rhetoric Review* imply), although there were always individuals who were expert writing coaches or editors and who helped neophytes. This rising interest can only incidentally be called intellectual; rather, it grew out of practical needs for dealing with open enrollment, just as the Conference on College Composition and Communication grew from the accommodation to the rush of ex-GIs in the late forties. Even though the initiating purpose may not define the resulting program, I propose to classify current efforts to include composition and rhetoric in our doctoral programs on a scale from utterly pragmatic to rationalized responses to market forces, allowing always that from the squishiest academic dung sprout health-giving vegetables. I will not try to repeat Tate's descriptions or the MLA survey, each valuable but limited by problems of acquiring and classifying the data. One suspects that some of the categories in those surveys contain both apples and love apples, despite the care of the surveyors, and some of the data are only statements of hope. Conversations at years of academic conventions and in random campus visits flesh out for me the abstractions of polls.

First, a road map. I suggest a scale with four categories of program for our doctoral students: (1) those that are incidental to the administration of a freshman program staffed by TAs or adjuncts; (2) those incidental to the interests of a senior faculty member and permissible under flexible requirements; (3) those really offered as "English Education" and sometimes found deported to schools of education; and (4) those claiming by explicit curricula to be real specialties, often interdisciplinary and sometimes closely allied to programs in literary criticism or in area studies. Many of the courses and faculty members for these programs come from other departments, and most of the people in English have other interests as well, so it is hard to judge the adequacy of staffing from a distance. I have not really tried to include programs of creative writing, except incidentally in discussing the second and fourth categories, because they introduce still another set of complications, but there are provocative parallels.

The most common way to inform graduate students about composition is in the elaborated staff meeting, an administrative convenience for those who are responsible for the transient employees of the basic composition program. If one hires neophytes, one must provide some sort of plausible indoctrination – regular staff meetings, perhaps a preservice workshop, a course or two, some knowledgeable observation by a person rationalized in a curriculum vitae as an expert. No big investment but enough to forestall criticism if not eliminate it.

Despite my cynical description, such programs are often pretty good even though they don't usually show up on our surveys – at least in a way to tell the good ones from the bad. My experience tells me, and the MLA survey partly substantiates, that in good circumstances a composition enthusiast – usually self-trained, even though more and more "specialists" are appearing – conducts a seminar or workshop (often as a prerequisite to appointment but without graduate credit). The required readings are sound and extensive, although frequently rather loaded toward nuts-and-bolts concerns. The leader challenges some rather moralistic graduate students – those who sigh when they say they want to teach – to rally to the flag and become unrecognized students of rhetoric and composition. Since in the end we believe that true education results from individual searching (even when it is inspired by a true teacher), we should allow that some of our doctoral students are far better trained as practitioners and scholars of rhetoric and composition than their credentials would suggest. Alas, it is hard to know which graduates are which, and even the best may have eccentric gaps in their knowledge, a weakness common to autodidacts.

From "administrator as teacher" I move to a second category also ordinarily tied to one person (who might even be the director of the freshman program) but more programmatically tied to our published doctoral curricula. Most of our doctoral programs have enough flexibility to allow emphases dear to any senior faculty member. We tacitly believe in apprenticeship, so whatever is a passion for a senior professor is also creditable work for a young person, especially if the resultant scholarship is helpful in getting a job. The maturing of CCCC and the Council of Writing Program Administrators (WPA) and similar groups in size and quality over the last decade suggests the increasing presence of people oriented toward directing good scholarship.

In the late sixties when I began to take occasional doctoral students (our "program" came later), they enrolled out of curiosity, a general passion to teach, and a specific interest in teaching the "new" students. Dick Braddock, who ran our freshman program, or Carl Klaus, who ran many summer institutes, piqued their curiosity until they sought out still more advanced work. At meetings of CCCC the absurd, the trivial, and the intellectually exotic were equally dispensed in loud voices at cocktail parties provided by publishers, who flooded the market with freshman texts. We who went found many ideas that were fascinating and beautifully complicated, but we were also fortified by the sense that our study was socially significant. We were on the edge of social change, whether our departments cared or not. We had more than collegial tolerance for silliness, if it was the product of a good heart, but we took our graduate students as colleagues, and we expected to enrich the lives of our students, especially those who were first-generation collegians.

Now, as I read between the lines of the Tate descriptions, I believe that this tutorial relationship remains the basic pattern of doctoral study, even though the MLA survey implies that more conventional curricular categories and professors are more prudently restrained by concerns for quality. What we offer are not "programs" developed by systematic analysis but modeling and apprenticeship, although in a proper sense such imitation may be the basis for most advanced study in the humanities. The dissertations usually reflect the standard methodologies of English extended to rhetorical materials – often literary nonfiction. The course offerings are a bit thin, and the lists of faculty members in the specialty are ordinarily filled out with people who have secondary interests somewhat related to composition but who are quite able to fill out committees.

The remaining two categories exist more concretely in documents, although that may lead to greater errors in classification. We in English seem to be casual about having the content of courses accurately follow the implications of titles or even programs, but documents do require corporate approval and thus represent a higher level of commitment. Schools of education might be expected to offer explicit curricula, partly because they are used to the explicitness of "empirical and quantitative studies" and partly because they deal in credentials. Credentials provide an abstract record of study of a specified quality; they are part of the practical machinery required to run our educational systems. Before 1960 most of the scholarly studies – usually called research because of the social-science base –

appeared as dissertations in education, and most were comparative treatments of teaching methods or error counts, and few were well done. The last twenty years have brought significant improvements in methods and subjects for study, as documented by George Hillocks; more importantly, however, traditional rhetoricians, linguists, philosophers, semioticists, psychologists, sociologists, neurologists, and even literary critics have contributed to the serious study of composition. I am by no means sure what "empirical" meant to people responding to the MLA survey, but I have a hard time believing that many departments of English concentrate on the kind of work reviewed by Hillocks.

At the same time I lack data on how many programs exist in education. Most of the empiricists I know are housed in such places, and their programs stress statistics, research design, linguistics (sometimes), and studies of human growth, learning theory, and measurement. They rarely mention foreign languages, usually ask for little more than master-degree-level literary knowledge. Since most of the graduates work in the schools or train teachers for the schools, the research is likely to deal with the writing of younger people or perhaps with the operation of particular writing programs, although current literacy research may go farther afield. Quite possibly programs in communications or technical and business writing or journalism should be crowded into this category with English education, but I think that would introduce more complications without significantly altering my general scheme. These programs respond to research imperatives far removed from literary study, and they do create credentialed "composition specialists," but we in English usually look the other way.

My fourth category seems to me to be thinly populated, even though it is the nominal home of our composition specialists. I hear in that term more an analogy to a surgeon or an orthodontist than to a Miltonist or a Victorian, because most departments hire composition specialists primarily to run programs and train teachers rather than to do scholarship or even teach classes of undergraduates. The programs may include alien materials. We might find graphics, or scientific epistemology, or organizational theory, or speech-act theory, or reading theories parallel to deconstruction and to reader-response theories, or even courses in editing that are not explicitly tied to journalism. We easily justify such materials in our courses of serious intellectual intent as examples or borrowings of incidental skills, for we are notorious thieves from other disciplines, but the materials may exist primarily to serve some practical need of writers and administrators. It is hard to tell from our surveys where the intellectual center of a program is, for terms like *rhetoric* or even *writing* are elusive. The plausible content is so inclusive that precise descriptions may be pointless, and no one person really "covers" the field of how writing is generated any more than he or she "covers" the body of fine literary texts. Maybe the design of a particular curriculum depends on what resources are otherwise available at a given university. Interdepartmental cooperation ekes out limited resources to make a responsible program on a shoestring. We at Iowa tend to stress literary writing, for example, because we have scores of creative writers in the Iowa Writers Workshop and because a number of our students have MFAs or at least course work in creative writing. When our communications studies department was staffed with remarkable rhetoricians and our linguists dabbled in discourse and social theory, we also stressed that kind of knowledge. In a world of many options practicality in commanding resources may govern program design just as practicality of goal may arouse the interest that justifies the program of general intellectual discovery.

Whatever the cause of the variations, all programs engage the serious study of how language is generated in speech and writing and include a secondary emphasis on how texts are interpreted. Student writing and literary masterpieces and even oral exchanges are all proper texts of study. In these programs literary criticism is extended into rhetorical criticism and propaganda analysis. These scholars ease into area or cultural studies because they see all language in context. In short, their intellectual concerns are those of a department dealing with English language and literature, even though the package may sometimes appear to be a bit trendy, the examples rather far from the canon, and the politics aggressively democratic. Still, the surface variety makes it hard for graduates of differing programs to claim cousinship and for departments to recognize when they've found a person they want to hire.

Promotion and tenure committees are also frustrated by the shiftiness and the inclusiveness of the categories. Young faculty members are pressed to demonstrate their competence through published discovery, but interdisciplinary research often takes extra time, and purists hate to see their delicate methods twisted for some alien goals. They are ready for knee-jerk reactions of disapproval. Also, since most composition people are hired not only to do lots of tutorial teaching but to run programs, good people are eaten up by "chores," and they are lost to tenure as suffering servants who are (alas) "nonproductive" scholars. So many chores have to be done that lots of nonspecialists are enlisted, and, although they may teach responsibly, they may muddy the waters of sound scholarship with the silt of side issues and popular prejudice. Deans – even colleagues – may have trouble separating the spurious from the true. The real test of a program may be in how the practical and intellectual imperatives are balanced in judging the faculty, for programs are too varied to admit easy generalization.

Our surveys probably overstate what we are doing to create doctoral scholars, but we are certainly doing much more than we used to in training teachers, and I suspect that other gains are hidden under old course titles masking new content. I don't trust our protestations of virtue or our jeremiads about failures to prepare our students to teach. We should expect all PhDs to avoid stupid prescriptions about teaching writing, but we don't need a specialist under every carpet. That is, we should all have a respectable level of knowledge about all the areas assigned to departments of English. We are distressed, say, when someone talks about climax in a Dickens novel without being aware of the constraints of serial publication. So also we should be distressed when our graduates identify dialects as inferior rather than possibly inappropriate in a situation or when they assume every student should make preliminary outlines or every paragraph ought to start with a topic sentence. To be sure, we'd like that understanding from our undergraduate majors, too, but what we hope for in undergraduates might be a measure of what we should absolutely expect of all our doctorates.

Development of doctoral specialties in composition is another issue. The force to create them may be pragmatic, simply another way to recognize the power of academic fragmentation. Their bias is toward the language processes of the ordinary person rather than the rare productions of the exceptional writer, but they share with our dominant literary programs an abiding curiosity about the way language works. Crafters – writers themselves – and theorists have much to contribute to the teaching; I have a hard time imagining a good program without both, even though I can otherwise see a broad expanse of legitimate programs. I assume that we all must at times examine particular texts very carefully, and we all need extensive knowledge about our culture and its past.

I worry about an administrative preoccupation with standardization, perhaps for the sake of credentialing, since such limitations deny the kaleidoscopic creativity generated by wordsmiths. Especially I worry about it when the surface descriptions of our studies seem at variance with the deep structures. For two or three decades, at least, we have not offered real historical coverage of a limited body of British literature as our essence, but we have seemed to. Anyone who constructed achievement tests to report what knowledge we added to our students would be frustrated and would probably miss the qualities that seem to please us when we hire new faculty members.

Mostly, though, I worry that specialization and division of study into composition and literature may lead to disabling and irrelevant differences within a department. Language itself depends on simultaneous processes of division and synthesis. Writing and reading are interactive processes. A department of language and literature needs to balance all these operations in its programs for all its students, so it probably should resist efforts to classify its doctoral emphases on composition too neatly. Even if we find the language to reveal the tacit reconception of English that has emerged, we might want to emphasize that mutability in representation is a virtue even of written natural language and should not be surrendered. The borderlines between processes of generating and interpreting texts are best understood as open, requiring no passports, exacting no tariffs, inviting the stroller to observe freely.

Some Problems in Graduate Programs

Robert Scholes
Brown University

Over the past century English studies in this country have obtained a measure of focus and precision by bracketing out certain domains of textuality to concentrate on others. First, we bracketed out all those uses of the English language that were utilitarian or speculative, retaining only those that could be covered by such designations as "oratory" and "belles lettres"–as I am forcibly reminded by the title of the English department chair at my home university: the Nicolas Brown Professorship of Oratory and Belles Lettres. Then, we bracketed out the oratory dimension, leaving ourselves with belles lettres alone, which we learned to call by the now focused honorific title of "literature."

Let us review what we have gained and lost as we made these adjustments. The first move, putting speculative and informational texts beyond our pale, enabled us to concentrate on those persuasive and aesthetic texts that used the expressive resources of language to the utmost–texts that relied on the effective attributes of language to bring readers either to desire particular textual objects or to make an emotional investment in textuality itself. As a discipline oriented to rhetoric and poetics, we came to concentrate more and more on the close study of certain highly valued texts for their own sake. This emphasis on major works of oratory and belles lettres gave our studies a certain coherence, which we enhanced when we made the second reduction of our field.

In this reduction we eliminated oratory and rhetorical studies generally. We did this, I believe, partly because these studies were tied to speech rather than writing, which we, like Jacques Derrida, consider by far the more important of the two, and partly because they smacked of practical application, conflicting with our ideal of liberal education as the study of purely impractical matters. This second diminishing of our field left behind only poetics (and its handmaiden, philology, which has since been dismissed or relegated to the basement). Free to concentrate exclusively on the literary side of English textuality, we were led, inevitably, to a greater and greater degree of formalism in literary studies: to New Criticism, to the Chicago school of generic criticism, later on to structuralism, and finally to deconstruction—which is the aestheticizing of all discourse, the denial that any really persuasive, or informational, or speculative discourse can exist.

Both those who despise deconstruction and all its works and those who embrace it wholeheartedly must recognize that it is so powerful among us (as it is nowhere else on the face of the earth) because we have deserved it, because our whole history has made us ripe for an intellectual conquest of precisely this sort. Deconstruction is the culmination of the dominant tendencies in the historical development of our institutional and professional discourse over the past century. By seeing all discourse as paradoxical or metaphorical—in a word, as literary—deconstruction has invited us to see the whole world of textuality as our particular oyster. There is a certain irony in this development. By progressive reductions we sought a tidy corner in which to interpret and reinterpret our major works, and now we find the entire universe of textuality invading our corner through a gap we cannot close.

It is one thing to retreat to one's private corner of poetic textuality; it is another to be told that all the world is in fact contained within that tiny space. Something will have to give—and it will do no good to retreat to the old days of literary study, crying, "Throw these rascals out," because they are our own rascals, acting on our own secret desires. We have wanted deconstruction—that is why it has come home to us and moved in with us. The Nietzschean figures who have dominated deconstructive discourse represent our private Mephistopheles, here to make us an offer we cannot refuse because we have sought it all along. "There is nothing outside the text," a voice is whispering in our ears, "and the text is always already literary."

Of this fruit we cannot choose but eat. Then what? Then, it seems to me, we either burst or grow—until, like Alice, we become too large for our present dwelling. Let me attempt to put our problem in less parabolic terms by focusing more specifically on our present graduate programs. Our graduate students are clamoring for more and better courses in deconstruction and other forms of literary theory. They also need—and often know they need—some preparation for teaching students how to read and write in and about a range of discourses that extend well beyond our traditional belletristic domain—though not, of course, beyond the bounds of the Derridean "general text." We must decide how to respond to these needs. To focus on a single aspect of a complex problem, I suggest that we need to decide whether deconstruction should have a decisive effect on the way we think about and teach reading and writing. (In my view we have no choice but to proceed through deconstruction and the textual situation that has accompanied its entry into our field. That is, we need to learn the analytical and critical methods developed by and around Jacques Derrida, and we need to accept a wider range of texts as objects for our critical and pedagogical attention.)

For our graduate programs, then, we need to evaluate and position deconstruction and other modes of textual theory as components of our field of study – an objective that we are singularly ill-equipped to accomplish, for at least two reasons: first, because deconstruction, as I have indicated, comes in answer to our own repressed desire for the world to be a literary text; and, second, because we, collectively, are so unfamiliar with philosophical discourse that we cannot even properly place deconstruction, probe its presuppositions, read its texts both generously and rigorously. This intellectual inadequacy – which, I repeat, is our collective problem, despite some unusual individual exceptions – is the result of a number of factors, which we should at least notice here. One, of course, is our departmental retreat into belletrism. Another has been the comparable retreat by American philosophy departments from the metaphysical and phenomenological tradition central to European thought, a tradition that has often been bracketed or marginalized as a field for serious study. English departments and philosophy departments in our universities have succumbed to the specialization that is endemic in our society, and they are now, in different ways, paying the price. Part of our problem is that in this country we have no tradition whatsoever of studying philosophy in the secondary schools, except for whatever logic may turn up in mathematics courses. In general, we Americans despise learning, despise abstraction, and value only the practical and the emotional, work and feeling, with no place in our scheme of values for thought. This orientation hurts us in our scientific as well as in our humanistic education. Most of us do not even understand our pragmatic tradition of thought well enough to incorporate it in thinking about how to teach reading and writing. Few of us have a clear grasp of the issues in the Anglo-American traditions of "ordinary language" and "speech act" philosophy, though they bear directly on some of our main concerns.

Our philosophical weaknesses are responsible for our helpless dependence on Europe for literary theories of any coherence and power. We have learned to read texts sensitively and have brought this activity to an exceptional pitch of subtlety – achievements we need not be ashamed of – but that sensitivity without rigor makes it impossible to perform a seriously critical act. While we can interpret texts within the range of our competence, we haven't a clue about how to evaluate anything other than their formal qualities. It is because we judge so badly that critical evaluation has been gradually eliminated from what we still call literary criticism – though our "criticism" is in fact simply interpretive. How many of you would trust your undergraduates – or even your graduate students, even your colleagues – to tell you why one text is better than another? Serious evaluation is regularly accomplished in this country only by feminists – which is just one of the things that make feminism so interesting.

To return to the focus of this discussion, I am arguing that our graduate programs must do something to counteract the philosophical naiveté that besets all Americans. This weakness is by no means the only one we need to correct or attend to, but it is one central area of our concern. If we, and our students, can learn to think more rigorously and to manipulate abstractions more felicitously –

goals, I would argue, that have been our proper objectives all along—we, and they, will become better readers, better writers, and better teachers of reading and writing. And if something in our present curriculum has to go to make room for this kind of study—so be it.

Our present curricula for doctoral studies in English are both too specialized and insufficiently rigorous. We need to aim at a broader grasp of our textual culture as a whole—all kinds of texts in all kinds of discourses and media—supported by a firmer grasp of the central tradition of Western thought. As it is, we spend far too much time shepherding graduate students through text after literary text—works they ought to be able to read on their own—and not enough time helping them master the discourses they need to position literary texts for effective critical scrutiny.

We must learn to cross the curriculum at the highest level as well as in freshman English. For our own good as teachers and for the sake of the future of our world, we must learn to engage in critical dialogue not only with such as Jacques Derrida but with such as Jurgen Habermas. We need to come out of our belletristic closet, and we must have the courage to do so by opening up our graduate curricula to wider ranges of thought and knowledge.

The Yale Curriculum

Patricia Meyer Spacks
Yale University

I want to reflect on the graduate program in English at Yale: not as representative of anything in particular, but as one example of the way current critical dilemmas can be both incorporated and evaded in classroom practice. Yale is not what people think it is. It lacks the tropical vegetation and dangerous thinkers attributed to it by the *New York Times Magazine*; Hillis Miller has gone elsewhere and Jacques Derrida – never, in any case, a member of the English department – no longer lurks in the Connecticut mist. As for graduate students in English at Yale, they resolutely eschew jungles, to follow a conservative curriculum designed to prepare for conservatively conceived doctor's orals: period and genre (Renaissance poetry, the eighteenth- and nineteenth-century novel) and major figures (Milton, Chaucer, Shakespeare).

Such arrangements of curriculum and examination did not result from the departure of Miller and Derrida. On the contrary, the presence of such figures never made the slightest difference to the fundamental order of things, which has remained more or less unaltered for a quarter of a century, the last major change being the shift from orals covering the entire range of English and American literature to an examination that focuses on nine preselected topics. But I do not mean to convey that graduate teaching at Yale depends on worn out assumptions or exemplifies antiquated approaches. We attempt as a department to achieve a delicate synthesis of old and new; I'll try to suggest its nature.

You will hardly be surprised if I say that undergraduates now appear to get ever worse educations. This fact is distressing in many ways – not least because, I assume, we all teach undergraduates ourselves and therefore must be somehow implicated in their apparent deterioration. The students entering our graduate program typically think well, often write well, are passionately involved in the life of the mind, profoundly committed to the study of literature, greedy for learning. But they don't know a whole lot about the course of English and American literature or literary criticism. Often they have studied the modern and postmodern periods more thoroughly than they have examined any pre-twentieth-century work except Shakespeare's; often they prove familiar with an apparently random assortment of literary texts. Although they may feel skeptical about the notion of a canon, their skepticism derives from no thorough acquaintance with canonical texts. Their two years of graduate course work at Yale directs them toward such acquaintance.

Students and faculty members alike intermittently raise questions about our program's orthodox configuration; indeed, we are currently engaged in a formal reexamination of that configuration. Orals concentrate on major texts and on historical coverage; doctoral candidates tend to elect courses in order to prepare for orals. (The doctorate requires no written examination.) Why not loosen up the orals, we ask ourselves, and allow more freedom for innovative courses? Our neighbor, comparative literature, lets students design their own orals, collaborating with faculty members of their choice to articulate a series of questions and devise bibliographies to help answer them. So far, though, we have stuck to our established patterns, with minor modifications such as the introduction of an optional topic–infrequently elected–on orals and considerable permissiveness about the selection of specific novels and plays as subjects of examination. We continue to believe that thorough grounding in canonical texts provides the best foundation for teaching. Yet this account is partly misleading, for the nature of "thorough grounding" has changed at Yale in the past ten years or so. Although many courses retain familiar titles, their content and approach have often shifted, sometimes radically. Let me tell you something about three specific recent course offerings, one my own, two those of younger colleagues. I supply this evidence not to epitomize the Yale graduate curriculum but to suggest kinds of innovation manifest within a traditional scheme.

My first case in point will sound from its title very traditional indeed: The Pastoral: Genre and History. Taught by John Guillory, this seminar begins with Theocritus and Vergil, works through predictable sixteenth- and seventeenth-century English texts, investigates Pope's pastorals, Gray's churchyard elegy, and poems by Goldsmith and Crabbe in the eighteenth century, and concludes with Lewis Carroll's *Alice* books and *Tess of the d'Urbervilles*. The final texts–Guillory refers to them as "postpastoral"–deviate from those one might automatically predict for such a course, but the weight of the syllabus rests firmly on the canonical. "This course," the summary description begins, "will attempt to describe the pastoral as genre by means of sequential historical readings." The student who elects The Pastoral: Genre and History will build just the solid foundation promised by the title.

Yet no such course would have been taught fifteen years ago. One important purpose of the undertaking is to interrogate the notion of genre, to demonstrate how genre gets constructed and reconstructed in response to specific social, intellectual, and political circumstance. "My ultimate aim," Guillory writes, "will be to understand the conditions of possibility governing the emergence, regularization, and decline of the pastoral genre (implicitly of any genre)." His seminar investigates genre and canon as concepts – not to destroy them, but to redefine their usefulness in relation to current critical preoccupations. It raises post-Empsonian questions about pastoral.

My second instance may sound at the outset more innovative, but it reveals a similar preoccupation with new ways to understand literary tradition. Margaret Homans recently offered, both at the undergraduate and graduate level (in two separate courses), a seminar called Gender and Power in Victorian Literature. Its primary texts include: Virginia Woolf, *Between the Acts*; *Tennyson's Poetry*; *Poems of Robert Browning*; *Alice in Wonderland*; Elizabeth Gaskell, *The Life of Charlotte Brontë* and *Cousin Phyllis and Other Tales*; Elizabeth Barrett Browning, *Aurora Leigh*; George Eliot, *Romola*.

That syllabus illustrates a canon stretching but hardly shattered. Tennyson and Browning have doubtless appeared in every Victorian literature course since the notion of Victorian literature has existed. Lewis Carroll shows up everywhere these days – as Victorian novelist, as satirist, as exemplar of the comic. F. R. Leavis long ago canonized George Eliot, if not necessarily *Romola*. Gaskell, like Carroll, has been fairly widely absorbed into the curriculum. *Aurora Leigh* alone distinctly announces an unconventional view of the Victorians.

The most innovative aspect of Margaret Homans's course depends less on its syllabus than on its procedures. Drawing on passages from Queen Victoria's letters and diaries and including in the secondary readings not only twentieth-century criticism (for instance Louis Montrose on Queen Elizabeth) but such Victorian commentary as Sarah Ellis's *Women of England, Their Social Duties and Domestic Habits*, the seminar attempts to establish for its participants a new historical universe, a world containing Tennyson and Gaskell not as equal members – their socially defined inequality, after all, is part of the point – but as simultaneous contributors to complicated literary and intellectual actuality. Considering the nature both of "literature" and of "history" as legitimate subjects for inquiry, the course tries to devise appropriate ways of talking about literature and history as mutually constituted. If it enlarges the traditional canon, it also draws on that canon.

My third example is my own graduate course on the eighteenth-century English novel. In it, last semester, we spent seven weeks on *Clarissa*, reading not only the novel itself but the recent books about it by Terry Eagleton, William Warner, and Terry Castle. In the remaining seven weeks we pursued a strenuous curriculum, making our ways through *Amelia*, *A Sentimental Journey*, *The Man of Feeling*, *Humphry Clinker*, *Evelina*, *The Italian*, and *Northanger Abbey*. The last three novels, the three written by women, are the least conventional texts here, but none of them seems really startling in such a course.

More startling, perhaps, is what happens during the semester. Both times I've taught the course (with a slightly less ambitious syllabus on the previous occasion), there has come a moment during our discussion of *Clarissa* when the class has unconsciously dramatized in its own operations the sexual antagonisms contained in Richardson's novel. The young men and women seated around the seminar table, after weeks of harmonious discussion, unexpectedly find themselves at odds; anger develops between the sexes. Everyone is shocked. The next week we discuss what happened. Such discussion leads to deeper understanding of the novel's psychological and social dynamics and creates a new vantage point from which to survey the eighteenth-century development of a narrative language of feeling. We move on to analysis of the relation between plot and sexual ideology, of the meanings and power of "sentimentality," of the emotional sources of the gothic. These familiar issues assume new immediacy–and so do the eighteenth-century philosophic and historical data that illuminate them–in the context of our collective experience of reading Richardson. I could not have imagined in advance how passionate a discussion of Edmund Burke can become.

The approaches suggested by these three courses–investigating the construction of genre, examining the relations of literature and history, using immediate personal responses to help clarify social and literary issues of the past–all lend themselves in modified form to undergraduate teaching as well. We take it–that "we," of course, masks varying degrees and kinds of commitment–as one of our responsibilities to prepare graduate students for pedagogical careers primarily as teachers of literature in a time when literature's value is often questioned.

It's hard, though, for a graduate program nowadays to achieve more than an uneasy union of concern for teaching and for learning. Perhaps the union has always been uneasy. Even in my time at graduate school, in the heyday of New Criticism, we students felt troubled about the discrepancy between the relatively esoteric concerns we pursued in seminar papers and dissertations and those appropriate to the undergraduate classroom. And if not as students, we experienced that discrepancy soon enough as teachers: our expertise at tracing symbolic patterns in "A Rose for Emily" did not equip us to fill the intellectual needs of the freshmen we confronted. The problem for budding deconstructionists or Marxists or new historicists or feminists may differ more in degree than in kind.

Yale's most formal evidence of commitment to the teaching of teachers consists in the teaching practicum offered each year as part of the graduate curriculum. Linda Peterson currently teaches it; roughly two-thirds of our students elect it. Combining pedagogical theory and practice, the practicum investigates strategies for effective instruction in literature and in expository writing. Students thinking about such matters find themselves intensely concerned with relations between critical theory and pedagogical practice. Many of these students in their own writing experiment with feminist, Marxist, new historicist, or poststructuralist procedures. Their first experience in front of the classroom tells them that beginning students profit most from training in the close reading of texts, with a formalist emphasis. Yet that perception only initiates a continuing debate about the place of contemporary theory in a contemporary undergraduate class.

Graduate students acknowledge the problem of terminology: the vocabulary of poststructuralism hardly lends itself to freshman teaching. Still, they seek ways to use the insights if not the language of their own ways of thinking about literature. With varying reactions, they discover the difference between the graduate student's endeavor to find something "problematic" in a text, something new to say about it, and the teacher's effort to lead inexperienced students to understand, for instance, that the narrator has an important role in *Paradise Lost*. Exactly what to do about that difference is another matter.

The gap between what literary scholars do on paper and what they do in the classroom, the cognate dilemma about the relation in the graduate curriculum of traditional and innovative course structure and content: these problems surely trouble us all. At Yale we preserve the form without the traditional content of "coverage"; we talk and talk and talk about the problems of teaching. The dream that someone has more satisfactory solutions, no doubt, is what keeps the faculty of every English department I know engaged in unending argument about curricula.

Conceptual Frameworks and Curricular Arrangements: A Response

James F. Slevin
Georgetown University

For reasons that are perfectly understandable, there is one crucial figure not present at this conference on doctoral studies: the doctoral *student*. Since graduate students are present at nearly all our other gatherings, their absence here is an uncommon occurrence. So, in reading the five preceding papers, I have been taken with our ways of representing this absent figure, how we have come to picture this student. As the authors make clear, their not altogether flattering portrait is ultimately a portrait of *our* failure, the failure of the programs of study we have devised. But significantly that failure is regularly figured in the character of the students who enroll in our programs.

With the occasional celebration of graduate students' untutored potential (their intelligence, energy, and commitment to study), here is what we learn about them. Their "ignorance" and "pitifully inadequate intellectual habits" offer "simple evidence that we are performing badly" for they "show scant mastery of the art of careful and respectful interpretation of texts or of rigorous construction of argument" (Booth). They are remarkably "ill-informed" about the profession, primitives who seem familiar only with "myths" about it (Cantor). Like the rest of us, to be sure, they are unable "to master the discourses they need to position literary texts for effective critical scrutiny" (Scholes). And "they don't know a whole lot about the course of English and American literature or literary criticism, ... [having] no thorough acquaintance with canonical texts" (Spacks).

As a way of expressing our frustrations about the condition of our programs, these representations depend on the image of student as victim, and hence perhaps ill-prepared to participate in the process in which we are here engaged. Such an image focuses our problems, evokes sympathy, and so may help to bring about change; but it risks further marginalizing our graduate students, ignoring their desires and subverting their potential to collaborate with us in transforming the profession. What role might they play—while still graduate students—in contemplating and answering the questions that concern us here? How do we provide them with opportunities for such contemplation? What are our responsibilities to them, to the colleges and universities they will serve, and to the profession they will inevitably be called on to lead?

It seems to me that we should bring our dialogue here into our graduate programs, and to that end I will try to open up some curricular space within which our graduate students can learn about and participate in this critique of the profession. I build on Gerald Graff's suggestion that we bring our theoretical disputes into the classroom, but I attend more than he to all we "profess" (not just "literature") and to our professional and not just theoretical debates. I want to develop the programmatic implications of these five papers, recommending a range of graduate course work that sets the English curriculum, scholarship, teaching, and even the graduate program itself in larger professional and theoretical contexts. Each of the courses I propose would make a significant contribution to any graduate program; taken together, they would form a core of advanced courses that would serve very well our doctoral students, their future departments and students, and the profession. My specific proposals can also be read figuratively, as tropes for curricular change that might take other forms. I welcome such alternatives. My ultimate concern is to suggest that, as in part a professional degree program, the PhD curriculum should incorporate formal occasions not just for developing scholarship and improving teaching but for inquiring about the profession of scholarship and teaching and about the institutions in which they occur.

Concern about the rigor, coherence, and scope of the undergraduate curriculum pervades these papers, and a rigorous inquiry into this concern is crucially needed in our doctoral curricula. This inquiry is of theoretical as well as practical interest, and it deserves a forum, like a graduate seminar, for raising questions about the curriculum and its professional, social, and political contexts. Such a seminar, which we might tentatively call The English Curriculum and Its Contexts, would do well to begin with Wayne Booth's insight that our undergraduate programs are in part shaped by the scholarly and pedgaogical training we provide our graduate students. Our students' research, constrained by the pressures of "specialization" and "coverage," does little to prepare them to breathe life into a neglected—dispirited—liberal arts curriculum. And the teaching opportunities we provide (opportunities that come too soon, demand too much, and occur in freshman courses that we have trivialized) only make matters worse. While the graduate seminar I have in mind will in some ways redefine the issues Booth raises, even in departing from his recommendations I am indebted to his vivid portrayal of our current professional circumstances.

A seminar investigating the undergraduate curriculum can begin "at home," then, scrutinizing the graduate training we provide and the teaching opportunities we allow. It would incorporate Booth's proposed "supervised, collegial experience in undergraduate teaching" to broaden the knowledge and inspire the teaching of our graduate students. But at the same time it would raise fundamental questions about the social contexts of undergraduate education. For example, it would explore how the absence of serious beginning courses for all undergraduates might reflect larger, social resistance to the kind of undergraduate education on which Booth rests his proposals for graduate reform. Does society in fact value those with critical discernment enough to support the education that produces them? Is the cry of "back to basics" just, as Booth says, a "silly" translation of what he means by a classical education, or is it, rather, a powerful political movement seeking a technically trained, mentally efficient, but uncritical citizenry? And when, to society's interest in such trainees, we add our universities' very real economic interest in a subordinate, badly paid caste of graduate-student and part-time technical "trainers," how, and exactly by whom, is change going to be made?

In addressing such questions, the seminar will find current theoretical conflicts between the ancients and the moderns, as Booth calls them, of indispensable value and not at all, as Booth seems to suggest, a "distraction" from our responsibility to "mind the liberal arts store." At their core, these conflicts are about the meaning of liberal learning, a meaning that is not and never has been a static, established thing. It has been a site of dialogue about learning and about the institutions of learning, a dialogue that we will genuinely honor by incorporating it into our graduate programs. The seminar would study the history of this dialogue and the forces, inside and outside the academy, now intent on silencing it. As part of such study, theory would help us both to imagine the rigorous undergraduate curriculum we need and to conceptualize the institutional policies and interests that resist it. One contribution of theory, then, Ancient or Mod, and one measure of any theory's validity, would be its power to confront and destabilize that resistance and to assist us in shaping institutional structures that will realize our aims. This course will thereby draw our theoretical unrest directly into the service of curricular transformation and provide an opportunity for new teachers to explore for themselves the contributions they might make to the formation of new educational structures. Among other advantages, a course so open-ended in its inquiries would ensure that the mentoring relationship between senior faculty members and graduate students is not a top-down apprenticeship but, rather, a truly collegial experience. Combining considerations both practical and theoretical, professional and intellectual, we would enable graduate students better to teach themselves, and thus to teach us, about a future that is partly theirs to shape.

Shaping their own futures and the future of undergraduate programs is intimately connected to the scholarly training we provide our graduate students. No one disputes this, and yet the graduate curriculum offers little opportunity for emerging scholars to explore the larger professional implications of their research. Paul Cantor's paper helps us appreciate the need for a seminar that sets scholarship in a larger context. Like Booth (though with a tight focus on the PhD dissertation and not Booth's broader curricular perspective), Cantor bemoans the gap between the teaching positions that new PhDs are likely to find and the research projects encouraged by our graduate programs. He urges that we better prepare our graduate students by helping them shape their dissertations to the requirements and needs of hiring institutions.

Although he does not develop his solution to this problem in great detail, his essay invites us to extend his deliberations. How (beyond the counseling of a prudent placement director) might our graduate programs help students consider in rigorous and informed ways the faculty positions that they will be assuming? Several graduate programs are now offering "dissertation seminars," often at the recommendation and under the leadership of rhetoric and composition specialists. These formal or informal occasions for dissertation writers to gather and discuss their work help to overcome that isolation of the dissertation years that so often delays the degree and impairs the quality of the product. This kind of colloquium would be all the more effective if preceded, during the period of course work, by a seminar that helped students begin early to grapple with the problems facing scholars in our profession.

Such a seminar, which we might title Scholarship and Its Contexts, would explore the professional and pedagogical, as well as the scholarly, implications of the research one plans to undertake. Recent efforts (I am thinking particularly of Graff, Ohmann, Lanham, Lentricchia, Fish) to situate scholarship and teaching within their institutional settings and larger historical contexts provide a solid framework for organizing such a seminar. This seminar could consider the origins of English studies in relation not only to the system of departmental governance but to the norm of specialization and the ideology of professionalism that rationalize it. It could examine historically how specific curricular arrangements were formed and how one's own theoretical inquiry into canonicity, periodization, genre, and authorship can be brought to bear in understanding and reconceiving those formations; how the profession's system of rewards and constraints (research expectations, teaching loads, evaluation procedures – about which graduate students know far too little) will affect students' own commitments to scholarship; how their research will and will not contribute to their teaching, with at least some attention to how their lives as writers can assist their teaching of writing. These hardly exhaust the possible topics of such a seminar; others can easily be imagined. Whatever the specific syllabus, the aim would be to pose those questions that will contextualize research and empower graduate students not as more desirable commodities in a marketplace but, through a critical grasp of their situation, as agents in reconceiving and shaping that situation. In the light of Booth's concerns, the seminar could explore how one might envision a career that unifies rather than atomizes one's scholarly, pedagogical, and professional commitments.

While early scholarly training shapes one's entry into a career in English studies, for most members of the profession – even most of the 28,500 MLA members – it is primarily through teaching that one continues to participate in the life of the discipline. Because most doctoral programs have recently been responsive to these professional choices of their graduates, the last twenty years have witnessed a significant rise in graduate courses designed to prepare teachers. But, lacking the rigor and breadth of other graduate offerings, these courses have generally received only marginal status in departments and frequently bear no graduate credit. The alternative I want to propose, called Teaching and Its Contexts, would resemble these fairly common "teacher-training courses," but it would contextualize teaching and scrutinize it from the perspective of current theoretical controversies. The papers by Robert Scholes and Richard Lloyd-Jones can help us grasp the larger and more rigorous aims of such a seminar.

Scholes's recent work epitomizes the investigation of teaching that such a graduate course could undertake, particularly as Scholes transcends the profession's atomistic tendencies by addressing, together, issues of theory and pedagogy. In the context of his other work, and especially his explorations of how composition research can contribute to both our graduate and undergraduate programs, his remarks here seem incomplete – questionable not for what he has to say but for what he leaves unsaid. At the critical juncture of his essay, when he moves from tracing the exclusionary processes of our discipline's past to addressing the circumstances of the present and needs of the future, he astutely characterizes the situation of current graduate students in two ways: he discusses their "desire" to study more theory and their "need" to be better prepared as teachers of non-literary discourse. In response to their desires, Scholes has much of importance to say, elaborating a program grounded in a wide range of texts and centered in rigorous philosophical scrutiny, a program much like Booth's "liberal arts education" and Lloyd-Jones's "language and literature" curriculum. In response to their needs, he is uncharacteristically silent. Without specifying exactly how it will do so, Scholes simply asserts that his broader and more philosophically rigorous graduate program will improve our reading and writing, hence our teaching of both.

But improved teaching does not necessarily follow from other improvements, no matter how dramatic; what we need rather are programmatic changes that provide occasions for graduate students themselves to relate their theoretical desires to the needs they anticipate, and particularly the kind of teaching responsibilities they will have. For many the teaching of writing will be a primary responsibility. Perhaps Raymond Williams's characterization of current critical trends bears on our graduate curricula as well: "it is significant," he notes, "that the tolerance accorded . . . 'reading-public' studies is usually *not* extended to studies of the economics and politics of writing" (216). The teaching careers that await many of our graduate students suggest the need for precisely those studies – a course that investigates how discourse is produced and that sets its own investigation in historical context.

The course I am advocating here does not simply provide hands-on teacher-training; rather, it considers seriously an expanded definition of our discipline's teaching responsibilities. As composition research has demonstrated, learning to produce critical discourse is not the inevitable consequence of wider or even more perceptive reading alone. The development of students' critical powers depends on how they are taught to write as well as to read, and powerful reading in many ways depends on writing. A graduate seminar preparing teachers to meet this dual responsibility, to integrate the teaching of reading and writing, would therefore want to begin with a broad historical analysis of our discipline. It would expand on Scholes's history of exclusionary acts to consider our abandonment of "rhetoric" not simply as a mode of textual analysis but as a disciplined inquiry into how a writer or speaker constructs discourse and makes its power felt. This revisionist history might trace our ever-narrowing (until recently) concern with reading and with the texts we deem worth reading, to the detriment of our understanding of how those texts, and our own, and our students', come to be and come to be considered worthy of our scrutiny. It would investigate not just methods of teaching writing but the history of writing instruction, including its role in socializing new student populations we have historically taken to calling "remedial." It would draw on the work of other disciplines (psychology, linguistics, and much of contemporary literary theory) as they contribute to our understanding of textual production. And it might even address the current preoccupation of nearly all humanistic disciplines with "discursive practices" by bringing to bear on this question major texts from the rhetorical tradition.

The range and intellectual seriousness of this graduate seminar can be further ensured by heeding the warnings of Richard Lloyd-Jones. His concern with rhetoric and composition programs is of special interest here because they are largely responsible for what improvement there has been in teacher training. Given our clear need to integrate the teaching of reading and writing, Lloyd-Jones raises critical questions about current tendencies in this field, rightly objecting that in recent years it has begun to narrow rather than expand the questions it asks and the courses it certifies. Insisting that the effective preparation of teachers depends on our keeping open the borders among our various fields, he formulates a paradigm for emerging rhetoric and composition programs that could serve as a compelling intellectual foundation for all graduate programs, no matter how diverse their surface forms:

> [Such] programs engage the serious study of how language is generated in speech and writing and include a secondary emphasis on how texts are interpreted. Student writing and literary masterpieces and even oral exchanges are all proper texts of study. In these programs literary criticism is extended into rhetorical criticism and propaganda analysis. These scholars ease into area or cultural studies because they see all language in context. In short, their intellectual concerns are those of a department dealing with English language and literature, even though the package may sometimes appear to be a bit trendy, the examples rather far from the canon, and the politics aggressively democratic.

He laments that this kind of program is "thinly populated," but there is sufficient reason to question such pessimism. Whatever the resistance to this intellectual structure within current institutional policies and practices, many in the
profession (like most members of this panel) now locate their research and teaching
within just such a paradigm.

Perhaps Lloyd-Jones's pessimism can be traced to his excessively modest estimate of the origins and intellectual foundations of rhetoric and composition programs. Since the future of this field, and particularly the possibility of its full
integration within our graduate programs, depends in part on how we conceive
of these origins, it is crucial to question Lloyd-Jones's historical account. His seems
to me an incomplete and blurred picture. By suggesting a gap between these programs' beginnings (depicted as little more than passive, practical responses to open
admissions and other political pressures) and what Lloyd-Jones considers merely
contrived intellectual "rationalizations" that accompanied or soon followed their
institution, his account ignores the serious intellectual concerns that link the recent
renewal of rhetoric and composition studies to coetaneous developments in English studies. Indeed, I would suggest that it was rather the serious theoretical
interest in literary and rhetorical criticism and in cultural studies, not so "trendy"
at the time, that led many directors of TAs, and many secure professors looking
for new challenges, to first take up their interest in composition. It was not solely–I
doubt even primarily–their desire to help out around the department, though
that they did, often contributing in astonishingly beneficial ways. However dim
the curricular and pedagogical implications of the moment of origin, intimations
of such a conceptual framework are what *caused* open admissions and other "aggressively democratic" movements, movements that in turn accompanied not only
the rise of composition but the formation of much of poststructuralist literary
theory. These historical developments are intimately related, and the questions
addressed three decades ago to certain forms of political domination and exclusion were also soon addressed, within our discipline, to forms of intellectual domination and exclusion, though these latter questions have taken longer to find their
way into the *New York Times*. The integrative paradigm that Lloyd-Jones virtually
dismisses as a mere rationalization of rhetoric and composition might more accurately be characterized as a recovery (or rediscovery) of original motives, a working out within the discipline of the implications of earlier, more conspicuously
political and institutional transformational projects. And in doing this intellectual work, the field of rhetoric and composition joins with other critical movements in contributing to the reformulation of graduate programs. Not simply
a vehicle for teacher training but an arena for disciplined inquiry about the aims
of English studies and the meaning of liberal learning, this field merits an important place in a reconceived doctoral curriculum.

Reconceiving the graduate program, as I suggested at the beginning, ought
not to be the work of the faculty only. I am concerned with how we can effectively involve graduate students in the consideration of the graduate curriculum
itself and, through this involvement, in the shaping of their professional goals

and the scrutiny of ours. A new kind of integration for our graduate programs could emerge from this involvement. What I hope for, at least, is a drawing together: of graduate faculty members and students in a shared exploration of issues; and of courses in the graduate program, where coherence, for the time being at least, might derive from a shared *process* of inquiry. That is, our courses, though proceeding inevitably from different and often competing critical perspectives, can be experienced by the graduate student as cohering in their shared commitment to examining their own theoretical, pedagogical, programmatic, and social implications. Patricia Spacks helps us imagine such a graduate program. Her paper examines three of Yale's innovative graduate courses to suggest how at least Yale's curriculum addresses the issues of this conference, issues she describes as the "cognate dilemma[s]" of introducing innovation within a traditional curriculum and of combining the scholarly and pedagogical preparation of PhDs.

As Spacks notes, these courses in themselves provide graduate students with examples for their undergraduate teaching, models for uniting canonical content and innovative approach. What is not made clear about these courses is the extent to which their "exemplary" role can itself become an issue in the course. Each course might all the more effectively resolve what Spacks calls the profession's "uneasy union of concern for teaching and for learning" by incorporating critical reflection on its own pedagogy, its own union of current theory with traditional canon, and its own possibilities and limitations as a model for undergraduate teaching. The course would in effect be turned upon itself to scrutinize its adaptability to undergraduates and (as a stimulating extension of this question) its possible relevance to institutions unlike Yale. To the extent that graduate students in the course could at the same time be experimenting in similar ways in the undergraduate courses they teach, Yale would be developing an exemplary program for teacher preparation.

By becoming an arena for self-conscious, sophisticated inquiry about teaching and learning, each of these courses would engage in specific ways the larger concerns of Yale's "teaching practicum." Described by Spacks as one site of "a continuing debate about the place of contemporary theory in a contemporary undergraduate class," it offers still another example of the kind of graduate course work we need. It provides a place for exploring fundamental connections and conflicts among scholarship, teaching, and the institutional structures they inhabit.

Spacks's argument about tradition and innovation would lend itself nicely to the concerns of such a course, which we might entitle The Graduate Program and Its Contexts. If we could imagine this graduate seminar taking up, as a subject, the very issues that Spacks examines in her paper, and taking these issues up in terms of her examples, we might get a better sense of how such a seminar can prepare doctoral students for the roles they might choose to play in the profession. How might this instance of Yale's "continuing debate" proceed? And what would be its purpose?

The debate would examine and contest the implications of current theory for the traditional curriculum. On one side, we would find a powerful case for conservation. From her presentation of these graduate courses and from her description of the difficulties that graduate students experience when bringing their advanced theoretical interests into their freshman classes, Spacks expresses caution about the pedagogical and curricular effects of radically transforming either the graduate or undergraduate curriculum. It is conceivable, she suggests, that our responsibility in the training of teachers requires the kind of conservative curriculum she describes at Yale, where the focus on canonical texts repairs the incoherence and modernist preoccupations of undergraduate programs and thereby (here she joins with Booth) prepares new teachers to restore breadth to the departments they will eventually join as colleagues. As Spacks presents them, these three courses illustrate and thereby defend a commitment to tradition.

But these same courses can be seen to challenge this fairly conservative conclusion. The other side of the continuing debate could argue that the traditional curriculum these courses inhabit no longer serves as a coherent articulation of the work that goes on in them, so that the very coherence Spacks desires is confounded by the energy of these courses' innovations. That is, graduate students engaged in such a debate would be free to question to what extent the department's traditional curriculum and requirements conflict with and thereby misrepresent the program's intellectual life, at least as it is manifested in these innovative courses. One could argue, for example, that Guillory's traditional course in the pastoral is concerned not simply with "the emergence, regularization, and decline of the pastoral genre" but with "the conditions of possibility governing" that emergence and decline. That seems a different genre of genre course. Homans's course, though generally canonical, "tries to devise appropriate ways of talking about literature and history as mutually constituted." That's literary history as *literary* history, and this seminar, in its existence as a "devising" of discourse, does much more than simply stretch and enlarge the canon. In Spacks's course in the eighteenth-century English novel, students at one point enact the sexual conflicts embedded in *Clarissa*. This enactment is hardly an accident and clearly not based on "immediate [in the sense of unmediated] personal responses." It is, rather, an arranged drama, a text authored jointly by the class and by Spacks herself, and of course by Richardson. These courses, in short, reflect conceptions of genre, history, textuality, and pedagogy that might in fact be in conflict with, and so not in any coherent way integrated within, the traditional conception of English studies articulated by the Yale curriculum.

You will hardly be surprised to learn that I think much can be said for this second line of argument, but it is the debate itself that truly matters. The seminar that enables this debate constitutes a continuing self-study of the graduate program, a study in which graduate students participate. Here they can discuss their graduate education, with particular attention to the relation between current intellectual movements and the department's curricular structures and program requirements. Obviously, such a course contributes in immediate ways to the vitality of the graduate program, but it has long-term benefits as well. It will prepare students to use what they have learned about scholarship and teaching in the reformulation of the departments they will join and the profession we are eventually to entrust to their leadership.

In effect, such a course does nothing more – and nothing less – than bring the aim and process of this conference home to our graduate programs and to the graduate students whose inquiry and choices are ultimately of greater consequence than ours. The seminar I have just envisioned, however constrained by the immediate issues that occasioned it, would be addressing a question that seems to me so central to this conference and the profession that all five of these papers have led us to ask it. Have new and potentially disruptive theoretical perspectives, which ten years ago we kept safely tucked away in "theory" courses, entered so profoundly into the substance and purposes of all our courses as to transform the nature of English studies? When would it be appropriate to conclude – and is it not crucial, if appropriate, to conclude – that the *curricular* structure of a program is only concealing from the unfriendly eyes of others (or from our own anxious, apprehensive eyes) a new *intellectual* structure waiting to find its appropriate institutional form?

In its various forms, this seems to me the question that marks both the crisis and the opportunity of English doctoral programs at this time, and it is the question to which the papers that follow offer responses, if not answers. But the danger is that we will make this exclusively "our" question, a question about graduate programs but not for them, and so a question that will not be formally addressed within our programs, by students as well as faculty members. It is to that danger that this response has been addressed.

Part 2:

The Transition

from Graduate Student

to Faculty Member

Doctoral Studies and the Fine Art of Teaching

Nancy R. Comley
Queens College, City University of New York

I've been asked to examine my doctoral training in relation to what I do now and to try to draw from this review some conclusions about the future of doctoral studies. First, a bit of autobiography is necessary. This is my sixth year as director of the English Composition Program at Queens College. In the academic year 1986–87, this program employed 63 part-time instructors and ran 117 sections of composition in the fall and 97 in the spring. I pursued my graduate education at Brown without a thought of ever holding such a position and without ever having taught a composition course. I was traditionally trained as a literary scholar who respected the text, researched, read, and acknowledged previous scholarship, and took seminars that would fill gaps in my knowledge of English and American literature. Until near the end of my graduate career I was virtually innocent of theory. In the job market of the late seventies, there were many others whose training was just like mine, with one major exception: very few had had the amount and variety of teaching experience that was available to Brown graduate students.

Brown's doctoral program in English offered no courses in pedagogy, but it did offer diverse opportunities for on-the-job training. Starting in the second year, we were assigned one course a semester (the pay was minimal, but tuition remission was included). One could assist as section leader in large literature or film courses; or teach a self-designed section of introductory courses in the novel, poetry, or drama; or design a freshman seminar in a particular mode of thought. One could also be assigned to a composition section, and I was very happy not to have been, since teaching methods were prescribed, and formulaic, and students were assumed not to be among the best and brightest. In literature courses, supervision of teaching assistants was of the benign kind; help was always available if we asked for it, but we were allowed to make mistakes because it was

assumed we'd learn from them. And we did, largely because everyone took teaching seriously, both students and faculty members.

Because of such respect, teaching at Brown was a pleasure. After an apprenticeship in the course Comedy and Laughter, I taught introductory sections of
the novel, mass communications, and, my favorite, poetry. However, the closer
I got to the end of my graduate studies, the more I realized (thanks to the MLA
job list) that my teaching responsibilities at most other institutions would probably include composition. Just how I would go about teaching it was not clear
to me until the semester when I participated in an NEH experiment in which
a semester's reading in the introductory poetry course was fed into a computer.
Students responded to the reading online, and each one produced about eighty
pages of writing during the semester. Not only had their ability to read poetry
improved, but so had their writing. The instructors had provided frequent feed-
back, directed solely to content. I had not known before how best to use writing
in literature courses and had proceeded in the usual way, doing what was done
to me, requiring a short paper and a final paper, and then being uncomfortably
aware that some students were not keeping up with the reading because they
weren't being asked to respond to it in writing. I didn't quite have a conversion
experience at that time, but I did begin to educate myself in writing theory and
pedagogy. I now saw that writing was a major element in teaching. The usual
term paper assumed much less importance, for it was only one practice in a repertoire of writing that would enable students to enter literary texts to find out how
they work, to practice making one themselves, and only then to appreciate or
criticize the professional's text. Once I discovered what intertextuality was and
how to use it, it was a relatively simple step from there to devise writing approaches to almost any kinds of texts. On the job market, however, it was my
work with literature and composition, and the fact that my publications were
in literature as well as composition, that made me, as they say, a viable candidate.

Nowadays, graduate students still enter doctoral studies with a "romantic vision of writing and solitary research," to quote a graduate assistant currently teaching composition at Queens, and with a vision of teaching as teaching the literary
works they love best to groups of entranced students. Ideally, doctoral programs
should enable students to spend much of their time in reading, research, and writing. That vision of "solitary research" should be part of the reality of one's graduate experience; as a vision, it reappears regularly in later years as one works toward
a sabbatical. The early vision of teaching is that of presenting what one loves
to an ideal audience; in practice, one retains the love and learns the art of cul-
tivating the ideal audience: students who are responsive as well as receptive. Doctoral programs should be as responsible for the nurturing and development of
the art of teaching as they are for the cultivation of scholarship. Such responsibility should involve the entire graduate faculty, if not in the sense of active (or
even benign) supervision of new teachers, at least in an awareness of their own
teaching, its theory and practice, and its politics.

Graduate faculty members are usually appointed because of their scholarly achievements; these confer prestige to a graduate program. Where teaching is concerned, some view their appointments as safe berths, a release from teaching, an opportunity to relax and tell anecdotes and to send the graduate students out to do the real work of the seminar. The best graduate teachers are no different from the best undergraduate teachers in their enthusiasm for their subjects, and the rigor with which they run the course is indicative of their desire that students function actively, not as mere containers for the professor's distribution of nuggets of knowledge. At the very least, then, a graduate faculty should provide models of effective teaching styles. In so doing they impart their respect for teaching as an art. Far better if, in addition, members of the graduate faculty function as supervisors or resource persons for graduate students' teaching responsibilities. This was my own experience as a graduate student. Now let me move on to more problematical scenes.

At too many institutions, graduate students function as the major source of cheap labor for the staffing of freshman composition sections. The better composition programs train and supervise new teachers through such means as seminars, workshops, and observations. Some programs, unfortunately, do little or nothing, leaving graduate assistants to infer that teaching – especially the teaching of composition – is a lonely and demoralizing occupation. The issue here is that when teacher training is foisted off on undergraduate programs, it is theoretically divorced from graduate studies. I am speaking of traditional graduate studies in English, and not of composition or rhetoric graduate programs, where the teaching of writing is integrated into one's graduate work. For, as may be obvious by now, the issue of teacher training and respect for teaching are closely related to the issue of the composition-literature gap. And is there a bridge in our future?

I like to think I see the future of doctoral studies in English (and comparative literature, for that matter) in the graduate students I've been working with in the Queens College composition program and in a seminar called The Teaching of College English. The burgeoning interest in theory has enabled these new teachers to see the connections between composition theory and literary and cultural theory and their practical applications in the classroom. While these students may not agree with Derrida's excessive privileging of writing, the current theoretical emphasis on the act and scene of writing and of reading as the production of texts works well with composition's emphasis on writing and reading as processes. Thus these new teachers see writing as far more than the ability to construct mechanically and syntactically correct sentences and paragraphs. They are learning how to interpret student writing with the same care they devote to literary texts, reading their students' work as writing in progress and not judging it as malformed artifacts of academic discourse. They see writing as the stimulation of thought and as a form of empowerment for students, an initiation into academic discourse. Reading Foucault was part of this lesson; reading David Bartholomae and Anthony Petrosky's *Facts, Artifacts, and Counterfacts,* a detailed account of a basic writing program, was another part. It is through theory, then, that these graduate students link their graduate studies and their teaching.

Taken together, the lessons of composition theory and literary theory have the force not only to change the way we teach, the way we think about teaching, and, possibly, even the nature of English departments. Such theory, in embracing the extraliterary as well as the literary, also moves writers and readers into a realm quite different from "pure" English studies, a realm of textuality where the literary text is but one part of the spectrum of textuality. The spectrum is also called rhetoric, and the future of doctoral studies in English lies, I think, in its redefining.

Welcome to Paradise!

Geoffrey Green
San Francisco State University

"Welcome to Paradise!" intones the university administrator. You are in the portico of the library of your new institution of higher learning, attending your first official university event as a full-time tenure-track assistant professor of English: the reception for new faculty members in the humanities. The ambience reflects an academic social occasion: among the autumn trees are tables of assorted fruits and appetizers and a seemingly limitless supply of wine and beverages. For the season, the afternoon is extraordinarily hot – everyone is perspiring – and the sun, to your heat-addled sensibility, appears to be expanding. It is the fall semester of the new academic year, and you have arrived at a town or city that may be unfamiliar to you, at a reception among visibly uncomfortable people – all smiling conspicuously – all looking similarly self-congratulatory at their good fortune. Paradise! As you examine this scene, perhaps the lines from Milton occur to you: "The mind is its own place, and in itself / Can make a Heav'n of Hell, a Hell of Heav'n."

You are eager to attend this event since you have hardly spoken to any of your colleagues for more than a few minutes, although you have been teaching your courses for several weeks. After the mandatory formal introductions, the conversation immediately turns to athletics – or, perhaps, finances. When one new recruit confesses that he knows and cares nothing about any form of athletics, the dean of humanities replies, "I think you had better learn quickly." There is a bright smile on his face, but there is nothing comic about the comment: an ever-present reality at your institution is the link between administrative budgetary largess and the fortunes of the home teams. At your next reception, you happen to hear that new recruit's revised comment to the dean: "What a performance by the home team!" He is learning, and so are you.

You have been summoned to paradise by either a voice on the telephone or a document, a letter informing you of your new appointment as a tenure-track assistant professor for the next academic year. Your first meeting with the chair of your department concerns your office assignment, or, perhaps, your keys, or the documents that await your signature in the personnel office. A subsequent meeting may concern the book list for one of your new courses, a literature course for general education students. During the summer, the chair may have written you that the students you will face shortly are unsophisticated readers who are taking the class to fulfill academic requirements. The problem with your book list is that it contains, in addition to established canonical authors, several other authors that have not been fully accepted within the canon and are viewed with some skepticism by your chair. Should these relatively inexperienced readers be exposed to such esoteric authors when author X might be more suitable? And is it appropriate for your students to be studying authors not yet admitted to the canon in what might well be their only literature course? Your chair does not seem to be intending to pressure your choice of texts. Your chair is an engaging individual who has had more experience than you in teaching this course. But it is true that the curriculum at your new institution has been characterized (by one waggish colleague) as consisting of "introductory, intermediate, and advanced survey courses." To state it more moderately, periodicity is the backbone of the course offerings. (Indeed, one of the chaired professors has proposed at a meeting that there ought to be a second level of graduate survey courses, one to present the primary texts, the second to consider the same texts in the light of literary criticism.) Authors such as those you have selected are thought to be more appropriate for English majors who might focus on them as examples of literature falling within a specific period. You decline, with thanks, your chair's well-intentioned suggestion – that you substitute more mainstream authors – but your reasons highlight the difference between your graduate education and your current professional situation.

As a doctoral candidate at your graduate school, you have had stimulating late-afternoon discussions with your instructors about Foucault and Derrida. The English department you attended as a graduate student contained a large and varied assortment of specialties and theoretical approaches to literature. In addition to its core offerings, the department encompassed smaller programs devoted to literary theory and a host of interdisciplinary courses of study.

(To be fair, let us stipulate that the situation might well be the other way around: your graduate school's emphasis might have been on canonical authors and its courses organized entirely on the basis of periodicity. At your new institution, the talk is not of Henry James and Jane Austen but of names you don't recognize, such as Jean-François Lyotard and Julia Kristeva. In either case, the sense of perplexity and cognitive dissonance is equivalent.)

You have been hired at your new institution as a generalist with a particular field of literary specialty. Yet immediately, you are asked to teach a course in English literature that is outside your field and a course within your field that contains an implied preference for canonical texts. As a result of the period emphasis of the course offerings, you may be impelled to design several new courses – to the great astonishment of your older colleagues.

A genuine surprise for you is how little the members of your new English department actually converse about literature or even teaching. Various committee tasks, tricks to arrive at a more convenient schedule, methods to deal with the school bookstore are more typical subjects of conversation. Or else, colleagues might discuss real estate, interest rates, vacations in Europe, fine dining, grants and sabbaticals, or the latest offerings in music, theater, and cinema. At your graduate school, from your graduate student's perspective, you had the impression that the often public intellectual disagreements were a veneer that covered a fundamental collegiality. At your new institution, from your assistant professor's perspective, the situation seems precisely the opposite: there are no public disagreements whatsoever (at first), nor is there much intellectual interaction. Everything is warm, cordial, and correct. Beneath this veneer, however, there may lurk a fundamental and widespread antipathy, a resentment among colleagues about rank, salary, treatment, policy, and privilege.

At the core of your department's ill feeling is the rivalry between the full and chaired professors (whose prolific publication records have enabled them to be hired at the senior rank) and the associate professors (most of whom have been at the university for a longer duration and who perceive their expertise as teaching). The tension comes to the fore annually with the ritual of assessing and assigning each department member's merit salary increase. Contributions are evaluated in regard to scholarship, teaching, and administration.

As an assistant professor, you are caught in the middle of this process. You are expected to achieve a standard of teaching excellence on a par with the very best associate professors *and* publish scholarly work that compares well with that of the full and endowed professors. If there is one aspect of professional life at your new institution for which you are inadequately prepared, it is the intensity with which the evaluation and retention proceedings are initiated – almost from the moment you arrive on the campus. As a new PhD, you tended to cultivate a vaguely self-congratulatory air of accomplishment. This sense is destroyed instantly as the merit, evaluation, and tenure machine calls out for data: what are your student-evaluation computer totals? what were your class visitations like? how many articles have you published? what? none yet? you're almost up for first year review! get on the stick!

Although new assistant professors at your institution are hired on a tenure-track line, you feel as if you were hired on a single-year contract with some possibility of renewal. The attitude of your department might be characterized as follows: if a mistake has been made in hiring a junior scholar, it will be rectified during evaluation proceedings – after all, there are lots of fish in the sea. With evaluation time at many professional journals now ranging from some six months to a year and the publication delay often another year, beginning scholars at institutions such as yours are in a quandary: how to do your best work and yet publish as prolifically and speedily as possible? With credit toward salary increases issued on the basis of completed work, new assistant professors like you are often in a permanent financial slump: for the first three years of your employment, your university raises the starting salary for first-year assistant professors beyond the amount assigned to second- and third-year faculty members through merit salary increases. This necessitates elaborate appeals to your dean under severe time restrictions in which you request a reconsideration of your meritorious service to reflect a somewhat higher dollar total.

Or else, the tension in your department may occur as a matter of ill feeling over previous tenure decisions, or hiring policy, or allocation of research funding, or vested procedures for organizing a curriculum, or the election of a new chair. In any case, as a new assistant professor you are pressured to become involved, pressured in ways that were not covered during your graduate education. The subtle pressure often takes the form of a vague insinuation that by doing/supporting/favoring X (as opposed to Y), you might improve your chances for tenure.

There are several points that I might draw from these generalized, hypothetical experiences. I would recommend that job-seeking graduate students receive some guidance so as to be able to inquire more knowledgeably about the tenure policy of their prospective institutions. Given the state of our job market, the likelihood of a newly hired graduate declining a tenure-track position on the basis of this information would be nil, but at least the shock to the system might be diminished. In the essays "Emotional Problems of Graduate Education" and "The Graduate Years: What Kind of Passage?" Peter Loewenberg describes the role conflict of the graduate student: being an apprentice/adolescent in relation to one's professors while being simultaneously a professional/adult in relation to one's freshmen students (48–66). It is important for us to take a hard look at hiring practices for junior faculty members. If we hire with seriousness, with rigor, and with a sense of purpose, then we owe it to our young professors to treat them as full members of the profession as opposed to prolonging their period of apprenticeship. Newly hired tenure-track faculty members deserve the feeling that their departments have a certain degree of confidence in their abilities to engage in research and to publish their results. A tenure-track appointment is no guarantee of promotion, naturally, but we ought to be wary of the extent to which our newly hired assistant professors may, on occasion, be used to revitalize departments and then disposed of, in favor of a still newer youth movement. Loewenberg, in his "Love and Hate in the Academy" (67–80), emphasizes the unconscious psychological transferences that occur in faculty relations; to minimize the effect of these inappropriate interactions, the transition from graduate student to faculty member ought to be achieved in accordance with clear and delineated expectations.

Graduate students need to appreciate the political implications of the canon: organizing a course, opting for a particular book list, even declaring a specialty are tantamount to favoring one mode of thought and repudiating another. Regardless of our intention, when we include writer X in a course of a set number of weeks, another writer Y must be excluded. Graduate students need to be aware of the reasons for such choices and to take responsibility for those decisions. Even the advocacy of an open canon is likely to be resisted by those future colleagues who view such a position as a threat to the concept of thorough curricular coverage of literary periods.

Similarly, the graduate student must recognize that the selection of a critical methodology affects one's identity in the profession as well as indicating one's approach to texts. All too often an instructor will expound on the virtues of a particular stance without sharing its liabilities. I believe that an open and flexible curriculum ought to be accompanied by rigorous standards of qualification: in this way, one hopes that the graduate student will actively participate in his or her education. The future of our graduate students depends on their awareness of the profession from the onset of their graduate study.

Finally, it is important to remember our shared endeavor: we all work with graduate students, and we were all graduate students at one time. Our love of literature, our sense of ourselves as being a part of the unfolding of the interpretive interactions in time bring us together as members of this profession. As fellow readers and writers of texts, let us welcome our newly hired junior faculty members not to a particular institutional paradise but (in Milton's words) to "a paradise within thee, happier far."

Advancement in Learning

Jeffrey Spear
New York University

Life you make
A whole lot of fools
'Cause you're always teaching something
That they never teach in schools.
Julius Dixon and Henry Glover, *Love, Life and Money*

Even as I agreed to provide my perspective on the transition from graduate student to faculty member, I heard a Ginsbergian voice declaiming, "I saw the best minds of my generation go into business." As a seventies PhD still in the life, I have something of a survivor's complex. I was encouraged to pursue graduate education by the offer of a National Defense Education Act Fellowship – *requiescat in pace* – at a time when the Ford Foundation was offering money to departments that would cut the doctoral program back to a guaranteed three years; when college presidents were calling for a national placement service to ration a shortage of PhDs; when the five-year projectors were saying that "salaries will continue to go up. As with the Loch Ness monster, there seems to be no end in sight"– and that the number of PhDs for the classroom, "despite vastly increasing enrollment in graduate schools, will continue to plummet" (Ness 145).

I entered graduate school quite naive about what precisely professors did to obtain employment and tenure. While my fondness for literature and the researching of things past had led me into graduate study, my distaste for any of the apparent alternatives society offered was as strong a factor, and I spoke with more confidence about how the government ought to behave itself at home and abroad than on how I proposed to sustain myself and family. In 1969, two years after those "bleak" tidings I cited about a shortage of professors generating ever higher pay were presented to the National Conference on Higher Education, disappointed graduate students returned from the Denver MLA meeting blaming the failure of many departments to recruit there on geography. Things would be better next year in New York, they said, leafing through the slender sheaf of flyers advertising for positions that someone had tagged the Book of Job.

But the Carnegie Commission report *Demand and Supply in U.S. Higher Education* soon told us what was really going on with "the American stock of degreed manpower and womanpower":

> The dynamics of demand and supply in higher education are influenced by two significant features of the technology of education: (1) the "durability" of the faculty, who form an important part of the capital stock of institutions of higher education, and (2) . . . the great length of time it takes to produce new faculty. . . . It typically takes more than 20 years to produce a new faculty member with the Ph.D. degree, and that faculty member may last for 40 years on the job.
>
> . . . Durability of the faculty member has the consequence that fluctuations in the *time rate of change* of the demand for total faculty (i.e. the demand for faculty *stock*) can cause significant fluctuations in the level of demand for *new* faculty. . . . A decline in the rate of increase of the demand for faculty stock will cause an absolute decline in the demand for new faculty with the Ph.D.–or possibly even a negative demand. On the other hand, the recent prolonged expansion of higher education has generated an increasing flow of students who aspire to a Ph.D. degree and who have expectation of obtaining academic positions. (Radner et al. 351)

In other words, as we waxed, jobs waned.

I made the transition from graduate school to faculty member because I was lucky enough to beat the odds. Win or lose, individual pieces of degreed "stock" experience the statistics of negative demand as circumstances. I happened to apply to Princeton when it was expanding its junior faculty to accommodate the recent admission of women, when new rules required searches to be truly national as well as representative in other ways, and, most important, when its chairman was a Victorianist with a lively interest in Ruskin, the subject of my dissertation. As so often happens, it is as much the knowledge of the interviewer as that of the interviewee that allows the candidate to shine. To be sure, I knew Ruskin's work and was conversant with almost everything ever written about him, but many of my equally competent peers in the "lost generation" of scholars never had the chance to demonstrate their skills.

As I look back on my time as an assistant professor, it is again the structure of things rather than any feature of my training that stands out. True, I had not been particularly encouraged to publish and participate in academic conferences as a graduate student, and I had little idea of how important not teaching (that is to say, leave time) is to a secure career in education; but these are not deep mysteries, and current job applications suggest that encouragement to publish at least is being given most everywhere. That most of my colleagues came from Ivy League schools, had, as often as not, stopped off at Oxford or Cambridge for an MA, and had an article in print before arriving at Princeton was less significant than the network of professional connections most of them had established along the way–something it took me three or four years to acquire and without which such things as grant applications look rather forlorn.

Institutions like Princeton had jobs through the lean years of the seventies because they turn over most of their junior faculty. Tenure slots are predetermined, often filled at the senior level, and only under the most extraordinary circumstances are new slots created to retain a particular individual. Of the seven of us swimming under a single precut hole in the ice, one made it through to tenure, two now teach at regional colleges. One, despite a book published by Yale University Press and articles in *Shakespeare Quarterly* and the like, is now an attorney; another, despite his edition of the Cornell Wordsworth and favorable reviews of his book on the poet, is now a financial analyst. One, at last report, is not working outside the home. Were it not for the offer of a year as a visiting professor at Columbia, I would now be managing a trucking company in Seattle.

I currently direct the Expository Writing Program at New York University. Did my graduate school prepare me for that? Yes, in that I taught writing at Minnesota for several years in a program in which the graduate students had a considerable voice–though I left just as a genuine faculty and real training in the field were being established. Yes, in that such experience was unusual at Princeton so that I was asked, as three-year-renewal time approached, to direct the department's one genuine composition course for a couple of years. Yes, in that what New York University wanted in 1983, for reasons peculiar to that moment in its history, was not a person specifically trained as a composition specialist but a tenurable literary person with enough competence in composition to direct the Expository Writing Program–preferably someone qualified to teach Victorian literature at the graduate level.

Looking back on my advancement in learning, with its odd blending of what I hoped to do, what I proved capable of doing, and what circumstances have allowed me, I feel no urge to promote or disparage a curriculum that has in any case changed since I left Minnesota more than a decade ago. My experience has been that no program, no set of courses, can outsmart the market or ensure that candidate X will fit job Y (assuming that there is a job Y to be had). There are too many variables–not to mention mere caprice. I have the advantages and disadvantages of traditional, historical training with full minor, but even in graduate school much of what I learned was not in the catalog. We are all engaged in extending our educations, and I never found myself wishing I had been schooled differently or feeling unprepared for a challenge except, perhaps, in academic administration, and there were no courses in that.

Administration even more than teaching makes us aware of the structural pressures and constraints under which we operate and how thoroughly we are bound by the world of getting and spending. As academics we may not do what we do for money, but it can't be done without it. I suspect that most of us as individuals and particularly as administrators spend more time than we would care to admit thinking about where money can be had within or without our institutions and how closely what we want to fund can be made to match the proclaimed criteria for getting the funding. This may not be our profession, but it is part of being a professional. Even in a university it is remarkable how rapidly the intellectual rationale for a proposal can become "merely academic" outside one's department. My contact with graduate students suggests that it is the extracurricular, structural aspects of the profession – our functioning in the world and the forces that make or constrain career opportunities in different specialties – about which they are most naive. (The more professionally aware graduate students often prove to have academic parents. The expansion of faculties in the fifties and early sixties has now produced a cohort of students distinct enough that, on my daughter's undergraduate campus at least, "fac brats" claim they can recognize one another across a crowded room.)

The tension between individual desires and professional circumstances is perpetual. I am not suggesting that the future of doctoral studies lies in substituting the Pragmatics of Professionalism or *Différance* in the Committee Room for the traditional bibliography or methods course. I wish rather to move beyond the pattern of desires and constraints that shaped my career to consider some of the forces and structures that shape the context of this conference.

The differences within the profession of English that might in some measure be mediated by curricular reform are clear enough from the inside. More than a decade of lean years for the English major and scant demand for literature professors has increased the percentage of faculty members teaching writing and spurred the emergence of composition as a graduate teaching and research field. But the nature of that research and its focus on student writing has often met resistance within departments of English, particularly where the New Criticism's disjunction between poetics and rhetoric remains even implicitly a methodological premise. In this same period, poststructuralist critiques together with feminism in a variety of critical guises reopened such basic questions of literacy as What happens when we read? Is the locus of meaning in the text or the reader? Is the gender of the writer or the reader an accidental or essential factor in the generation of meaning? On what grounds do we privilege one text or reading over another? Is Literature itself the creation of Curriculum and Criticism in the service of ideology?

Given the notorious longevity of faculty stock to which I have already referred, the administrative response to the many and conflicting voices of contemporary criticism has generally been to secure one of each behind an office door as vacancies occur. The consequent curricular confusions are summed up in the now notorious student question: "Is there a text in this class?" At issue are the basics, the very name and nature of "English," and the debate will not be confined to departments or the profession.

The MLA convened its conference on the future of doctoral studies at a time when the president and some of his men, particularly Secretary of Education William Bennett, were making regular pronouncements on curricular matters. Like *A Nation at Risk* before it, Bennett's NEH report *To Reclaim a Legacy* has in-

spired both professional grumbling and paragraphs in the latest university grant
proposals dedicated to restoring the humanities to that good eminence from which
many shades of political opinion would agree they have fallen. I don't want to
belabor the question of whether it was the new careerism of the students or bad
teaching of a "bazaar" curriculum and pandering to student opinion by the
products of our graduate schools that led to the decline in humanities enrollments
that in turn exacerbated the bad job market of the recent past. Such an either/or
proposition manifesting the will to blame is itself dubious, and the report's citations denigrating current pedagogy come down to the claim that my anecdotes
can lick your anecdotes. I'll settle for a pop quiz. Given the present state of American undergraduate education, select the most plausible ending to the following
sentence: I am choosing a major in business rather than the humanities because
(A) My English professor keeps asking what I think about the assigned readings;
(B) I might graduate without reading Aristotle; (C) I will graduate $40,000.00
in debt.

To Reclaim a Legacy is the fifties revival in academic garb. The repressive days
of my childhood were, it seems, the halcyon days in the teaching of the humanities before, as Bennett has it, the teaching of skills like critical thinking came
into vogue and "the desired ends of education changed from knowledge to inquiry" (20). Despite rather more subtle points made by some members of the
NEH commission and others quoted in the report, the emphasis is back to the
basics in a finer tone. Humanistic knowledge comes down to great books, supplemented by great paintings and great musical scores, embodying great souls,
whose great ideas will be implanted into grateful students (albeit from ever more
greatly diversified backgrounds) by enthusiastic but entirely objective professors
untainted by ideology who doff their prejudices when they don their teaching
robes. In like manner, these objective, but nonetheless impassioned, teachers for-
bid students to "chew over their feelings, emote, or rehash their opinions" (8).
This vision of passive literacy is of course non-ideological, though some might
say that a defining feature of ideology is that it is invisible from the inside.[1] Iron-
ically enough, while Bennett implicitly blames the decline of the humanities
on a 1960s mentality, the statistical high point from which he dates the decline
is 1970. Given the collapse of the job market, it seems that at the college level
at least, the heroes who taught humanities to increasing numbers and the goats
who gave away the store are pretty much the same people under different
circumstances.

The Bennett report denounces "relativism" without any acknowledgement
of the intellectual trends that have undermined the Arnoldian foundations of the
traditional humanities curriculum. While the same cannot be said of the best-
selling works by academics that have followed in its wake, Allan Bloom's *Closing
of the American Mind* and E. D. Hirsch, Jr.'s *Cultural Literacy*, these books resemble
To Reclaim a Legacy both in holding the educational system largely responsible
for a decline in literacy and in looking, with differing degrees of hope, to schools
to repair the cultural deficiencies of modern students. The very assumption that

schools should teach rather than enrich what the authors call culture suggests that American society has already marginalized it. The "deficient" students who most concern Bloom and Hirsch are not products of minority culture. They are children of the students who went to college in Bennett's good old days but nonetheless grew up with lots of television and very few books. They are a generation for whom rock music, in which Bloom hears a barbaric appeal to sexual desire that "ruins the imagination of young people and makes it very difficult for them to have a passionate relationship to the art and thought that are the substance of liberal education" (79), is as likely to be a link between the generations as a sign of rebellion.

The most publicized feature of *Cultural Literacy* is Hirsch's sixty-three-page list of "what literate Americans know," representing in provisional short form the "few hundred pages of information [that] stand between the literate and the illiterate" (143). Literate Americans, it seems, know Manet, but not Monet; Constable, not Turner; they know penis and vagina, but neither vulva nor clitoris; they know nymphomania, not rape; abortion, not orgasm; MIRV, not AIDS; and potato famine, Irish, but neither homeless nor hungry, American. The Black Panthers, among others, appear in the text, but not on the list. This is a game anyone can play. Indeed, the very ease with which this list can be shown to be incomplete or biased suggests that something is wrong here that can't be corrected by reactive revision or the sale of dehydrated encyclopedias as dictionaries of cultural literacy. The tree of culture is being conjured from the leaves down rather than grown from the seed up.[2]

I am not here defending American education against all the strictures of Bloom and Hirsch, which would be to deny things my own children have suffered through. My point is that just as my career was bent and altered by forces that had nothing to do with what I proposed to study and write about, the entire educational system is part and parcel of the larger culture. It is shaped by factors as crude as the translation of values into funding and as various as the fact that the teachers and administrators of the system are themselves products of our culture and not simply of its schools. Commerce with the mighty dead and the contemplation of transcendental values cannot remove the humanities from historical contingency or produce objective teaching (as opposed to teaching that at least aspires to ideological self-awareness).[3]

I conclude with three points for discussion concerning graduate curricula derived from my remarks about context and from my experience as a teacher of literature and the administrator of a writing program.

1. It is clear from the MLA survey of doctoral programs that in contrast to writing programs, the education of graduate students as teachers of literature is receiving little attention. Though such training was certainly not a feature of Secretary Bennett's golden age of the humanities, I would have no hesitation in citing *To Reclaim a Legacy* in arguing that my school should find ways of incorporating such training into the curriculum directly or as part of any provision of teaching assistantships, with particular attention to the ways in which writ-

ing can enable more critically aware reading. Such training has become more urgent as a practical matter, since university students *are* coming from ever more diverse backgrounds, and as a response to contemporary critical theories that suggest the importance of starting interpretation with the reader's understanding of the text. In addition, the rise of theory as a field in its own right also increases the potential gap between how the graduate student is trained and what the new assistant professor is likely to be required to teach.

2. The business of "the Decline and Fall Off," as Silas Wegg would put it, may seem clear to outsiders counting numbers and to those in the profession, polemically dubbed "antiprofessional" by Stanley Fish ("Profession Despise Thyself") who see the diversification in study areas and critical approaches as the loss of a central tradition of literary study and a consequent trivialization and marginalization of the humanities. Looking at recent trends in the humanities and social sciences generally, however, the English department's concern with text seems to be everywhere. Philosophers like Richard Rorty are arguing that "textualism" converts writing in all fields into literary genres. Psychologists as distinguished as Jerome Bruner are saying that "like Clifford Geertz and Michelle Rosaldo, I think of the Self as a text about how one is situated with respect to others and toward the world–a canonical text about powers, skills and dispositions that change as one's situations change from young to old, from one kind of setting to another" (130).

Bruce Robbins argues that far from declining, "the profession is making new claims for itself, staking out new territory" (8). In theory the study of language and literature is becoming once again the core of the liberal arts, though in a very different manner than that imagined by William Bennett. The rub is that the theory places no limit to what in practice the Teufelsdröckhian Professor of Textuality might be expected to know. This interest in all forms of text does, however, provide the potential for a common discourse linking the various and sometimes contending branches of our profession from composition to criticism to editing. There is always a risk that graduate students might learn only about intertextuality without mastering texts to connect, and this is a tension that curriculum might mediate. There may be some disputes over turf, but I don't think we should shy away from the cross-disciplinary or cultural-studies aspects of textualism, which, as Robert Scholes's brief history of the profession reminds us, only restores in a new mode territory we abandoned earlier in the century in pursuit of belles lettres.

3. In recent years, willy-nilly, we have found ourselves educating many people for jobs that do not exist. In response we have evolved placement procedures that reach beyond the academy and a corresponding interest in reading and writing in the broader world. While the prospects for new hiring in English and American literature held out by the MLA survey of departments are more than welcome, the rekindling of hope is already producing a new wave of applications to graduate school, even from people who have already entered other professions. I now have young attorneys applying to teach in my program for tuition remission and

$7,000 a year. We will continue, I think, to train people who for one reason or another do not become faculty members. Far from abandoning the tenuous links we have developed with the world beyond the academy, we should keep them in mind as we evolve new curricula. There has been talk at this conference about the "death of coverage." If the new curricular focus is the study of reading, writing, and textuality, providing—to borrow a colleague's favorite term—"metacognition," academic training in English can do more for people who do not or cannot work in the profession than immersion in traditional genre or period study could ever do. It can bring into the general culture powerful tools of analysis and critique that supplement the aesthetic and historical awareness that outside the academy almost necessarily becomes private appreciation and cultural consumption.

While we may seem to debate the future of doctoral studies in professional isolation, we are in fact playing a role in a broad and politically charged reconsideration of education and curriculum at all levels of schooling. The outcome of this debate will influence both the climate in which our institutions operate and, practically, the kinds of projects and reforms in the humanities that are apt to be funded. Reduced to simplest terms, that wider controversy poses a question at least as old as Plato's *Meno*: Is education at root a drawing out or a jamming in?

Notes

[1]In this context it is noteworthy that the Study Group, an officially constituted NEH body, was balanced with some care. The thirty-one members represented a wide range of schools and one newspaper. There were nine women and at least one black and one Hispanic male. When authorities are invoked within the report, however, at least twenty-eight men, living and dead, are cited, some several times, but only four women, all members of the Study Group itself. A humanities sequence built on the sample list of authors and documents Bennett provides would feature the Bible, thirty-five works by white males, two by women, and a few pages of Martin Luther King, Jr.

[2]My disagreement with Hirsch centers on his use of schema theory, the contention that as we read, through a process below consciousness, we bring to mind contexts and instances that make sense of the words. Reading is thus an interactive process and not simply a decoding of incoming data. Each individual from the dawn of consciousness constructs a set of references that can eventually be enlarged by formal education. Schema theory suggests, to me, that the scholastic implantation of lists in the attempt to bring individuals into "mainstream" culture will not take very well and that we will be far more successful if we foster development outward from the cultural situation the student brings to school.

[3]For a consideration of theory, ideology, pedagogy, and the restructuring of English, see Widdowson; for discussions of gender and literacy see Flynn and Schweickart; for the postulation of a feminine space outside the master narratives of the dominant sex-gender system and reactive reconstructions of it, see de Lauretis.

The Informal Curriculum

Susan Wolfson
Rutgers University

In her letter of 15 October 1986, Phyllis Franklin, on behalf of the MLA Commission on Writing and Literature, invited me to serve on a conference panel "charged with describing the transition from graduate study to faculty status." I was asked to speak specifically about the ways the graduate school curriculum at Berkeley did or did not prepare me for what I am now doing as a literary critic and as an associate professor of English at Rutgers University in New Brunswick. The commission wanted me to "identify courses that helped, courses that were supposed to help but did not, and courses that might have helped had they been offered." More generally, I was asked to comment on the assumptions relevant to that curriculum implied by the available programs.

As I was preparing this assignment, I was unaware that the commission had given the conference in Wayzata a specific agenda for discussion: the reorientation of doctoral curricula away from traditional coverage of literary history and toward the study of rhetoric – broadly conceived as an interdisciplinary subject focused on discursive structures, cultural codes, and signifying practices – and the value of this reorientation in synthesizing graduate course work with undergraduate curricula and pedagogy. The commission's enthusiasm for this agenda derived, in large part (I was to discover at the conference), from a pervasive feeling that "coverage" was an impossible goal, that the methods of achieving it were dubious, and, most important, that the study of rhetoric under discussion promised greater relevance in preparing graduate students for careers in undergraduate education. As challenging and provocative as this subject proved to be for the chairs and associate chairs of graduate study at the conference, all of whom were tenured and none of whom was tenured recently, I confess that I was struck not only by how little this issue had occupied my own reflections of my transition from graduate student to full-time faculty status but also by the fact that none of the several assistant professors whom I interviewed in preparing my paper for the conference mentioned it at all. The issues that we discussed were of a

decidedly practical rather than theoretical bent. My paper may thus seem anom-
alous in relation to the recommendations animating the other papers and reports
in this volume, but I believe that anomaly itself is compelling–in no small part
because assistant professors were not included in the conference. Indeed my advancement to tenure in 1984 marked me as one of the most "junior" attendees.
The conference organizers, I realize, made a conscious and caring decision not
to invite untenured professors, thus sparing them the possible consequences of
having spoken their minds on controversial issues while their situation in the
profession was still unsecured; but the absence of their voices produced certain
disadvantages of perspective that I hope my report may redress.

Let me begin with the first item Phyllis Franklin asked me to consider, graduate
curriculum. The assistant professors with whom I spoke and I all had more or
less the same thing to report. We learned about teaching in and out of our fields
by working as assistant professors and by talking to others about their experiences;
this is also the way we learned how to work effectively on various committees
and how to participate in professional meetings. Our critical and scholarly work
developed the same way: although we were energized and educated by the courses
we took and especially by writing our dissertations, few of us can say that any
one course we took as graduate students, or even all of them together, taught
us how to write a book, an article, or a review. I'm not convinced that course
work can or should specifically teach these skills, although the community of
a department and graduate program can certainly provide intellectual stimulation and a supportive atmosphere. Things may have changed at Berkeley since
I was there in the seventies, when, aside from Fred Crews's noncredit seminar
for teachers of freshman composition, the curriculum was devoted to matters
critical and literary; the closest thing we had even to a service course was a required seminar in "bibliographical and research techniques," a course that rarely
fulfilled the promise of its title. The implicit assumption that the business of the
graduate program was to teach subjects, not methods, marginalized discussion
of pedagogy and of orientation to the profession. This is not to say my education at Berkeley wasn't thoroughly informative and stimulating; it was, and all
I could wish for in retrospect was more specific attention to my writing at stages
before the dissertation and more freedom to think and read for those of us struggling with a full course load and a substantial work week (without, that is, the
support of fellowships or lucrative teaching assistantships) in the early years of
our education. The only course I would have welcomed had it been offered is
one introducing us to and assessing various critical procedures. Now, of course,
seminars in theory are standard, and they form a different atmosphere from the
one that in 1971 had us all agitated about deconstruction, though few of us knew
what it was. I can say, however, that such innocence was not crucial; as we know,
critical and theoretical sophistication is not to be won in a semester but must
develop through wide reading over time.

While specific questions about courses and curricula in relation to our present
professional lives did not occupy me and the assistant professors with whom

I talked, other matters did. These tended to concentrate on our state of relative innocence about the facts of professional life during our graduate-student years and, consequently, our inadequate preparation for the transition that awaited us. I want to address this issue in response to the MLA commission's questions concerning how I would educate graduate students who will be accepting positions similar to mine. I have little to say here about the formal graduate curriculum and propose that what is needed in addition to an excellent education is a richer elaboration of informal resources for those making the transition from student to faculty status. My discussion is based on my past experience as a tenure-track assistant professor in a PhD-granting department of a research-oriented institution. To provide a check for possible idiosyncrasies in my experience and to develop some modest, valid generalizations, I interviewed others with similar appointments, some who have degrees more recent than mine and whose experience, therefore, may have more immediate relevance to the situation of junior faculty members today.

We all feel that we were given too little help in getting oriented to the facts of professional life. When I was a graduate student at Berkeley, formal and deliberate discussion of the business of the profession was considered by many faculty members to demean the mission of a PhD program: "we guarantee the quality of your degree and you figure out the rest" was the tacit assumption – so much so that even the existence of our placement committee was lamented by some faculty members for degrading vocation to business. (Not coincidentally, the most effective member of that committee was the person with the most recent PhD.) This committee was still a very limited resource, and, in general, practical advice was hard to come by, not only because of our teachers' idealistic, antibusiness attitudes, but also because of their unfamiliarity with the grim job market of the seventies, which stood in stark contrast to the bull markets of their experience. Yet making that transition from advanced student to beginning professional is one of the most difficult stages of our lives. Most of the people in my generation foundered, or picked up advice randomly and anecdotally, and tried to gauge their circumstances through circuits of gossip about the fates of others. A better alternative is for our departments to assume a more conscious and responsible role in helping junior colleagues and graduate students with their entry into the profession. Indeed, providing information about and assistance with that transition ought to involve the cooperation of the faculty members in all departments that produce PhDs and all departments that hire them. And that last group also needs the cooperation and support of administrators, for universities that advertise themselves as places where teachers and scholars may begin and develop their careers need to remain sensitive to the value of providing encouraging circumstances and meaningful resources for so doing.

One of the most difficult aspects of this transition for the junior faculty members with whom I've talked is the sudden change in status: having succeeded on the job market, they now worry about tenure. We all know instances of fine teachers and scholars who did not secure tenure and have had to accept appointments marginal to their professional and scholarly interests; some have had to leave the profession altogether. To some of my older colleagues this concern may seem to debase our professional dignity. But my many conversations with assistant professors in both my own generation and the next one have convinced me that not having tenure, or having to worry about securing it, is deeply demoralizing. My department has been able to hire faculty members who also had offers from Ivy League departments, in part because tenure at Rutgers is a more visible possibility. And it is well known that in more than one Ivy department the warmest faculty recommendations have been chilled by administrative review – so that even when those revolving doors do yield tenure tracks, success can remain cruelly elusive, a fact not lost on PhDs with a range of offers to consider. Moreover, junior faculty members in Ivy League departments – or any department in which promotion from within is unusual – often have an acute sense of their transience. In one such department, about half the junior faculty members who have yet even to be reviewed were on the job market in 1987 – a year in which that same department was unsuccessful with all its offers of assistant professorships.

Circumstances in traditionally tenure-track departments can be uncertain as well. This is true especially at universities that make a deliberate effort to improve their national ranking with prestigious new appointments at the senior level and corresponding, and often abrupt, escalations of the standards for tenure from within, especially for publication and research. In such cases, it is particularly important for our department chairs to keep a close watch on shifts in administrative criteria and to advise junior faculty members as far in advance as possible about what they need to do in order to present a strong candidacy for tenure. Such advice is necessary even in relatively stable departments. Some assistant professors with whom I have talked who did not receive strong support for tenure from their departments complain, rightly, that they had not been advised accurately and adequately, if advised at all, during their first five years about their senior colleagues' expectations and evaluations of their work. At Rutgers we now have an informal second-year review and a formal, and quite rigorous, third-year review (conducted on the model of the sixth-year tenure review) precisely for the purpose of providing specific and copious advice to our assistant professors about how they are managing their careers and how they might strengthen their records. Our midterm report to the candidate and the administration covers teaching, publication, work-in-progress, other kinds of professional activity such as conference work, as well as the record of service to the department, the university, and the profession. These are the same categories discussed at the tenure meeting, so the midterm review is helpful both to the department and to our assistant professors. This process, of course, is nerve-racking for our junior faculty members, but it is emphatically preferable to the alternative, which leaves everything to informal inference or misapprehension. To enhance the effectiveness of this review and all others, department chairs need to take care with their reports to administrative review committees, in order to explain clearly such matters as why it usually takes those of us in the humanities five years to write a book, why we may publish only one or two articles a year when scientists publish half a dozen, why a controversial book or article is valuable and healthy in literary studies even though controversy may be a cause for caution in the sciences, how the paperwork in our classes differs from what obtains in mathematics or the sciences.

For these reports to seem as fair as possible and to serve the best interests of both the faculty and the university as a whole, their methods and consequences should be presented as part of an assistant professor's orientation. The most important information any new faculty member needs, and deserves, in making a successful transition into professional life is a clear statement about what is expected during the probationary term and on what sort of schedule. This statement will vary according to departments, especially depending on whether the department is located in a teaching-oriented college or a research-oriented university. The chief, and quite stunning, revelation for me and others in many places was how little dedicated teaching counts in the big picture. Short of breaches of contract, casual approaches to class preparation, tutorial work, and paper reading are not only tolerated but seemingly not noticed, or covertly rewarded if such an approach enables publication to proceed at a brisker pace. Most universities and colleges are on record as according teaching and publication equal weight in all review processes, and most of us support the values such criteria are supposed to uphold, but it seems equal balance is often treated as pleasant fiction: junior faculty members soon become aware that their senior colleagues' salaries are related much more predictably and rewardingly to excellence in publication than to excellence in teaching. Moreover, we can all point to cases in which a candidate for tenure who was an outstanding teacher with a somewhat less distinguished record of publication did not get tenure, while another candidate secured tenure with an outstanding record of publication and merely adequate teaching (or worse, whose teaching evaluation was conveniently inflated for the occasion).

It is clear that such criteria have a degrading and demoralizing effect on collegiality and teaching and that university communities as a whole will benefit from encouraging and rewarding dedicated teaching and service. But until that revolution, responsible department chairs have to instill a certain skepticism in their untenured faculty members about the rewards, at least at research-oriented universities. I am not recommending a cynical attitude about teaching. Most of us entered the profession because we enjoy teaching, take it seriously, derive great satisfaction from teaching well, and work hard to be good at it. For this very reason, chairs must protect junior faculty members from being exploited, as can happen, sometimes scandalously so, at less affluent universities when they are called on to teach large lecture courses (sometimes numbering in the hundreds) or demanding service courses (for instance, freshman composition with a teacher-to-student ratio of 1 to 30) without adequate (sometimes without any) staffing for paperwork and consultations. No chair, I realize, likes to tell a new assistant professor that while time-consuming, energetic teaching is admired and appreciated, it is writing and publication that will decide tenure in the institution at hand. Communicating this information is necessary, however, even as we try to educate administrators about the value to our universities and our society of recognizing and rewarding excellent teaching.

This is not to say that teaching is not rigorously evaluated at many of these universities; moreover, those with whom I have talked who have taught at colleges with strong traditions in undergraduate education report the frequency with which teaching evaluations are conducted and the weight these evaluations carry. In any circumstance – whether evaluation occurs semiannually or biannually and whatever the degree of importance – this process may add to, rather than ease, anxiety about making the transition from graduate student to faculty member. At Berkeley, my teaching experience consisted entirely of freshman composition. Graduate students at many other universities are similarly limited (indeed, at Rutgers, freshman composition is taught almost entirely by graduate students and visiting part-time lecturers, that is, non-tenure-track teachers who are not eligible for benefits). The advantage is that we are all familiar with composition pedagogy. This is a valuable asset, and departments at Berkeley and Rutgers, like many others, offer an array of workshops, support groups, and advising systems for teachers of these courses. The usefulness of such pedagogy is not confined to freshman composition. I have found that student writing in every undergraduate course I have taught at Rutgers, including my senior honors seminars, requires that I teach students to pay attention to logic, clarity, coherence, organization, style, and usage. Preparation to teach composition is not, of course, the same thing as preparation for a lecture course in one's field of specialization, a broad survey, or a seminar. Decently paid apprenticeship as a graduate student in such courses would be valuable experience, but such opportunities are expensive to fund and hence rare. As a consequence, most of us find our ways by imitating the best and most productive aspects of the classes in which we were students, and we improvise, amend, and develop from there.

Because it takes a while to get oriented to a new job, a new department, a new student body, a new set of courses, junior faculty members ought not to be evaluated in the first year, unless they request such service and advice. Confident and effective teaching sometimes takes a few semesters, yet a number of departments not only solicit student evaluations from the first but allow these to constitute the sole evidence for assessments. Such evaluations are useful, but, as we all know, undergraduates are capable of confusing good teaching with being entertained or with having easy access to desired grades. It is important, therefore, for departments to broaden the range of documents they consult in their deliberations about promotion and tenure: at Rutgers, to cite one possible approach, a junior faculty member invites a colleague, with whom he or she shares syllabi, assignments, and other course materials, to visit one class meeting or two; the visitor writes a report that is shared with the one reviewed, who in turn has an opportunity to comment or who may ask for further review; we also solicit faculty members' own statements of teaching effectiveness. The full-

ness and breadth of the resulting reports underscore the value we place on effective teaching – not that our values are always credited at higher levels of review,
but at least our care demonstrates our seriousness. And as with everything else
pertaining to evaluation, the procedures, expectations, and consequences are defined clearly.

The whole matter of publication and professional activity needs to be clari-
fied, too, especially because of the wide diversity of standards and expectations.
Even such basic issues as "a book" or "some articles" can be ambiguous. Do com-
missioned articles count as much as refereed ones? Some universities think not.
Is one expected to publish in general journals as well as specialty, field-oriented
ones? And what is appropriate for "a book"? A lightly revised dissertation of
modest length? Or a substantially revised and developed dissertation? And in
what stage of completion? Is a finished manuscript enough? Or must it be under
contract? Or must one have a book on the shelf – or a book on the shelf that
has already received reviews? And published where? Junior faculty members at
my institution, for instance, are impressed with the fact that, their colleagues'
attitudes aside, our administrative committees think little of books that have not
been accepted by one of a dozen or so nationally prestigious presses. Criteria will
vary, of course, from department to department and from institution to institution, but the constant is the expectation of publication and of distinguished quality.

PhD-granting departments can stress this fact of professional life and take
an active role not only in conveying information about the whole business of
publication to their advanced graduate students but in helping them in the first
stages of the process – by identifying potentially publishable units of their dissertations, or advising them about how to develop promising seminar papers. To
demystify what is involved in submitting papers to conferences and preparing
articles for publication, departments can put these students in touch with recently
hired junior faculty members for a series of colloquiums or informal meetings.
They can also assist their junior faculty members with information about grant
and fellowship resources within the college or university and in the profession
at large. At Rutgers the chair regularly distributes notices to the appropriate candidates; we also have a meeting every other year or so on the subject (to which
we invite both graduate students and junior faculty members), and we maintain
a file of successful fellowship proposals by our colleagues. It also helps enormously
to provide graduate students and junior faculty members with financial support
for the submission of papers to conferences (MLA as well as regional and specialty ones). Not only is this an ethical act of generosity to those about to enter
the profession or taking up their duties, but it is a positive encouragement to
the reluctant. Such support, to be effective, needs to be offered a priori: if you
get a paper accepted for a conference, we will enable you to attend.

It may seem that I have been emphasizing the "business" of getting professionally established at the expense of talking about the more intangible pleasures
of beginning one's career. Yet for all the junior faculty members with whom I
have talked, getting so established (that is, getting books and articles accepted

for publication, getting tenured) is a primary concern, and despair over such prospects tends to dilute other potential pleasures. Not everyone agrees with me, I know, but I think – given the present, very professionalized situation of most junior faculties – that one of the best things we can do for our graduate students is encourage them to attend and participate in conferences and begin their publication careers while they are graduate students.

There are at least four good reasons for this recommendation. First, the traditional one: it is fun to discover the profession. It is encouraging and exciting to learn that there are audiences for our ideas, people with whom to correspond, and resources to nurture and challenge our thinking and writing. But there are more practical reasons. Publishing is professionally necessary and participating in conferences is a valuable enhancement. These days, most search committees, even for assistant professors, take note of conference papers, and many look for some record of publication – one article out or at least accepted, perhaps a review. I don't think these appearances are necessarily as informative about the quality of a candidate's work as is the complete dissertation (which is usually the subject of the interview), but publication may be what gets one an interview in the first place: it establishes a credential and indicates a professional beginning, and so search committees tend to accord it value; some even use evidence of publication to make the first cut. When I entered the job market about ten years ago, one article accepted by a major journal was sufficient, along with a degree from a major department, to distinguish a job candidate. Now an article is standard, and the exception is the candidate who has not yet published anything. Graduate students need to be encouraged to acquaint themselves with the journals of our profession – not only the general ones, but ones in their particular fields of interest. Such acquaintance is of course a valuable resource for their own development as scholars and critics, but more immediate values are those of learning what constitutes publishable work, of feeling enabled to make a contribution, and of developing a businesslike, rather than emotion-charged, attitude about the flux of acceptances and rejections. All graduate students, in any event, need one writing sample, sometimes two, to present to search committees; preparing an article for publication can accomplish two purposes at once.

A third reason for beginning to publish as a graduate student is the sheer factor of time. As any assistant professor knows, the business of relocating, developing new courses, learning about a new department and a new university is quite time-consuming, and it is often at least a year, sometimes more, before one has a chance to resume one's writing. As a graduate student, one frequently has time to write as well as teach, a luxury that vanishes as one begins full-time employment. This is a crucial issue, because successful midterm reviews in some departments require a record of noteworthy publication. Let me tell you about the third-year review in my department in the winter of 1986: of six assistant professors, three had each published a book, along with several articles and reviews; one had a book under contract and several articles out; and another had enough articles out, all in prestigious places, to constitute a book's worth of writing. In

1983, when I was reviewed for tenure, such records were enough for promotion. And my senior colleagues tell me that in previous years full professorships had been secured with even less. The remarkable record of my six assistant professors is in part an accident of four of these people having moved to entry-level positions at Rutgers from other positions, rather than directly from graduate school (and indeed many PhDs these days do not go directly from graduate school to the tenure-track appointments they desire). But that one of those with a modest but excellent book on the shelf (her dissertation) came to us directly from graduate school is a sign of the times, and the group as a whole is not the aberration it seems: early records of accomplishment (and not just quantity for quantity's sake) are becoming typical not only at Rutgers but at other research-intensive universities as well. As you may imagine, we worry that such midterm records will raise the stakes for tenure – all the more reason to favor graduate students who have begun to publish. The pace may be different at other universities, but clearly more, not less, publication is required at earlier stages than most of us are used to.

The last reason to begin publishing as a graduate student is partly practical, but mostly pleasurable: it is, simply, the comfort and availability of collegial resources and advice – that is, conversation and critical exchange with one's classmates and savvy advice and rigorous scrutiny from one's teachers (who sometimes can also create opportunities for publication). These resources are potentially available in any department, but for advanced graduate students they have reached a state of cultivation that is remarkably different from one's circumstances as a stranger in a new department.

That status as stranger in a new world is a critical phase of the transition from graduate student to faculty member. New faculty members, especially junior ones, may feel odd and isolated – not only in terms of their strangeness in and to a new department, but more elegiacally, in terms of their loss of the community they enjoyed as graduate students. This strangeness can be acute at a university such as mine, where most faculty members commute from elsewhere and are around only on teaching days. But it can obtain even in cozy in-residence departments of the hourglass shape – that is, a body of tenured professors, a few associate professors tenured from within, and a group of assistant professors, most in a revolving door. Assistant professors in such departments are often quite collegial with one another but just as often feel isolated socially and professionally from their senior colleagues, who are hesitant to form friendships with people whose stay in the department is usually temporary.

Department chairs can ease this situation in a couple of ways. First, they can make a point of welcoming new assistant professors to the department's community of researchers, scholars, and teachers, introducing them to the junior and senior people in the field, distributing a writing sample, the curriculum vitae, and an informal biography. Second, they can involve junior faculty members in the business of the department by assigning them to committees that include senior faculty members and that seek and value junior faculty perspectives. I suspect that with few exceptions, these committees will not be concerned with graduate curriculum, senior job searches, personnel matters, or promotion – and sometimes, it is unwise for new faculty members to take a highly vocal and aggressive role in meetings that have complicated departmental subtexts not always visible to a newcomer. It is important, of course, not to exploit junior faculty willingness to serve on time-consuming committees, because, as we know, such service counts little if the record of publication suffers. But two kinds of assignments are productive both for new faculty members and for the department as a whole. The first is the placement committee for job candidates: recently hired assistant professors, more than anyone else in our departments, can be informative and helpful in advising graduate students who are about to enter the job market and begin publishing and submitting conference papers. Service on this committee not only benefits the graduate students but also helps establish new faculty members as part of a department that values their advice. The second assignment is to a committee with a focused pedagogical mission. In my department, this means the Honors Committee and the group that runs the introduction-to-the-major course. The Honors Committee at Rutgers has a good mix of teachers from all ranks; the work is interesting and respected by the administration. The sophomore course is also one taught by almost everyone in the department; the committee decides on the reading list and undertakes the revealing process of working out common essay assignments for the dozen or so sections that run every semester.

As the dynamics of these committees sometimes demonstrate, however, one last issue that makes the transition into professional status difficult for women is the sexism that lingers in some departments or among some of their members. As the demographics of even this conference suggest (women administrators represent about 20% of those in attendance), most of us enter departments where women are still a minority population, especially in the upper ranks. Most departments and most administrations, that is, still look like men's clubs, and most of the assistant professors with whom I've talked have felt that new men are welcomed more readily than new women. This situation is partly cultural: some senior men are not used to having women as colleagues or according them respect as such; moreover, because most departmental offices are staffed by women, some senior men may also regard their women colleagues, particularly those of lower rank, as secretarial adjuncts. Not all our male colleagues are men's clubbers, and the perception of sexism does not emanate just from women. Many men acknowledge and supply the evidence of sexist attitudes and recount the relevant anecdotes as readily as do their female colleagues. Many departments such as my own have hired quite a few women in recent years and appoint women to important administrative posts and committees. Even so, one hears comments, casual as well as calculated, at meetings and observes behavior toward women, apparently accepted, or at least tolerated, that indicate the force of the older bonds, older ties, older attitudes.

I've been talking about what departments can do to ease the transition from graduate student to faculty member. New teachers, of course, have to exercise initiative too. It is important for them to talk with their chairs at least once a year about goals and expectations, especially if their departments do not yet have a formal mid-term review. And they need to take active roles in exploring their new collegial resources. Many junior faculty members lament the loss of their graduate-school mentors—not only for intellectual and psychological support but for help in getting established and discovering opportunities for professional activity. This loss can be remedied in part by developing closer contacts with their new colleagues: sometimes chairs will put new faculty members in touch with the community in their field; sometimes there are study groups to join; but if not, the newcomers might take the first step: an invitation to discuss work in progress is a good way to begin. Such exchanges help rebuild the community we all leave behind in graduate school, and they can be supplemented by participation in professional conferences: contacts, friendships, and acquaintances developed at these meetings provide a constant that may steady some of the more distressing fluxes of making any kind of professional transition. All these individual initiatives deserve deliberate and conscientious departmental and institutional support: junior faculty members provide a constant source of fresh ideas and enthusiasm, and we need to do everything we can to nurture this resource for the advantage of us all.

Part 3:
Exploring the Future:
Proposals for Change

Convergent Pressures:
Social, Technological, Theoretical

Richard A. Lanham
University of California, Los Angeles

I want to discuss three pressures that are converging on English departments at the present time – social, technological, and theoretical. Our response to these pressures will largely determine changes to the graduate curriculum for some years to come, and we ought to have them clearly in mind.

Since I have been talking about the social pressures on English studies for several years and since these pressures have now been accepted into the professional conversation, I shall only summarize them. First, our student body has become multilingual, multiracial, and mixed in social class. This development has led to a literacy crisis – to an awareness that our humanism must be Eastern as well as Western, to our sense of English as a world language rather than only an English and American language, to the expansions of the canon, to a sense that foreign language teaching must be integrated with English teaching in new ways. Second, we have begun to think systemically, sequentially, in a way that we did not do before. Most obvious and important, we have begun to acknowledge that educating secondary teachers stands as a legitimate item on our agenda. Beyond that, we have started to think about the English secondary curriculum as our concern as well, to realize that we are part of a paideia that runs from kindergarten beyond graduate school to lifelong learning. Third, we have had to face an enrollment drop caused partly by demographics but substantially by a resurgence of that long-standing American preference for education that is practical and income enhancing, and we have had to ask ourselves what, if any, claims we can advance in this direction. Fourth, we face continuing pressures from business and government to produce citizens at least minimally literate and not grossly stupid and to devote to this end money we would prefer to spend on graduate seminars in our special fields.

These pressures, and many more of course, have come together as a social pressure on English studies to become more rhetorical, and less poetic, in emphasis and scope. This is familiar ground, the great lit.-comp. street fight, and I need not dwell on it here.

These social pressures on our profession are intensifying at every step because of the technological pressures created, really in the last half-dozen years, by the personal computer and by the digital videographic techniques that have accompanied its arrival. We are so used to fixing on commercial television as the great enemy of literacy as we know it that we have not attended to the electronic presentation of words, which is now upon us and which affects us much more nearly. But we and our students will all increasingly do our reading on an electronic screen, and this will affect our profession in the most intimate and immediate ways.

What happens when we display a written text on the electronic screen of a capacious personal computer with, say, a color monitor and good graphics? First, unlike a printed page, the text is no longer fixed. We can interact with it, change it in all kinds of routine and nonroutine ways. The very nature of the machine invites us to do this. We *want* to do all that it *can* do. All the impulses of game and play move us this way. We want to reformat, revise, do global searches, change type size or font, squeeze columns or fatten them, play around with background colors – all that neat stuff. But when we do, we have discarded the center of Western humanism since the Renaissance – the fixed, authoritative text. For Renaissance scholars, establishing the original text was their main task, and generations of textual editors since have renewed their labors. The aim of all this was to fix the text forever. This unchangeable perfection immediately puts us into a one-way hierarchical relationship with what we read. The text can influence us but we cannot influence it. Surrounding it with glosses is the best that we have ever been able to do, and surely nothing so graphically allegorizes the master-slave relationship.

The electronic screen changes all that. And with the change in hierarchy comes a change in the canon, the fixed list of fixed texts that, taken together, constitute the fixed wisdom of our culture. Our relation to this accepted wisdom now is a two-way street, and this interactivity changes the balance of power absolutely. We can fight back, draw a mustache on the *Mona Lisa* if that is how we feel about her. No more must we gaze in breathless adoration at a changeless perfection. Changeability is the name of the electronic game.

These two related and consequential changes – in the fixed text and the fixed canon – bring fundamental changes to humanistic teaching and inquiry. The great humanistic computer accomplishment to date – the gigantic concordance – pales in comparison, and even word processing seems secondary. The fixed canon lent itself to political and religious hierarchy. Only a special class of creators, divinely inspired, could produce such a canon, and once they created it, our job was to find ever-new Arnoldian ways to celebrate its perfection. The electronic canon is not canonical at all in this way. Instead of lending itself to hierarchical ways of thinking, it dissolves them, radically democratizing art.

And not only art but ordinary discourse. Imagine all the constraints, and all the implied messages, alphabetic and imagistic, that conventionally printed prose conveys. We can now change all those conventions, tabulate sequential information or vice versa, highlight the "print" itself rather than desecrate it with a yellow highlighter, boldface or paleface at will, and so on. Gloss and text start to interpenetrate at every point. The reviser's pencil can go into global action. All the conventions of typography suddenly become possible avenues of meaning, activated either by the first author or subsequent reader-authors.

We can hardly exaggerate what stands at stake here. Eric Havelock has pointed out, in a series of pioneering articles on the Greek alphabet, that Western literacy, in the full sense of the word, required two things: an alphabet simple enough to be learned in early childhood and thus pushed beneath the level of consciousness; and a printed text transparent enough so that we do not notice it for itself, for its size, shape, aesthetic stimulus of any sort, but simply read right through it to the meaning beneath. The final development of this transparent verbal surface is our conventional printed text today: no color, linear progression without regression, a single type size and font—or a very restricted repertoire of them—no pictures where words could substitute, paper all the same color and unchanging in size and texture, and so on. This transparent conception of the codex book is the foundation stone of true literacy. It underlies what we are accustomed to think of as "real" conceptual thought. And more than that. It implies a whole theory of motive and human behavior. The transparent, unselfconscious text, as Havelock has made clear, breaks away from all the qualifications of thought imposed by surrounding political reality, imposed by all the impulses of competition or self-pleasing showing off, and looks at things as in themselves they really are.

Now, with the electronic screen, all those political and rhetorical qualifications crowd back in. The electronic display of words breaks that "literate compact" which underlies literacy and thus everything that we think the humanities to be. The oral, as against literate, personality crowds back on the scene with a vengeance. And orality brings with it a definite conception of Homo sapiens as an essentially dramatic being, whose self is social, not central, and who is surrounded by a society that is equally dramatic in essence. Electronic print, that is, implies a different kind of seriousness.

We need only think of the motivational environment that the computer has occupied from the beginning. Every step of its journey has been galvanized by the tutelary deities of the oral world, game and play. Every time ordinary practical purpose has stepped in, it has been rudely shoved into the wings by the hackers, hacking just for the hell of it and, of course, to impress one another, to compete. The computer encourages an electronic persona, an online self that may seem soigné and thirty but turns out to be freckle-faced and fourteen. And the dramaticality goes yet deeper. The habit of mind and thought that the computer encourages above all others is modeling, creating a rehearsal-reality that we then tinker with. And this kind of modeling has stood at the center of humanism from the beginning, whether we dress it as mimesis, the romantic imagination, or something else. Modeling reality has been what art is all about. Now, the electronic screen takes rehearsal-reality deep into every phase of human intelligence and contrivance. As much of postmodernism has been telling us, art and life thus interpenetrate in altogether new ways. The dramaticality of the computer is fundamental and pervasive.

Consider what else the computer does to literature. If we think of a software genre like interactive fiction, with its blending of criticism and creation, of reader and writer, we soon have to think of a completely new kind of critical theory. We simply have no categories for, say, collaborative reader-writer authorship, although some work in literary theory has made a beginning here. And we don't know how to handle the new mixture of information from the eye and the ear. Our criticism, that is, depends as fundamentally on the basic literacy compact as does our Arnoldian high seriousness of purpose, self, and society. What happens when iconographic information and alphabetic information are radically mixed? What happens when chirographic information can become allegorical, letters turn into icons, backgrounds for the written alphabet turn different colors according to the moods of the story or become pictures, stage sets against which the written text is projected?

The real change will come, however, in the attitudes and expectations of "readers" who have grown up reading electronically. For they will carry their habits to the printed text as well. And they will not like what they find. They will find the conventional codex book awkward to hold and read, colorless for a start, gummous and intractable, resisting any kind of manipulation even for ease of reading—transposition into a larger typeface, for example, or change from an unreadable sans serif to a more readable type. As for what reading has come to mean to them—a full collaborative and interactive game—it simply will not be possible in such a system. They will do one of two things. They will either, like Paolo and Francesca on a happier occasion, that day read no further, or more likely they will scan the printed text into a computer and set to work giving, perhaps, a fully colored background to the similes in *Paradise Lost*. The electronic reproduction of words will work as enzymatically on the literature and art of the past as on that of the future.

With these technological pressures, as with the social ones, none of this is prophecy. Although electronic text stands at the beginning of its life cycle, it is out there right now, as insistent in its pressures for the democratization of art as is the vastly changed student body we now teach. Like the social pressures, the technological pressures of electronic text all push literary study in the direction of rhetoric—away from the purity of Arnoldian seriousness toward the mixed-motive world of present dangers where rhetoric has always dwelt. Electronic text is rhetorical through and through in a way that print never was. Put words on a CRT display, and the poetics of black-and-white fixed linear print become rhetorical before you've put your fingers on the home row. You don't have to think about it at all; it just happens.

But, of course, people have thought about it. For what we have sketched is nothing but the postmodern aesthetic, electronically driven, electronic "theory" if you like. The explosion of the fixed text starts with Filippo Tommaso Marinetti and the Italian futurists at the beginning of this century. Typography as a self-conscious expressive parameter has been around almost since the beginning of writing, as the Winter 1986 issue of *Visible Language* makes abundantly clear, but it gained a renewed focus with Marinetti's alphabetic paintings. It was Marcel Duchamp who challenged Arnoldian seriousness with R. Mutt's famous urinal and showed the way to postmodernism's radical democratization of art. It was so appreciable an accomplishment that Duchamp, on the strength of it, rightly retired for life. The combining of creation and criticism in interactive works of art, the obsession with rehearsal-realities, the pervasiveness of game and play motives were all contributed by the extension of futurism we usually call Dada. In fact, so fine is the congruence of postmodern aesthetics and the electronic word that we might be justified in considering the personal computer the ultimate post-modern work of art. Literary theory has restated this aesthetic at length and in ways too familiar to need restatement here.

So literary study feels three strands of pressure – social, technological, and the-oretical, all of them modern restatements of classical rhetoric; all of them ap-plied and didactic (the essential didacticism of postmodernism from Dada onward has usually got lost in the "outrage" that masks it), and self-conscious and radi-cally democratic. They all turn their backs on Arnoldian seriousness and em-brace instead a self-consciousness that we might call rhetorical seriousness. This transformation could hardly be more radical and total. And clearly it is being felt in other fields as well, where rhetoric rather than philosophy is being reas-serted as the dominant seriousness. (I am thinking of books like Donald McCloskey's brilliant *Rhetoric of Economics* and James Boyd White's writings on rhetoric and the law, *Heracles' Bow* and *When Words Lose Their Meaning*.)

Many things would seem to follow from this fundamental alteration in fig-ure and ground between poetic and rhetoric. I can here list only the most impor-tant ones. First, the quarrel between literature and composition seems not so much unnecessary as cosmically silly. Second, the present administrative and disciplin-ary arrangement doesn't make much sense – literary study in one place, compo-sition in another; the historical study of rhetoric, if there is any of that, left to forensics on the one hand and advertising on the other; the study of electronic communication stuck off in "comm studies" and more often than not in the di-vision of social science; "literary theory" isolating itself even within literary study; and none of these pigeonholes in contact with any other. Keep everything out of everything else, as Kenneth Burke once said, and then complain that the world is in pieces. Third, the effort to put the pieces together for humanistic inquiry – the search for a core curriculum – must find that elusive center where it has al-ways been, in the rhetorical paideia. Fourth, we must recognize, *pace* the anguished cries of some recent educational philosophers, that we are now an applied not a pure discipline; we can't go on talking about power and politics in literature and still assume that poetry makes nothing happen. Fifth, to accommodate this basic shift in the plate tectonics of literary study, we will need a new kind of educational administrator, someone who understands this theoretical shift and its historical dimension. The dean and chair as we now conceive them, tactful and savvy referees of the career game, will need new conceptual strings to their bows. Sixth, a completely new administrative structure is implied here, one calling into question the interface between English and the foreign languages, especially that between the Western and the Eastern languages, and the relation of literary study to the fine arts. We are going to need systemic thinking of a high order, an order not always found today in university administration.

In discussing this reappearance and reintegration of the rhetorical paideia, we are talking not about something that may happen but about something that is happening right now. The central question is how English departments will align themselves in accordance with it; whether they will try to lead these convergent forces or leave the task to some other academic integer yet to be devised. There are compelling arguments on both sides of the question. But it is not, we should remember, an administrative question only; it concerns literary study in its deepest interiority. When Western literature ignores rhetoric, it ignores half of itself, doing for all Western literature what C. S. Lewis tried to do for the English Renaissance; it wounds itself mortally, from the inside, in whatever administrative structure it finds itself.

Whether English studies is likely to confront this reassertion of the rhetorical paideia as a dominant vision, and if so, what changes will follow for the graduate curriculum, chairpersons may know much better than I. But is it being too bold to suggest that, at the least, our graduate students ought to be *told about it*? For if we don't tell them, we shall be graduating students who, for all their hyperkinetic theoretical sophistication, will be only the last clerks of a forgotten Arnoldian mood.

Imagining Changes

Jonathan Culler

Cornell University

We are here to reflect on the shape of graduate programs in English at a time when a number of different changes present potentially rich opportunities, a time when we ought therefore collectively to explore possibilities that different institutions may individually pursue.

The changes that create these opportunities are, I think, four:

1. Signs are that the period of retrenchment is coming to an end, so instead of wondering how best to fend off cuts and make them least damaging, we should be asking what developments would be educationally most valuable.

2. A significant number of departments have recently established doctoral programs in rhetoric and theory of composition, so we ought to have a range of new and specific educational models to evaluate, particularly for their success in integrating the traditional areas of literary study and the teaching of writing. There should be promising models among these experiments.

3. Work in literary theory has recently stressed connections among different sorts of texts or discourses, literary and nonliterary, instead of insisting on the unique character of literature, thus creating opportunities for broadening the work of English departments and linking interpretation of texts with study of the production of texts.

4. Finally, what many regard as a problem or threat, the questioning of the basis of the traditional literary canon, is also an opportunity to create new kinds of combinations. At the very least, it provides an opportunity to reflect with greater freedom on what we think should happen in graduate programs.

We are assembled here not because there is a crisis but because these developments offer opportunities for departments to rethink and reshape programs, and this endeavor should be based on a broad dialogue within the profession so we know what others are thinking.

The MLA's recent survey of graduate programs shows that there have been significant changes in recent years, both in courses offered and in courses required, but statistics cannot reveal what may be the most important aspect of that change. A key question for any graduate program is, what holds it together – what makes an intellectual community out of an assortment of graduate students? A university was once perspicuously defined as a miscellaneous assortment of programs and enterprises united by a common parking problem; an English graduate program may sometimes seem united by a wall of mailboxes and a common question: "Is the Xerox machine working?"

Previously the canon of English literature, from *Beowulf* to Virginia Woolf, with some American literature thrown in, may have seemed to create a common enterprise. Today that is considerably less true: coverage of this canon is not nearly so pervasive a general requirement. Women's studies, black studies, cultural studies, and literary theory have given us multiple or expanded canons, including not only neglected literary works but interesting groups of nonliterary works as well, and have placed on the agenda questions about canon formation – its mechanisms and costs. In many places requirements have adjusted to meet this situation, where traditional coverage can no longer be required and students are in fact held responsible for different areas or groups of works. In some programs certainly, what now brings students together and creates an intellectual community is not a common literary canon but problems of literary theory and questions of method – debates about the virtues and possibilities of deconstruction, psychoanalytic criticism, feminist criticism, Marxist criticism, and the new historicism. Concern with these questions unites people writing on Shakespeare, George Eliot, and Joyce, the Renaissance, Romanticism, and postmodernism.

Now whatever proposals we might make, it seems to me unlikely that we can return to a common literary canon, even a judiciously expanded or selected one. Although there will no doubt continue to be a shifting collection of literary works that most of our graduate students will have read (or will be ashamed to admit not having read, which is the real definition of the canonical), "theory" of various sorts is likely to continue to play a significant role as a unifying concern and space of debate, if not a common ground. The question about the shape and focus of graduate programs in English is in part a question about theoretical issues to be raised, and if we are particularly interested in integrating the teaching and study of composition with the study and teaching of literature, then this integration needs at least to be posited as a matter of theory if it is to have any chance at all of becoming a matter of practice. We already have a name – *rhetoric* – for such a perspective of integration, and it is striking that such different literary theorists as Paul de Man and Terry Eagleton have proposed that literary studies be reconceived as (or give way to) an expanded rhetoric: a study of discursive structures and strategies, in their relation to systems of signification and human subjects (their role in producing subjects).

My first proposal is that we actively try to work out ways of integrating the study of cultural practices under the heading of rhetoric and place such a course or colloquium at the center of the program – perhaps as a seminar designed to bring together in their second or third year students with different interests.

Psychoanalytical criticism, deconstruction, and the new historicism, in their moves back and forth between literary and nonliterary texts, provide starting points for exploring what it might mean to bring the study of literature into a generalized rhetoric. For me, one of the more promising approaches or topics is the study of plot structures in writing of different kinds, including the arguments of student papers. The point is not that there is a single model for integration but that we think of a rhetoric course as a potential integrative device, drawing on the experience of new rhetoric programs.

But, second, if we are to succeed in bringing together, under the heading of rhetoric, the study of literary and other discourses in a way that may enrich approaches to the teaching of composition, we must, it seems to me, succeed in displacing the massive, imperious assumption that now governs literary studies: that interpretation of individual works is the goal of all literary study. The problem is not, as some assert, that academic literary interpretation is elitist or that it has become supersubtle – like most intellectual activities, interpretation is valuable only when it is pursued to the utmost, with all the subtlety and resourcefulness one can command. The problem is, rather, that interpretation excludes other goals. The tradition of rhetoric, however, does provide us with alternative goals, such as studying literary works to learn to imitate them, an exercise that has a good deal to be said for it as a way of finding out about discursive structures and effects. The popularity of creative writing courses suggests that a reorientation toward imitation might not meet massive resistance among students (although we might eventually discover that much of the popularity of creative writing courses is due to an ideology of self-expression – as demonstration that there is a self – rather than an interest in gaining proficiency in a literary mode). But whatever the case, I am convinced that the emphasis on interpretation is a major obstacle to the integration of literary studies and the teaching of writing under the rubric of rhetoric.

In many places the link will no doubt be made by courses on the theory of discourse directed toward the practice of teaching in which students are currently engaged. There is much to be said for this, but I want to add a caveat that to me seems more important than any proposal for curriculum reform. There is a danger that in our desire to prepare our students more fully for their role as teachers – an admirable socially and pedagogically responsible goal – we may lose sight of what I take to be the single most important problem in graduate studies today. Our graduate students teach so much that they have little occasion to be thoroughly and productively students. In many programs, they even teach two sections of freshman composition at a time. This is the dirty secret of our profession, so seldom discussed that I – a naive young man untutored in the ways of large state universities – spent five years as a professor of English in the United States before I learned that graduate students in some institutions taught what would in other institutions be regarded as a full-time professorial teaching load. I taught for a semester in a program where graduates taught two sections of composition simultaneously; the effects were immediately apparent: when one recommended interesting reading to a graduate seminar, no look of eager anticipation could be discerned on any face; the students all had two sets of freshman papers awaiting them. They had no time to throw themselves into an intellectual investigation, pursuing whatever interesting issues might arise. The immediate obligation of a class to meet tomorrow necessarily takes precedence.

We ourselves are all too aware of the difficulties of pursuing sustained research while we are teaching. Even we for whom teaching is familiar find it hard to do more than work toward limited objectives, and we wait for vacations or leaves when we can devote ourselves wholeheartedly to some investigation. Graduate study in English ought to provide an opportunity for students to immerse themselves as fully as possible in English literature and the myriad of questions that its study can raise. The originality of their work is likely to depend on the possibility of pursuing unorthodox interests or unusual connections – on having the time to profit from serendipity – instead of holding interests in check in order to keep to a tight schedule of short-term requirements imposed by their own teaching and their seminars.

There are considerable differences among graduate programs, in style and substance, but a variable of overwhelming importance, in my view, is how much graduate students are required to teach; consequently a reduction of graduate teaching is the most important single change that can be made. This is my third proposal. We do not often speak of this matter because of the discomfort such talk provokes: professors in the programs where graduate students teach a great deal are embarrassed or defensive about it; professors in institutions where more fellowship support is available are embarrassed to raise issues and make claims that suggest elitist values and draw attention to their institutions' superior wealth. Coming from a department whose students teach too much but considerably less than at many other places, I am uncomfortably aware that I may seem to be making a virtue of a situation that depends more on institutional wealth than on anything else, but it seems to me important to raise these issues. Only if there were a general outcry against exorbitant loads for teaching assistants would institutions that now require so much teaching have to reconsider their priorities. One role of a conference such as this one – one charge to the Commission on Writing and Literature – might be precisely to tell graduate deans what we deem unworthy of a serious graduate program. In other fields the standards articulated by national organizations do command administrators' attention, and we might at least make a start here, recognizing that graduate programs operate under a variety of budgetary rules but declaring that graduate students ought not in principle to teach more than one section of composition per term.

At issue is not just the amount of teaching but its distribution over a graduate student's career – to speak now about what might be desirable rather than what might be a standard. All too often such fellowship support as is available comes in the first year, when students are adjusting to graduate school, and then in a dissertation year. Freedom to pursue one's studies is certainly important at these times, especially in the first year, but a dissertation year fellowship is generally designed to permit students to complete an already defined project, in principle well under way, rather than to engage in the wide-ranging intellectual exploration that may best take place once a student has settled into graduate school life, gained some sense of current issues and of the institution's resources, but before he or she is committed to a particular thesis project. The student most needs freedom, I suggest, in that formative moment of the second, third, and fourth semesters.

In my own institution there has seemed to me over the years a palatable difference between the work done by those who enter on packages with three years of fellowships and those who come with only an initial year of fellowship support. I would be interested in knowing whether this corresponds with people's experience elsewhere. Those who teach more are less likely to have had time for broad, serendipitous reading and to have come up with truly exciting projects.

In planning for the future we should not let our desire to integrate preparation for the teaching of writing with literary study, under the rubric of a generalized rhetoric, lead us to neglect the importance of reducing the teaching that budgetary constraints impose on our students. Let their teaching be not a way of supporting themselves during graduate school but an integrated apprenticeship that takes place, perhaps, in their sixth and seventh semesters. This is my fourth proposal: we should explicitly provide such training in teaching as we can give, making students' teaching part of their training. Extensive experience will come later. Students can be teachers throughout their lives but graduate students only briefly. This policy will require a good deal of financial support, but money is already available in the sciences, and at a time when there is such interest in encouraging effective undergraduate teaching, we ought to make clear our view that teaching assistantships be considered not a means of support or source of cheap labor but an appropriate training program within the larger graduate program.

Crossing the Boundaries: Interdisciplinary Education at the Graduate Level

Helene Moglen

University of California, Santa Cruz

At the beginning of what has now become a landmark essay, "Beyond Interpretation: The Prospects of Contemporary Criticism," Jonathan Culler observed that "what is good for literary education is not necessarily good for the study of literature in general" (245). He went on to distinguish between the benign educational effect of the New Criticism, which had made the autonomous literary work available to students so that they could discover its truths by analyzing the complex interrelation of its formal elements, and the deleterious effect on criticism of this same emphasis on interpretation. Insisting that to read a text as literature must be to read it in relation to other texts – literary and nonliterary, cultural and epistemic – Culler called a moratorium on literary interpretation: a moratorium intended for critics but not apparently for students. Critics were now to consider the function of literature in society and "its historic relation to other forms of discourse through which the world is organized and human activities are given meaning" (246). The serious critic would desirably theorize about the activity of interpretation and the nature of textuality. If also a teacher of undergraduates, he – or, very occasionally, she – would apply the benign but now anachronistic mythology of the New Criticism, leading students through networks of irony, paradox, and ambiguity to meanings no longer considered to be significant. Culler did not even allude, of course, to the third function proscriptively served by members of our profession: the teaching of writing – in its lowest form, composition, or what Robert Scholes has called "pseudo-non-literature" (7). The exclusion was appropriate since the responsibility for teaching composition was delegated increasingly by the secure and respected to teachers – usually women–who were marginal to the institutions that patronized and exploited them. Viewed neither as theorists nor as interpreters, they had become the proletariat of the profession.

Culler's sense in 1976 that the radical division between literary education and literary criticism was both inevitable and desirable can be seen as representative of the literary establishment's response to the social and academic changes that had taken place in the late sixties and early seventies. It is important to remember, after all, the nature of the power-knowledge relations of the New Criticism. It was a methodology that contradictorily affirmed the student's ability to grasp the intended meanings of a text through the rational analysis of stylistic elements, while it assumed that–through the interpretive process–he or she would come to acknowledge both the superior interpretive skills of the teacher and the ultimate authority of the writer. While New Critical methodology had been absorbed as common practice, its ideology–so expressive of the social relations of the fifties–could not be sustained through the substantial political challenges of the sixties and early seventies, challenges that undermined authority generally: the authority of the teacher and writer no less than the authority of the state and the university. The ahistoricity and cultural elitism of the New Criticism–its aestheticism that rationalized and harmonized social conflict and contradiction and its validation of a canon that perpetuated through its principles of exclusion the white, male, middle-class, Europocentric values of the dominant culture: all this came to be revealed and then rejected under the pressures of a new spirit of pluralism that emphasized historical contexts and cultural difference.

Of course, that form of pluralism had little place in the emergent literary theory of the late seventies that, while rooted in the European consciousness of resistance represented by Derrida and Foucault, moved rapidly in a conservative direction. The radical potential of poststructuralism was soon lost. Cultural pluralism was appropriated by the playful pluralism of interpretive strategies celebrated for their own sake, and self-conscious self-reflexivity replaced self-conscious self-criticism. The descent into the fog of textuality that absorbed and erased the writer and reader–along with history, social reality, and the subject–represented the literary establishment's dramatic and effective response to the demands of two dissenting groups. On the one side were the students who were questioning traditional social and academic values and hierarchical structures. On the other were insurrectionary colleagues, not only junior faculty members who identified with their students, but also blacks and women who demanded a stronger institutional voice, greater representation in the curriculum, and a deauthorization of the canon. The move "beyond interpretation" sidestepped resistance. It allowed men who represented the elite culture of the profession to separate themselves effectively from their students–permitting them to believe that teaching and criticism had become, as Culler suggested, incompatible. It depoliticized the undergraduate curriculum by maintaining it in its earlier ahistorical and disciplinary form. It relegated to marginal segments of faculties and programs engagement with the social realities that continued to exert pressure on the academy in the form of ill-educated students, mostly nonwhite and working-class. Feminist and minority colleagues, intimidated for the moment, were encouraged to ghettoize themselves in their own intellectual, academic, and social communities. For their own reasons, they assented.

Perhaps the dilemma currently facing our graduate students most clearly emphasizes the seriousness of the crisis that has been created by the ideological schisms within our profession. The graduate curriculum at most universities necessarily reflects our own absence of clarity about our scholarly and pedagogical purposes. Courses in critical and cultural theory are offered alongside, but with no real connection to, conventional canonical courses focused on genre, period, and major authors. A single course on the teaching of writing may also be offered – may even be required – but it remains an isolated fragment of the graduate student's program. The contradictions and inconsistencies that, for those of us who are professionally established, are matters for lively debate – the stuff of departmental meetings – are for the graduate student matters of survival. Status within the profession is achieved by those who function successfully in the world of high theory. Jobs are usually available, however, at state colleges and universities where there is substantial hostility to theory on the part of the faculty members and where familiarity with interpretive methodology is far less important than is the ability to teach basic courses in writing and reading to ethnically diverse students who are not only mystified but also alienated by literariness. It becomes achingly clear to our former graduate students who are placed in this situation that the theory and practice of literature do indeed have little to do with each other and that their teachers and mentors have failed them as they are likely to fail their own students.

By reproducing versions of our own schizophrenic selves through our graduate programs, we ensure the impotence of the next generation of undergraduate teachers, the increased marginalization of certain groups within the academy of literary studies, and our own separation as citizens and intellectuals from social engagement and commitment. It is true that we can continue to debate the existence of the subject while we ignore the subjects in our classrooms, and we can smugly agree that reality cannot be known and that history cannot be retrieved while we are undone by our personal and collective pasts. But we do have other options, for the form of our abdication also contains potential forms of creative resistance that could allow us to integrate critical practice, pedagogy, and social responsibility.

It is probably the challenge to disciplinarity – phrased first by Marx and Freud and further articulated by structuralist and poststructuralist theorists of the last twenty years – that has most radically affected our sense of the nature and function of literary studies and of the relation of literary studies to other fields in which language, knowledge, and culture provide the foci of interest. Attentiveness to the open text has replaced analysis of the closed work, and the recognition of the interconnection of documents and institutions – literary and nonliterary, social and epistemic – has centered the role of interpretation in the social sciences and the humanities, even in the natural sciences with the publication of Thomas Kuhn's *Structure of Scientific Revolutions* and Evelyn Keller's *Reflections on Gender and Science.*

The move to interdisciplinarity – in its current form, an overriding concern with textuality and interpretive studies – is now sufficiently mainstream to have been appropriated as "news." In a recently published article, entitled "Scholarly Disciplines Breaking Out," the *New York Times* reported that faculty study groups have emerged at Bryn Mawr College, Berkeley, the University of Virginia, Stanford, Wesleyan, and "other respected schools," where faculties are frustrated by the narrowness of the departmental orientation. Musicologists, philosophers, lawyers, anthropologists, theologians, art historians, and literary critics are said to be talking to one another; "groups and committees are being formed all over the country to break down the departmental system"; and new interdisciplinary journals are being published. Undergraduate and graduate programs have appeared at such prestigious institutions as Yale, Johns Hopkins, University of Pennsylvania, Brown, Carnegie Mellon, and Santa Cruz, advertising themselves with such titles as Interpretation and Human Studies, Literary and Cultural Theory, Semiotics, and History of Consciousness. Steven Levine, one of the originators of the Bryn Mawr study group, is quoted as having said that "students may eventually major in reading or writing rather than in things called anthropology, history of art, or French. . . ."

What all this seems to suggest is that scholars trained in a number of disciplines, with a broad range of interests – certainly not all theoretical – are experiencing a *need* to understand one another in order to do work that is not readily categorized according to traditional fields. Furthermore, the work that they're doing is making them wish to change the form and substance of both undergraduate and graduate education. If we don't take advantage of this moment of opportunity, we will simply be reinforcing the alienative separation that has so ill served our students and our profession.

With hindsight, we might say that the avidity of our current concern with textuality marks the return of the repressed. The long history of belief in the specific representational forms of knowledge that we have called "disciplines" has given way to an obsession with the crisis of representation itself. History is textualized, as are the complex experiences of gender, race, and class, and oppositional consciousness has been appropriated as an elegant rhetorical strategy. To rescue literary studies by moving beyond the stasis of the polite pluralism of interdisciplinarity without getting mired in the new formalism would also be to extricate ourselves from an unflattering defensive position. We might be able to achieve this by aligning ourselves with those discourses that were marginalized in the late sixties and early seventies, particularly claiming the legacy that has matured in feminist literary theory and criticism – and enriching it through a politically defined textual practice.

Certainly it seems clear that while debates were raging over the cultivation and care of deconstruction, the home-grown plant of feminism was overrunning the garden. In its first stage, feminism provided a compensatory critique that was fundamentally oppositional. It placed a female tradition against a male canon, discovering female-authored texts that had been lost or suppressed; it explored the social, psychological, and historical relations of reading and writing from a woman-centered perspective, and it illuminated the ways in which sexual politics had pervaded interpretive, methodological, and rhetorical practices. Multidisciplinary in nature, the compensatory critique in its many forms made use of feminist scholarship rooted in fields across the humanities and social sciences.

When feminists began to seek theoretical structures in which to ground their work, their critiques became transformational – not simply because they drew on the transdisciplinary models available in psychoanalytic, Marxist, and deconstructive theory, but also because they reconceptualized those basic paradigms, rejecting their male-centered, gender-based assumptions. Further, this transformative effort involved a radical deconstruction of what had become the dominant categories of feminist theory itself. Having struggled to define the ways in which the differences of sexuality had been translated into the oppositions of gender, many academic feminists found themselves confined by the basic terms of their analysis. Theorizing oppression, they had been attracted at times by the view of women as victims, constructs of male desire, knowing – as, of course, they did – that male and female are not pure categories and do not stand in simple opposition to each other in cultural discourse or in our mental lives. Finally, while they rejected as a cultural construct the male representation of Woman as a universalized sign, they tended to reconstruct that sign in their own dominant image: heterosexual, Western, middle-class, and white.

The project that has now emerged for feminist critics and theorists is the reconceptualization of difference in a context that transforms the relation of the abstraction to its object, encouraging the reading of theory against experience to allow the appreciation of differences: differences within women and differences among them; the differences that align women with and separate them from men. The project involves as well the reconceptualization of power relations in order to acknowledge that resistance and conflict – as well as contradiction – are always inscribed in discursive practice and that we are all situated in many different places in those intersecting and often conflicting discourses. Understanding *how* we are situated, we can begin the process of re-situation: of resistance and change.[1] Obviously, it is also this project that links feminism to other self-conscious discourses of marginality and colonization that are concerned with interpretation as a social practice with material consequences.

The pedagogical and curricular implications of the feminist analysis can be interestingly explored through an adaptation and extension of the textual practice that Robert Scholes advocates in his important book *Textual Power*: a practice that assumes reading and writing to be reciprocal activities that mediate between experience and theory, teaching and learning, and the verbal and social text. Designating three stages – reading, interpretation, and criticism – that are performed by reader-writers at all levels of sophistication, Scholes maps a movement from submission to the meanings of a text to an interpretive process facilitated by the methodology of deconstruction, to a critique of themes and cultural codes that represents a form of ethical and political resistance. The process he describes is useful here because it supports our sense that, while power is invested in discourse, it is not monolithic but, as a property of relations, flows in more than one direction, with its directionality determined by the particular discourse in operation and the positioning of individuals within that discourse. So, in pedagogical relations – graduate and undergraduate – the authority of both the text and the teacher must be recognized, but that authority is shared and its directionality changed in the interactional processes at the heart of textual practice. Since students occupy at each successive step of the process a position of increasing distance from the text, they can – with the help of their teachers – come to read and finally to resist not only their written texts but also themselves and their social worlds *as* texts. The shared goal of both the pedagogical and the critical projects then becomes the reconstitution of the subject as a reader-writer who is capable first of recognizing points of resistance within the text as self and other and who is able then to achieve transformational rereadings that will open possibilities for psychological, intellectual, and social change.

We might recommend, therefore, that a graduate program intended to prepare students for the intersecting roles of teacher and critic should emphasize the reading, interpreting, and criticism of verbal and cultural texts within historical contexts in a core program oriented to critical and cultural theory. The categories assumed as central in conventional literary studies – genres, canon, narrative form, literary history – would be problematized and the positions of writer, reader, and critic relativized. (We might, for example, wish to ask in period courses such questions as, For whom was the Renaissance a renaissance? Who was not allowed to be enlightened in the Enlightenment? For whom was Romanticism romantic, and for whom not romantic? We might define current surveys of English literature as courses in white Western male literature and require that they be taken in conjunction with black, women's, and world literature courses. Letters, journals, and interviews might be read along with fictive narratives of any period, and a genre course in the gothic would include contemporary horror films as well as a case history or two by Freud.) The historicizing of texts, while involving the analysis of institutional, cultural, and discursive determinations of systems of thought, would also rely on the study of social practices engaged in by anthropologists and social historians and the practice by students themselves of what has come to be called the "new history." Feminist theory, theories of colonial discourse, semiotics, theories of language and of the subject, theories of aesthetic production, representation, myth, and ideology would be incorporated into the core program, but attention would always be paid to the implication of specific theories for pedagogical, social, and political practice. Finally, departments of literary studies would maintain strong connections with women's studies and ethnic studies programs, for it is there that those who resist social, psychological, and epistemological forms of sexism and racism will continue to engage important questions of curricular and pedagogical reform.

Just as the effort to authorize students through a shared process of writing, reading, and revising would contribute to the democratization of the undergraduate classroom—with student papers serving as texts along with official literary and nonliterary documents—the changed focus of the graduate program, and of the larger intellectual effort that it represents, might well help to redefine the relationship of faculty members to graduate students and of graduate students to one another. Here too it is the writing—produced by both students and faculty members, all participating in an exploratory and innovational project—that could allow individuals and groups that formerly viewed themselves as being in hierarchical and competitive relationships to redefine themselves genuinely as colleagues. The scholarly work, now the result of individual effort and proof of individual agility, might be replaced by a multivoiced, collaboratively produced text that makes use of synthetic methodologies that have been defined through poststructuralist theories. The authority of the individual critic, who appears at once so arrogant and so impotent, might then be replaced by a collective power claimed and exercised in acts of significant intellectual, institutional, social, and political resistance.

Note

[1]This is a central argument in Julian Henriques et al.; see especially 116–18 and 284.

Thinking Change, Changing Thinking

Janel Mueller
University of Chicago

If the remarks I make here prove of any use, it will not be because I can pretend to any expertise or representativeness in addressing the concerns of this conference. (Let me briefly document the oddity of my situation. I chair an English department with equal numbers of undergraduate majors and graduate students: there are 160 in each category. The larger setting of this English department is a private university of 8,000 students: 3,200 in the college, and 4,800 in the graduate and professional schools. Our graduate students outnumber our undergraduates overall, by a proportion of 3 to 2.) As chair of the English department of the University of Chicago, I knew that I would be attending very much as a listener and a learner and that I would be given a good deal to think about. This prediction has proved true. And now, although my thinking is far from finished, let alone settled, it is my assignment to offer some reflections on the topic Proposals for Change. I have interpreted this to mean proposing some thoughts about change – above all, as we are experiencing it; next, as we may initiate it.

Arguably the most important of recent changes affecting curricular philosophy and practice, certainly at the University of Chicago, has been the revision of the qualifying examination in the doctoral program. We are among the sixty-six percent of departments reporting substantial changes in this examination, and I have gathered from our discussions here that our pattern of change has been typical. Our revised qualifying examination supersedes the coverage model and the organization by periods of literary history to hold the student responsible for intensive command of four fields – one, typically, nonchronological – selected from among fifteen that include history and theory of genre; linguistics, stylistics, and language theory; and film, to name just a few. Dissertation projects have reflected this new opening up of fields for advanced research. I myself welcome our situation of change and consider that it has already afforded important sources of renewal for our profession – the advancing place of feminism in the academy being the one that has affected me most closely. I am optimistic in the face of the changes we are experiencing. I echo the feelings of Milton, who in *Areopagitica* envisaged a London full of "pens and heads . . . , sitting by their studious lamps, musing, searching, revolving new notions and ideas" and generalized to his nation, "Where there is much desire to learn, there of necessity will be much arguing, much writing, many opinions; for opinion . . . is but knowledge in the making."

Negative outlooks on present changes, however, have arisen in influential quarters; the Carnegie Foundation devoted its recent report to our "crisis in education." We should, I think, take the attitude that crisis is ongoing and that vitality in teaching and learning depends on how effectively we cope with new situations, new subjects, new students. During my experience as a teacher of English – going on twenty years, all but one of them spent at the University of Chicago – the single most sweeping change I have seen in the discipline concerns the emphasis in defining a new professional as a person specifically qualified to teach writing. Job descriptions from many more prospective employers are pointed about making this demand of PhDs in English – and hence of the programs that train them. If I recollect rightly, figures cited at the conference indicate that almost 15% of the jobs announced in the MLA listings for 1987 were in writing, and almost 20% more were in composition combined with introductory literature.

During the same twenty years there have been many accompanying changes in English as a discipline, not restricted to the teaching of writing. There have been revisions of our literary canon, proliferations of theory, multiple challenges to traditional critical and historical approaches, and significant shifts in the class, race, and gender makeup of student bodies and faculty constituencies. The most publicized – and perhaps the most convulsive – changes have affected graduate programs in their literary dimensions: courses in new subject matters and methodologies, older courses transformed from within. Virtually of equal importance, as the 1986 MLA survey of English doctoral programs shows, is the incidence of new courses in rhetoric. Here I want to add my voice to the calls that have already been issued at this conference for clarification of "rhetoric" as a covering term, whether applied to a body of knowledge, or to a complex of functions performed in language, or to the profession of English teaching as a whole. Our present uses of this term are far from transparent in their range of contexts, and the term is having no more success as a talisman to conjure up quick consensus among us.

In acknowledging that the new professional in English must be able to teach writing, we likewise acknowledge the impact of this specification, which is eliciting responses right now. As always, some responses to change are pretty much necessitated; others can be freer and more considered. I have been trying to sort out for myself which are which, at least in a preliminary way, during this conference.

What seems to me most profoundly necessitating is the magnitude of the task of teaching English composition both in colleges and in universities nation-wide. This has long been a sizable task, if we are to take the word of William Riley Parker who laid down this historical generalization: "It was the teaching of freshman composition that quickly entrenched English departments in the college and university structure" (qtd. in Chapman and Tate 124). Declines in the numbers of undergraduate English majors on many campuses keep Parker's generalization current. At this conference we have been informed that the greatest single impetus to the creation of separate doctoral programs in rhetoric and com-position has been the challenge of mounting required undergraduate writing courses under the open enrollment policies in effect in many institutions. Data gathered by David Chapman and Gary Tate corroborate the connection at several specific points. Among the thirty-eight institutions they list as offering doctoral programs in rhetoric or composition, all but four appear to be publicly funded. They remark that the graduate faculty members in such programs, despite their small numbers, commonly serve as directors of the freshman writing program or as directors of writing centers as well. They also remark that the only course currently found in all doctoral programs in rhetoric and composition is "the ped-agogy course for teachers of freshman composition" (128, 129).

If it is true that doctoral programs in rhetoric and composition have frequently originated as responses to the massive enterprise of teaching writing to Ameri-can college students, we can be confident of the element of practical necessity in their existence and we can also infer something about the practical necessities of their nature. However abstract, theoretical, or long-range some of their research projects may be, these programs will constantly feel pressure to generate applica-tions, to transmit norms, concepts, and strategies to their graduate students that they in turn can transmit to students at more basic levels. (See Bettina Huber's table documenting a marked correlation between the existence of a graduate rhet-oric program at a given institution and enrollment levels in its undergraduate writ-ing courses in the appendix, "A Report on the 1986 Survey of English Doctoral Programs in Writing and Literature.") But because these programs are chronically understaffed and cut or kept to the bone in their course offerings (Chapman and Tate 129), the pressure to cultivate not just a cohesive but a standardized approach might often amount to something like a necessity. I confess to knowing much less than I would like to know about doctoral programs in rhetoric and composi-tion and simply cite at this point Huber's remark to the effect that program descrip-tions suggest considerable agreement about the appropriate course content for a doctoral training program in rhetoric, writing, and composition as opposed to far less agreement about courses required for the literature degree. This difference makes me apprehensive for two reasons that my ignorance undoubtedly exacer-bates. I wonder, on the one hand, whether we have sufficient cultural consensus to be able to affirm to our students at large, "*This* is how you should write," and, on the other, whether we have methods proven to be able to say, "And *this* is how you will learn to do it and teach others to do it."

I raise these worries in good faith, because of what we have been learning in recent times from changes affecting the study of English literature – namely, the healthiness of competing theories, alternative outlooks, contested norms. This diversity is by now as much incorporated in programs and courses in English literature as it is in the range of academic publications. I do sense a comparable diversity in academic publications on rhetoric and composition, but it may not hold as well in a number of the programs. If I am even roughly right that rhetoric and composition programs are frequently less diverse than literature programs, and also right about the practical necessities that conduce to a channeled approach, then there is a very serious difficulty here. We don't have to fear so much for the vitality of the field of rhetoric and composition overall, for theory and method and testing will develop apace and get written up and critiqued and evaluated. But in the meantime it does seem that programs in rhetoric and composition will risk being splintered and polarized according to the dominant approach adopted by each and that holders of doctorates from these programs will also risk being all too programmatically produced.

I hope I have not created a misunderstanding. Anyone who contracts to grapple for a time, let alone for a whole career, with the difficulties of teaching writing to undergraduates – or the difficulties of researching in the teaching of writing – commands my respect for being willing to work immensely hard and to put his or her training constantly on the line to foster essential capabilities. In our small discussion group yesterday, John Fenstermaker made a very apt remark to the effect that teachers of writing courses distinguish themselves systematically from teachers of literature courses by their willingness to work under and be judged by "the criterion of an immediate pedagogical payoff." To take a broader view for the moment, I agree with social, political, and moral analysts who connect inarticulateness with a lowering of cultural standards and who link responsible participation in society with a grasp of issues that in turn requires appreciation and effective use of language. I also believe, less somberly, that the pleasure and interest we take in society lessen when both the media and private communication fail to engage us at the level of discourse. This is why I express concern with possible constriction to programmatic aims in doctoral work in rhetoric and composition all the while that I register its necessity and hail its potential. I think these programs are something worth doing that is worth doing well; and to me, well means diversely. One of the most constructive things for me about this conference thus far has been the offering of suggestions about how this diversity might be fostered. Gary Waller has sketched for us the larger objectives of the present two-track doctoral program at Carnegie Mellon (his paper appears later in this volume). Jim Slevin has hazarded a formulation of what needs integrating in rhetorical study: how texts work on readers, how the social text works on writers, how a text originates in writing.

With this stress on diversity I have brought myself to a second aspect of responses to change on which I want to comment in connection with the teaching of rhetoric and composition – namely, those responses that can be relatively more free in designing courses and programs. Although I think their internal diversity sets a good example, I think their still preponderantly historical orientation is likely to set a bad one. What I am about to say is not impossibly paradoxical. Because I have been a student of Renaissance and classical texts for so much of my professional life, I am wary of approaches to the teaching of writing grounded in the history of rhetoric – unless this history is submitted to a careful critique of the social conditions and consequences in which it is implicated. I have recently found that my wariness is not shared by most of the members of my profession, for an article by William Covino, Nan Johnson, and Michael Feehan, "Graduate Education in Rhetoric: Attitudes and Implications," records strong support for teacher preparation that includes a course in classical rhetoric: 81.1% of general faculty members, 79.8% of general graduate students, 83.7% of rhetoric faculty members, and 76.5% of rhetoric graduate students take this position (391). My misgivings initially attached to the question of how much the technical apparatus of this tradition really promotes the acquisition and development of writing skills. I have since realized that what I find objectionable – and what I hope others will find objectionable – is the perpetuation of the classical rhetorical model for discourse: the winning out over and dominating of others that is graced by the term persuasion. I do not despair of our eventually having the requisite critical consciousness to rehabilitate the notion of authorship within a model that will replace its long-standing authoritarian emphasis with one based on the contractual, transactive, cooperative character of discourse. But to that future moment – I speak now as a feminist and a professor of English – the history of rhetoric seems to me to constitute mostly a negative preamble.

On the slim basis of what I now know, I am inclined to think much more promising the approaches that locate the study and teaching of rhetoric and composition within a matrix of connections to psycho- and sociolinguistics, discourse theory, and cultural studies. My thinking in this matter has been helped by one of my graduate students, who ensured through his dissertation that I would get some extended exposure to the thought of Antonio Gramsci. To characterize Gramsci's view very briefly and broadly, societies are sustained by labor. The psychophysical complement of this labor is language, which, through its cognitive modeling systems, helps to undergird the social order. The strategies we advocate for writing can be conceptualized and taught as a subgrammar, or secondary modeling system, that builds more intricately on the grammar and primary materials of natural language. This outlook on language as constitutive of our human capacities to live and work together is all too abstract as I have stated it, I know. Let me borrow more down-to-earth wording from a recent remark by Richard Lloyd-Jones: "What we are all really talking about and concerned with is language, the glue that holds society together." I concur; and this is as far as I see at present.

Let me close by reasserting as fact, not forecast, that programs in rhetoric and composition are with us as a major professional necessity. Will they be encouraged as a discipline within English departments, as 83.7% of general faculty members, 83.6% of general graduate students, 90.9% of rhetoric faculty members, and 90.8% of rhetoric graduate students have indicated (Covino, et al. 393)? That depends on whether English departments will continue to be responsive to a diversity that has already reinvigorated the study of literature in our midst over the past two decades. I believe that we must find and that we will find common institutional ground for our shared commitment to studying and teaching the reciprocity of reading and writing, the instrumentality of the English language as shaped by the multifarious concerns and purposes of its users. Beyond this I find myself incapable of pronouncing on the specific curricular shapes to be assumed by a future that, like our knowledge, is in the making.

Liberal Education and the English Department: Or, English as a Trivial Pursuit

Don H. Bialostosky
University of Toledo

The advent of literary theory has changed the boundaries of English departments, but we are not yet sure how. Some would say that the walls have come tumbling down to open a space of literary or linguistic studies that privileges no single language or its literary history. Others imagine that the theorists have walled themselves into a specialized enclave, cut off from literary experience in English or any other language. I argue that literary theory has reopened three doors in the city walls of our English departments, directed attention to three roads that enter through them, and pointed the way to the common place where they meet. Those roads are the medieval liberal arts of grammar, rhetoric, and dialectic, and their meeting place is the trivium – literally, the place where three roads meet – the common place of the verbal liberal arts. Literary theory, in other words, has trivialized English, or perhaps revealed its inherent triviality, or made it, whether we will or no, a trivial pursuit.

I shall return to the demeaning suggestions in this wordplay, but first I want to call a witness and adduce some evidence to substantiate my claim that the rise of literary theory has been the return of the repressed trivium. The most comprehensive and self-conscious witness I can call is Paul de Man, whose essay "The Resistance to Theory" describes contemporary literary theory as "one more chapter" in a discourse provoked by the "unresolved tensions" within "the classical *trivium*, which considers the sciences of language as consisting of grammar, rhetoric, and logic (or dialectics)" (13). De Man loads his own rhetoric when he calls that discourse "infinitely prolonged" and of "endless frustration," and he produces a crucial and unargued displacement of its terms when he renames the literary branch of the *artes liberales* the "sciences of language," but he has precisely identified the field of debate we call theory on the terrain of the old literary liberal arts. Although de Man locates his own position within that field by conflating grammar and logic and opposing them to rhetoric, which in his view "undoes the claims of the *trivium* (and by extension, of language) to be an epistemologically stable construct" (17), I am less concerned at this point to test de Man's account of the trivium than to show just how right he is that the arts of the trivium are the focus of current theoretical debate.

De Man identifies the principal opponent of his rhetoric as the grammar that informs structuralist analyses of language and literature. Grammar has provided the model for Gerald Prince's narratology, Michael Riffaterre's semiotics, Kenneth Burke's dramatism, Northrop Frye's anatomy, and other important theoretical projects, many of which have shared de Man's disposition to shift the status of their discipline from art to science – Burke, I think, is the only exception. Rhetoric has been returned from the repressed not just by de Man but by the other principal deconstructionist theorist as well. Jacques Derrida mobilizes rhetoric both against dialectic, which he identifies with Western philosophy generally, and against grammar as embodied in such projects as structural linguistics and speech-act theory, but he, unlike de Man, is careful to avoid calling rhetoric a science.

Rhetoric, however, has informed other early and recent theoretical projects besides that of the deconstructionists, who sometimes speak as if rhetoric, theory, and deconstruction were one and the same. Burke is the only modern theorist to have produced correlative theoretical works explicitly on both grammatical and rhetorical principles. Wayne Booth, whom even Jonathan Culler has conceded to be "a man of considerable achievement in the realm of literary theory" (*On Deconstruction* 7–8), has produced both his early and important theoretical examination of the novel and all his later works on irony and critical theory under the sign of rhetoric. Frank Lentricchia has announced a rhetorical theoretical enterprise through an extended engagement with the theories of de Man and Burke, while Terry Eagleton has brought forward rhetoric as a neglected alternative to the whole enterprise of literary theory that he has satirized in *Literary Theory: An Introduction*. W. J. T. Mitchell, editor of one of the principal forums in which the theoretical debate has been conducted, follows Stephen Mailloux in suggesting – in answer to an argument Mitchell's journal published "against theory" understood as a dialectical philosophy of interpretation – that "theory be understood rhetorically" (5). Richard Rorty, another major voice in the recent debates, affirms a similar position without explicitly naming it rhetorical. It is not surprising, then, that at this conference on Graduate Study and the Future of Doctoral Study in English, rhetoric has been the most frequently mentioned candidate for a unifying model of literary study.

But dialectic, too, has had its recent advocates in literary theory, opposed both to one another and to the advocates of rhetoric and grammar. Fredric Jameson announced a dialectical criticism at the end of *Marxism and Form*, and in *The Political Unconscious* develops that criticism to the point where it claims to subsume all theoretical alternatives. Jerome McGann has outlined a materialist dialectic that works toward the impingement of facts on theoretical systems, while Evan Watkins has arrived via Benedetto Croce and Giovanni Gentile at a critical dialectic that allows the poem's autonomous voice to resist the dominating voice of theory. Hans-Georg Gadamer, too, has made dialectic the name for the hermeneutic practice he advocates. Despite their many differences, all these theorists have pursued their projects on the debating ground of the liberal arts, and no one of these arts–not even rhetoric–can claim that ground for itself alone.

Feminist literary theory, too, has been reevaluating the liberal arts to discover the extent to which they are compromised by their association with patriarchal institutions and values, for most of the institutions that have carried the tradition of the liberal arts and many of the institutions in which they have been practiced have been open only to males until this century. Toril Moi shows in her recent critical survey of feminist literary theory that feminist theorists differ over whether grammar, rhetoric, and logic are fatally gendered or innocently available for feminist purposes. She advises a "political and theoretical evaluation of the various methods and tools on offer" and of the contexts of their use, even as she is aware that "all forms of radical thought remain mortgaged to the very historical categories they seek to transcend" (75, 88). Moi herself turns to Julia Kristeva's semiotics as a supplement to the traditional disciplines of linguistics and rhetoric, but she is also clear that grammar, logic, and rhetoric should not be simply categorized and dismissed as "masculine." Her book shows that feminist theory is deeply engaged with arts of the trivium though it too is not to be identified with any one of them.

You may well be able to point to theoretical enterprises that cannot be included in these trivial debates, but I will be satisfied if you agree that recent theory has brought the verbal liberal arts back into the purview of English departments and brought those departments back to the trivium where those arts encounter one another. That meeting of three roads, you will recall, was not in the first instance a point of advanced study and specialized knowledge. "Trivial" has come to mean commonplace and ordinary and even trite and hackneyed because all students were expected to master the verbal liberal arts on their way to other specialized and distinguishing studies. The trivial studies themselves were not unimportant, but knowing them did not make you important or different from any other educated person. They were not like either specialized scientific knowledge or like highly cultivated aesthetic taste or poetic skill. They were "prosaic"–another word that has suffered the demeaning fate of "trivial"–and prose was the medium of their practice.

In bringing these trivial arts back to our attention, literary theory has also brought back prose as a medium of our reflective practice and as an object of instruction to our students. The experience of reading theory has taught us that we cannot take a trivial thing like clarity for granted, and it has made us more aware of the figures that cast shadows on our own prose works. I think the advent of theory has also led to our teaching more prose–not just the belletristic prose that gives writers a distinguished place among the poets, but the workaday prose of our own critical production and the argumentative prose of the trivial tradition that offers without embellishment reflections on the practices of the verbal liberal arts. Theory has even begun to teach some of us to read our students' prose with rhetorical and dialectical eyes that supplement the grammatical eyes we have all along brought to it; we are learning to read the rhetorical complexities of students' figures and the dialectical investments of their commonplaces instead of chastising their mixed metaphors and slapping the wrists of their "low" diction.

Theory is teaching us, in short, to take interest in the trivial and to suspect our tendencies to identify our field with "good" taste and "fine" art at the expense of the prose we and our students have been speaking all our lives. It has reinvigorated our interest in the arts that inquire into the mysteries of simple predication and the figurativeness of ordinary discourse, the political prose of the public forum and the specialized prose of the scientific and philosophical argument. It has not displaced our interest in distinguished poetic achievements, but it has reconnected that interest with interests in the more common verbal productions of the open forum where three roads meet. It reminds us that those distinguished poetic achievements are the specializations of widely shared verbal potentialities and that the discovery and cultivation of those potentialities is, at bottom, a trivial one.

I find a tantalizing passage under the *OED*'s first sense of "trivial": "belonging to the trivium of medieval studies." The quotation from Alexander Barclay's *Eglogues* of 1570 reads: "If they have smelled the artes triviall, They count them Poetes hye and heroicall." I imagine Barclay is declaring contempt for the ease with which neophytes in the studies of the trivium imagine themselves as accomplished poets. He sounds the way we sometimes do when we turn up our noses at the quantity of "poets" produced by our introductory creative writing courses. But I find something heartening in the passage as well. It suggests that even a beginning acquaintance with the trivial arts and the verbal potentialities they cultivate leads to poetic interests and ambitions. We do not have to repress or exclude the more ordinary or common verbal interests in order to cultivate poetic interests. The roads of rhetoric, dialectic, and grammar may be left unimpeded and their intersection may bustle with the clash of their interests and poetry may still thrive. Literary theory, then, may inform our thinking and our teaching, and poetry may still thrive. Our trivial pursuits may lead to our hye and heroicall achievements.

Replacing Coverage with Theory: Toward a Heterogeneous Field Model of Graduate Study

Paul B. Armstrong
University of Oregon

"Coverage" could act as the organizing principle of graduate study only as long as it was possible to assume unity in the canon of works to be studied and in the methods by which mastery of them could be attained. Such unity meant that students could be given the simple injunction "Read everything," and teachers could expect that coherent knowledge would result. This expectation now seems strange and unreasonable to many students and teachers. Not only has the field expanded incredibly because of challenges to the canon and a multiplication of interpretive methods. This extraordinary recent growth has also exposed a diversity that already existed but that had been largely repressed or ignored. The expansion of the canon has lengthened the list of texts students must know to the point where the demand for complete knowledge seems impossible (cover *Beowulf* to Virginia Woolf plus women's literature, minority literature, English literature outside the Anglo-American sphere, and . . .). By insisting that a broad range of truths and values be granted cultural authority, these challenges have helped call attention to the internal diversity of the previously existing canon that the myth of a unified tradition had covered over. Even the traditional "great books" are a heterogeneous collection of styles, beliefs, and ways of seeing. Adding Frederick Douglass and Zora Neale Hurston to the canon makes it harder to claim that all its members speak with the same voice.

This destabilization of the subject matter of literary study has been accompanied by a denaturalization of the act of understanding. The notion that "covering" a group of works would result in coherent, complete mastery seemed reasonable when reading was viewed as a simple, unproblematic activity. But understanding could seem like a "natural" act only as long as consensus reigned

about its goals and procedures. No new consensus has emerged in the wake of
the New Criticism. Instead, a proliferation of methods has exposed the inherent
contestability of interpretation – the variability of a text's meaning according to
the presuppositions and interests that inspire the interpreter's hypotheses about
its patterns. In addition to mastering an expanded canon, our students must also
become familiar with feminism, deconstruction, psychoanalysis, the new historicism, reader-response criticism, Marxism, phenomenology, and so on. An even
more serious complication, however, is that this multiplication of ways of reading has fatally undermined the injunction "Read everything." How students should
read is no longer self-evident, and the advice that they should try out many different ways of interpreting merely adds to their burden. It also risks confusing them
rather than clarifying the bewildering diversity before them.

Under these circumstances, it is hardly surprising that many leaders in our
profession have sought a new center around which to organize literary studies,
and "rhetoric" has seemed a plausible candidate for that privilege. If rhetoric is
the study of discourse, then perhaps it is the common denominator uniting us
all despite the divergences in the texts we prefer and the procedures we follow.
Renaming our field will not unify it, however. Calling literary studies rhetoric
will not resolve the problems we and our students face. Rhetoric cannot provide
the unity and coherence that coverage once did, because discourse is a diverse,
controversial concept. We are unlikely ever to find a univocal, universally accept-
able definition of discourse, because its domain includes a variety of contestable
matters: language, signification, textuality, culture, and so forth. What these terms
mean and how they should be studied have been among the most hotly debated
issues in contemporary critical theory. Whether the adversaries are structuralism
and phenomenology, psychoanalysis and Marxism, deconstruction and the new
pragmatism, different methods of interpretation define themselves by their differing views about discourse.

There is little consensus or prospect of agreement about a range of issues that
would have to be settled in order to give rhetoric more unity than the coverage
model provides – such issues as the status of signs and their referents, the role of
conventions in creating and establishing meaning, the determinacy of meaning,
the authority (if any) responsible for the origination of meaning, the possibility
of new meaning, and the importance of figures and how they signify. Critics hold
widely different beliefs about all these problems, and their disagreements result
not only in different ways of reading but also (at least sometimes) in different
configurations of the canon. To seek in rhetoric a center for literary studies will
displace rather than settle the question of how to make coherent a diversity that
seems confusing to those who complain that we need a new unifying principle.

Diversity need not be debilitating, however, if we understand its causes and
consequences. I would argue that theory should replace coverage as the foundation of the graduate curriculum because theory – defined broadly as reflection about
textuality, language, and interpretation – can help students find their way in the
multifarious world of literary studies. Our discipline is a heterogeneous field, a

diverse but bounded enterprise characterized by fundamental disagreements about what to study and how to study it, as well as by many complex convergences and resemblances in our goals, assumptions, and procedures that resist reduction to a core of common principles. Our enterprise is not a neatly organized structure held together by a center we have lost and need to recover. Rather, it is better conceived of as a disparate set of concurrent, sometimes overlapping conversations. These discussions are devoted to a variety of more or less related topics, sometimes between partners who share presuppositions and interests and who agree about how to read, but often between adversaries whose disagreements are too basic ever to be resolved.

Such a heterogeneous field of argument and exchange may seem confusing and incoherent to outsiders and even, at times, to the participants. Theory is necessary navigational equipment to keep one's bearings. Training in literary theory alone will not, however, allow students to become productive participants in the conversations of the profession. Although coverage is an impossible and misconceived goal, students should still develop competence in a variety of subject matters so that they have an understanding of the dimensions of the field and can move around within it. They also need to acquire expertise so that they can contribute significantly to the discussion in a particular area. Widely distributed reading in an expanded canon and deep, detailed specialization of some kind should be required. But so too must a solid understanding of the basic issues of literary theory. If only to avoid getting lost in the maze, students need to know how the conversations of the profession work, what the participants' options are, and what recourse is available when one becomes confused or dialogue breaks down.

Literary theory can provide orientation in several ways. Theoretical questions are everywhere in the discussions of the profession. Having a firm sense of the major controversies of literary theory can help a stranger understand and appreciate interlocutors in a relatively foreign part of the field even when they are talking about unfamiliar texts. Wide reading in a range of literary periods, genres, and traditions (defined not only by nations but also by race and gender) is necessary if one is to be a cosmopolitan citizen of the profession who can talk readily and productively about common problems with others in the broadly defined community. But gaining access to an unfamiliar conversation is often more easily and effectively accomplished if one has a sophisticated theoretical understanding of the issue at stake than if one has an outsider's necessarily superficial acquaintance with the authors or works under discussion. Students should still read Henry James, for example, but they will better appreciate the controversy over his late style if they know about the theory of language and representation than if they possess only a first-time reader's comprehension of *The Ambassadors*.

It is more important for our students to develop the ability to acquire new knowledge about an unfamiliar period, genre, or literary problem than to cover hastily and thinly everything the profession talks about. Serious study of such theoretical issues as the determinacy of meaning, the workings of literary change, the status of texts, or the politics of interpretation can enhance students' ability to make sense of unfamiliar conversations. Knowledge of literary theory cannot, of course, provide immediate, transparent understanding of a foreign world. All students have to make for themselves the imaginative leap that inhabiting a different perspective requires. But familiarity with theoretical issues can give members of our profession a variety of hypotheses to try out to make sense of unfamiliar terrain, and this can increase our mobility and expand our appreciation of conversations different from those we ordinarily contribute to.

No one can participate in all the discipline's conversations, especially because some of them are based on mutually exclusive presuppositions about how to read. One of the most important functions of literary theory is to help an interpreter choose between alternative modes of understanding by exposing their assumptions and implications. Theory cannot make this choice for an interpreter precisely because it is a choice—a wager about what it will turn out to be better to have believed. Choosing one's interpretive position requires a declaration of faith in certain principles and a decision about which purposes to value and which goals to pursue. Theoretical reflection can ensure that a student's commitment to a particular way of thinking and reading is not blind or coerced but, rather, freely declared for lucid, coherent reasons. Theory cannot ensure the correctness of this choice, any more than it can guarantee right readings. Nor can it promise that a student will not some day, in the light of subsequent developments, come to regret previously-made commitments and decide to change them. But to act effectively in a heterogeneous world, we need to be able to make informed choices, and theoretical reflection can help to clarify the significance of our alternatives and their probable implications.

In a world where what one understands can vary so much according to what one chooses to believe, we and our students especially need to know when to change our minds. Here again theory can offer vital assistance. Our choices may have unforeseen, unwanted consequences, or an unexpected obstacle may suddenly block our investigations. It is not always easy to differentiate between an anomaly that will give way to persistent effort and a dilemma in which our presuppositions and procedures are faulty and need to be revised. But the ability to move from practical problem solving to theoretical reflection about the possible sources and implications of problems can stop us from banging our heads against the wall, at least momentarily, and help us clarify the available options.

For interpreters who may come to doubt their work because other critics find fault with it, theoretical reflection can sometimes sort out which disagreements spring from different, perhaps incommensurable beliefs and which locate genuinely mistaken or improbable hypotheses. Such distinctions may be difficult or even impossible to make, but the effort is useful because it can guide us in deciding whether to redouble our commitment to our presuppositions or reconsider and perhaps revise them. Impasses occur in conversations for many reasons, and the ability to reflect theoretically about them can help us discover why they have happened and what, if anything, can be done about them (and sometimes the answer is "nothing").

Many kinds of course offerings can cultivate in students an awareness of theoretical issues and an ability to reflect rigorously and precisely about interpretation, literature, and language. I would prefer a series of four courses during the first two years of graduate study that would examine the act of understanding, the workings of language, the notion of genre, and the problem of history. The first course would explore the reasons for interpretive conflict and its implications (is interpretation simply relative, or is it still possible to judge the validity of a reading? how does one choose between different ways of understanding? to what extent can hermeneutic disagreements be resolved?). The course on language would examine various theories about signs (including the relation of linguistic differences to differences of gender, race, and class) and their implications for literary understanding. Serious study of "genre" seems desirable because many interpretive disputes revolve around disagreements about how to type texts. In addition to asking about how literary kinds are identified and what follows from these definitions (different evaluative criteria, for example, and rankings of canonical works), this course might also raise the question of whether "literature" is a unique, determinable type of textuality (this might also be a theme in the course on language). Because many kinds of literary inquiry are historical in one way or another, it also seems advisable to introduce students to the debates about what history is, how change occurs, and whether understanding the past is itself a determinate or a historically variable activity.

This would not be a "core curriculum" in the sense that it would disclose the hidden unity of our disparate enterprise. The goal of these courses would be, rather, to help explain why literary studies are heterogeneous in subject matter and methodology and to offer students guidance in deciding what conversations they would like to join and what assumptions about language, literature, and interpretation they wish to embrace. This curriculum would provide a foundation for future work, but not by giving students an indubitably certain ground on which to stand or by showing them infallible procedures for generating right readings. Rather, it would familiarize them with a variety of important conceptual problems that they are likely to find debated in many of the profession's conversations, and it would cultivate their ability to reflect self-critically about basic hermeneutic and literary questions. In these ways, it would help provide students with the navigational equipment they will need as they try to acquire a coherent, distributed knowledge of the field and as they decide which specialization to pursue and which presuppositions and procedures to adopt.

What we need to teach our students is what we ourselves need to learn—how to find our way in a heterogeneous field that resists unification. We cannot do without theory in such a world but, indeed, need it more than we would in a homogeneous, harmonious field where consensus made the subject matter seem finite, objects stable, procedures self-evident, and coverage a possible and desirable goal. No one can cover the field of literary studies today, but theory can help us and our students participate productively in its diversity.

The Place of Rhetoric and Composition in Doctoral Studies

Janice M. Lauer, *Purdue University*
Andrea Lunsford, *Ohio State University*

While Wayzata conferees often invoked the concept of rhetoric and while more than half of the doctorate-granting institutions reported at least some offerings in rhetoric and composition, a number of participants expressed uncertainty about the meaning of the terms rhetoric and composition. What is included in doctoral programs in rhetoric and composition? More important, exactly what would doctoral studies in rhetoric and composition contribute to English studies? This essay addresses such problems of definition by describing, as concretely as possible, common features of these doctoral programs and by summarizing the contributions such studies can make to an English program.

Scholars of rhetoric and composition study written discourse as a complex set of processes by which writers and readers coconstruct meanings in historical, social, and ideological contexts. This field takes responsibility for both understanding and enhancing the growth of multiple levels of literacy, examining the linguistic, cognitive, and social knowledge writers need to coordinate the tasks of a literate society (Phelps). Doctoral students in rhetoric and composition study the largely tacit acquisition of lower levels of literacy that depend heavily on spontaneous, unself-conscious, and deeply contextualized learning. They also study the means by which writers develop complex higher levels of skilled performance, levels that entail sustained critical and intersubjective attention to language forms, purposes, and effects. Reconceptualizing literacy as the power to act in the world, rhetoric and composition scholars view writing and reading as intricately related instrumentalities for participation in, and critique of, the culture and thus extend the site of their investigations from school to home and workplace.

To study the complex domain of rhetoric and composition, scholars engage in multiple modes of inquiry, including historical scholarship, rhetorical or theoretical inquiry, and empirical research. In fully developed doctoral programs, these modes of inquiry and the issues they examine constitute the core of study. Historical scholarship in composition and rhetoric bears many resemblances to historical work in literature: scholars seek to reclaim those who have been marginalized or excluded from rhetorical history, to trace intertextual conversations across primary texts, to embed various historical constructs in a more complex ideological framework, and to examine the ways in which literacy has been defined and achieved in different historical periods. Very much at issue in current historical work are several deceptively simple questions: What has it meant to be a reader or a writer in, say, classical Athens or medieval London? Why do few (if any) women figure in traditional histories of rhetoric? What matrix of events and forces surrounded the gradual separation of rhetoric and poetic or the increasing valorization of expository discourse? As with other graduate English courses, graduate courses in rhetorical history go beyond surveys of primary texts to offer critical readings of, and readings against, these texts and their commentaries, using methods often familiar to literary scholars. As a guide to this scholarship, historical reference tools have been published, including two bibliographic texts edited by Winifred Bryan Horner; essay collections such as the one by Robert J. Connors, Andrea Lunsford, and Lisa Ede; and journals such as *Pre/Text*, *The Rhetoric Society Quarterly*, and *Rhetorica*.

Rhetorical or theoretical research, a second typical mode of inquiry closely related in method to traditional literary research, seeks to develop new theories of written discourse, often deriving them from other disciplines, and to argue for the viability of these new theories (Lauer). While a discussion of even the major figures and of the new theories themselves is beyond the scope of this essay, the following questions seem of particular importance because they raise issues of interest to other areas of English studies: Can we construct theories that will account for all the genres, processes, contexts, and facilitation of written discourse? for the ways writers and readers cocreate meanings? for the ways in which reading and writing are related? Over the last twenty-five years, rhetorical inquiry has generated a rich and diverse set of potential answers to these questions, which students in graduate courses examine critically, seeking to enlarge, qualify, or repudiate them. This mode of inquiry is essentially constructive, devoted to advancing and elaborating new explanations of discourse, rather than primarily finding gaps and inconsistencies. Several kinds of reference tools identify this scholarship: bibliographic volumes edited by Erika Lindemann; Gary Tate; Michael G. Moran and Ronald F. Lunsford; and Ben W. McClelland and Timothy R. Donovan; and journals such as *Rhetoric Review* and *CCC*.

A third major mode of inquiry in rhetoric and composition, empirical research, is less familiar to literary scholars and did not appear at all in those discussions at Wayzata that related even peripherally to methodology. Such research proceeds from systematic collection of data to analysis of these data, using either descriptive or experimental designs. Descriptive studies, which entail observation of writing phenomena and analysis of data, with as little restructuring of the situation or environment under scrutiny as possible, include case studies, ethnographies, survey research, quantitative descriptive studies, prediction studies, and program evaluation studies. In short, descriptive researchers isolate and define important variables for further study. Some behavioral and social sciences view descriptive research as "prescientific," to be conducted only at early stages of an investigation when the researcher is seeking hypotheses to test. Ethnology, anthropology, and rhetoric and composition, however, accord descriptive studies higher status because such research allows investigators to take multiple perspectives on any question. The research has been particularly helpful in shifting our attention from textual products to the *processes* of writing and reading. Descriptive studies have also been especially provocative in suggesting the ways in which student writers and readers become a part of–or are alienated from–various discourse communities.

A second kind of empirical inquiry–experimental research–aims to establish cause-and-effect relations between variables such as methods of instruction and the quality of writing produced. As such, experimental research is particularly linked to questions of pedagogy. Researchers typically assert hypotheses, assign writers or readers to treatment and control groups, administer contrastive methods of instruction, and assess the results by means of measurement instruments and observations that are both reliable and valid. In experiments, the value of the findings rests on the validity of the measurement instruments used. Because the conclusions of any experimental study can apply only to the groups studied, a new type of research design, meta-analysis, has recently been used to examine the cumulative results of many experimental studies on writing. Meta-analysis holds out the promise, for example, of being able to determine the effectiveness of writing instruction methods over a large number of experiments with a variety of students and settings. Descriptions of empirical studies and bibliographies can be found in Beach and Bridwell; Cooper and Odell; Hillocks; Lauer and Asher; and Scardamalia and Bereiter; and in journals such as *Written Communication* and *Research in the Teaching of English*.

It goes without saying that in neither experimental nor descriptive studies do the data speak for themselves. They have all been coded and interpreted; their conclusions must be argued. Graduate courses in empirical research have two general objectives: to study the body of research already accumulated and to examine the features of each research design and its claim to probable knowledge about written discourse. At their best, these courses take a perspective Pierre Bourdieu calls dialectical, revealing the conditions under which descriptive and experimental research are conducted and probing the presuppositions and theories that guide each type of researcher.

In rhetoric and composition, empirical, historical, and rhetorical studies work together. Historical research keeps the field from reinventing the wheel, providing it with discussions about good and bad solutions and possible causes of the contemporary problems it studies. Rhetorical inquiry suggests aspects of writing for empirical study; prompts coding schemes, questions for surveys, and evaluative criteria; and provides hypotheses for experimental research. Empirical research refines rhetorical theory, helping to verify or repudiate it, and identifies important new dimensions that contribute to theory formation. Using several modes thus helps rhetoric and composition to avoid the nearsightedness that can lead to overlooking major problems because they fall outside a particular pattern of inquiry. The use of multiple modes also cultivates a fruitful reciprocity. Rhetorical and historical inquiries help empirical researchers avoid the fate of some social sciences, which have become so mesmerized by good instruments that their investigators sometimes merely seek problems to fit their tools. Empirical research, on the other hand, helps to keep the field from the fate of some areas of the humanities that have lost touch with practice and human affairs. A major responsibility of doctoral programs in rhetoric and composition, therefore, is to engage students in a critical examination of scholarship that emanates from these three modes of inquiry. Another goal is to prepare students to conduct such research on their own, to create new rhetorical theory, historical knowledge, or empirical conclusions.

But what can such research, such new knowledge, add to the field of English studies? Why should the concerns that drive research and scholarship in rhetoric and composition have a place in English programs at all? We offer four responses to these questions, each of which relates to issues raised persistently at the Wayzata conference. First, work in rhetoric and composition offers a model for the integration of reading and writing called for by many at the conference. In practice, the field views reading and writing as reciprocal acts, studies the nature of this relationship, and aims to help students learn to move confidently between them.

The inherently interdisciplinary nature of work in rhetoric and composition offers another benefit to English programs and answers critics who claim that research in English studies has become too narrowly focused. The blurring of disciplinary boundaries characteristic of the postmodern academy (a tendency noted by Lanham, Scholes, and others at Wayzata) has always been a feature of rhetorical inquiry, which commonly builds on work in philosophy, communications, psychology, and linguistics. This cross-disciplinary feature can be seen in many doctoral dissertations in rhetoric and composition that use more than one mode of inquiry – for example, a study of the genesis of discourse building on rhetorical theories of *status* and on research in cognitive psychology on problem formulation; a Heideggerian interpretation of the Gorgian *kairos*; a new reading of Aristotle's concept of *techne*, drawing on Derrida, Bourdieu, and Castoriadis; a theory of *relevance* in discourse, building on work in linguistics, rhetoric, and language philosophy; a critique of writing-across-the-curriculum programs, using Said, Foucault, and Weber; an examination of the rhetorical-poetic binary, using Bakhtin and Burke; and a study of graduate student writing in English, drawing on work in ethnography, psycholinguistics, and literary theory.

Through its interdisciplinary connections and its study of the interactive nature of reading and writing, the field of rhetoric and composition also contributes to English studies by broadening its base of textuality, allowing us to interrogate and interpret a wide range of discourse, from fiction to public policy statements and advertisements, and from technical reports to texts produced by student writers. Doing so responds directly to Scholes's calls to reconceive the object of our study in broad and provocative ways and, more important, to connect theory and practice at all levels of study.

Finally, connecting theory and practice is possible, in large part, because of the emphasis rhetoric and composition place on pedagogy as an integral part of any program. In this view, pedagogy becomes not the service "burden" of a department but, rather, the arena in which theory and research are enacted, tested, and refined; teaching becomes a field of symbolic action, a network of primary discourse acts, of layers of discourse about discourse. Composition specialists study competing pedagogies to determine their underlying tacit or explicit assumptions about the nature of language and art, the relation between discourse and knowledge, and the hermeneutics of student texts. Subjecting our own pedagogies to rigorous scrutiny thus becomes a way of advancing research – and of answering critics who decry our failure to take responsibility for the teaching of teachers.

Conceived as the systematic study of the production and interpretation of all kinds of texts in their varying contexts, the field of rhetoric and composition contributes to English studies by integrating reading and writing, by establishing interdisciplinary frameworks, by broadening our textual base, and by viewing pedagogy as an enactment of theory. In addition, the field provides English studies with an opportunity to enter into and affect public policy debates and discussions about the way English is taught and assessed at all levels, about issues of literacy in general, and about the relation of literacy to particular social, political, and ideological agendas. But addressing such issues in the most fruitful and effective ways calls for a strong alliance among all areas of English studies – literary criticism and history, theory, language study – and rhetoric and composition. At some universities such an alliance is already in place; in others it is forming. It is the conviction of scholars in rhetoric and composition that such an alliance forms the richest base for doctoral studies in English.

Note

We wish to thank the following readers for their comments and advice: Jacob Adler, James Berlin, Janet Emig, Leon Gottfried, Sharon Hamilton-Wieler, James Slevin, Patricia Sullivan, and Art Young.

Polylogue:
Reading, Writing, and the
Structure of Doctoral Study

Gary Waller
Carnegie Mellon University

In our metaphors, we reveal (or betray) our futures. The Wayzata conference, along with the other major disciplinary conference of 1987, the English Coalition Conference at Wye Woods, Maryland, deserves to be put in a broader context in part because of particular proposals for change in doctoral study in English, but, more important, because of the emergent metaphors of dialogue, or "polylogue" as it might better be characterized, that rose to challenge the residual metaphors of battle, separate development, or loneliness that have been all too prevalent in the profession's debates (see Sinfield 35; Corder and Baumlin; Lucas). Even if what English is about is, as Alan Sinfield puts it, "no longer self-evident" except to "those who have been trained to regard it" as such (36–37), the Bakhtinian insistence on opening rather than resisting the possibility of change is an exciting one. Metaphors are always where our deepest cultural values (and, to take an even more upbeat view, the emergent values of a culture) can be located, and it is significant that at both Wayzata and Wye Woods, the emergent metaphors were not of expulsion or heresy or (on the other hand) appropriation or absorption but of energized, interactive communication: speaking, listening, restating, relistening, reopening dialogue.

One of the most striking metaphors in recent thinking about the profession is what Gerald Graff calls the "conflict" model of the discipline. It looks divisive (and may often be interpreted so) but should be read precisely as opening up such a polylogue as I'm referring to. In this paper, I want to argue for the institutionalization in our doctoral programs of such a model, suggesting that the very issues and debates of the profession become the focus of the structure of the graduate curriculum. I advance a general argument for a particular model of PhD studies in English and critique a particular example, the evolving dual program in rhetoric and literary and cultural theory at Carnegie Mellon. The inevitable question one always finds directed to utopian schemes of curricular reform—"Ah, yes, but would they work?"—can therefore be answered not merely on grounds of principle or desire but from a concrete, developing, although (confessedly) by no means perfect, example.

The goal of such a model is today all the more urgent, I believe, because of the dual revolutions within the professions of language and literary studies that have occurred in the past twenty years. These revolutions, too, were vividly engaged in the polylogue of Wayzata. First, we have seen that programs in rhetoric have risen to respectability, prestige, and, in a few places, dominance. When Carnegie Mellon established its PhD in rhetoric in 1980, it was one of a handful of schools that had recognized the justice of the struggle to legitimize writing not merely as a service activity but as the valid focus of intellectual inquiry. By 1987, we learned at the Wayzata conference, almost half of the departments represented had incorporated an option in rhetoric into their PhD programs, and about twenty departments offered exclusively rhetoric programs. But it has been a long struggle, and many reactions at Wayzata suggest that it will be a continuing one. The dominant model's reluctance to grant rhetoric and composition anything more than marginal status (even though most of our PhD graduates will be required to teach writing courses) has provoked a variety of responses. Representing the side of rhetoric, Maxine Hairston advocates secession from English, Richard Young and David Kaufer argue for equality, Andrea Lunsford calls for the necessary interaction of reading and writing at all levels of the curriculum, and Richard Lanham seeks a new *paedeia*. But for many traditional programs, "writing" is seen not as an intellectually demanding focus of study but, rather, a response to a perceived crisis in general literacy. Hence many universities, such as the University of Southern California, the University of California at Los Angeles, and the University of Texas at Austin, marginalize composition researchers and teachers and relegate their graduate courses in composition theory to the status of electives.

By contrast, a decade ago, Carnegie Mellon's English department, then headed by my colleague Richard Young, developed—within the university's aggressive policy of establishing a "comparative advantage" in all its departments—a PhD in rhetoric. Instead of asking how the residual conception of English might simply be served by adding options in rhetoric—what I have termed elsewhere the "classic park-bench" model of curricular change ("Working" 7)—those developing the program asked, What problems and issues related to writing and the production of texts across our society need addressing? Further, what qualifications, skills, and interests are involved in addressing them? The answers to such questions initially took the department beyond the traditional boundaries of English into, for instance, speech, cognitive psychology, computer science, philosophy, design—disciplines in which some of the faculty members who were hired had graduate training, thus avoiding certain of the problems of being in "English." The department also began to make more central some interests that have been traditionally marginalized in the discipline of English, such as sociolinguistics. The program has become distinctive for a special focus on cognitive rhetoric, an umbrella that covers classical rhetoric, critical thinking, theories of invention, educational software design, writing processes, and audience analysis. Not all faculty members are equally enthusiastic about the concentration of the program. All, however, would support the structural principle that the curriculum should introduce students not to a random sampling of courses but to a set of problems and issues that the faculty believes define the ways the discipline at large should think about the study of writing. These include the inclusion of quantitative and empirical research, the study of composition process, the history of rhetorical theory, invention, protocol analysis, the importance of educational computing, and discourse analysis.

As I have implied, the program has been criticized (inside as well as outside) for its narrowness and for its desire to remain independent of any literary study, issues to which I will return since they have significance to my general argument, not merely to my particular department. But regardless of such criticism, the PhD in rhetoric represents a distinctive challenge to the residual PhD models mounted by the rise of the "new" rhetoric and is remarkable for the commitment and enthusiasm of its faculty members and students. It has produced important research and publications—in cognitive rhetoric, expert and novice studies, educational computing, protocol analysis, and curriculum design, among other things. The publication of two highly regarded textbooks—one by Linda Flower, the other by David Kaufer, Christine Neuwirth, and Cheryl Geisler—in itself indicates one important direction for the program as a whole: textbooks not only reflect the program's interest in curriculum and pedagogy but often contain some of the most innovative work being done in the discipline.

Similarly dislocating to the old paradigm of the PhD in rhetoric has been the rise of the new literary and cultural theory. Within the literary establishment, and on both sides of the Atlantic, the standard concept of "English" has undergone a major challenge by the retheorizing of such matters as the making of canons, the gendered and ethnic diversity of our histories, the role of the reader, the historical and cultural determinants of textual production, and the study of language as a site of cultural struggle. The Carnegie Mellon literary and cultural theory PhD, established in 1985, like its counterpart in rhetoric, attempted to structure its curriculum by focusing on such currently significant questions as, What is it we do when we read complex texts? Who is the "we" in that question? What constraints and pressures—cultural, gender-specific, as well as cognitive—are operating? Building on our undergraduate core's framework of language, history, and culture (Waller, "Working"), we proceeded to lay down a core of courses built around the issues of the discipline, matching the problem-centered focus of the rhetoric PhD. Just as the rhetoric program reached outside the boundaries of traditional composition studies to pose its central questions and establish its intellectual core, so the new developments in literary and cultural studies reach out to philosophy, history, sociology, or politics. Thus semiotics (the study of sign systems in their sociocultural contexts), feminist and gender studies, theories of historiography, hermeneutics, reading theory, and the history of the discipline itself became core areas of concern, expressed in required courses and implicitly throughout the program. As the literary and cultural theory PhD has developed, it is focused, like the rhetoric program – though, with somewhat different methodologies – on the cognitive and cultural interactions involved in the reading and writing of texts. Like the rhetoric program, too, it has emphasized questions of curriculum, pedagogy, and the development of textbooks (see Waller, "Powerful Silence"; McCormick and Waller, *Reading*).

I have dwelt briefly on a particular case not because I offer our two PhD strands as universal models, but because they seem to me to represent a first stage in an ongoing and multiple shift in the profession in general. In one way, however, they do offer a model, not merely a random movement: both programs have curricular and pedagogical self-consciousness at their hearts. Required courses in both programs (The Process of Composition, and Theories of Reading) introduce students to the theory and practice of college teaching; both tie these theoretical courses to workshops and classroom experience for teaching assistants; both see curricular and pedagogical application – workshops for high school teachers, the development of textbooks, the influencing of educational, professional, corporate, or government bodies – as part of the essential, diverse, material practices in which the discipline must continually interest itself.

Nationwide these two revolutions – the new rhetoric and the new literary theory – have gradually, at the level of theory and increasingly in institutional practice, broken the structural (and, beyond that, the ideological) dominance of the residual model of PhD studies in English. The old model was – and in many places remains – always adaptable, able to absorb change by acceding to it piecemeal while retaining the traditional structures, if only under the guise of pluralism. What programs like those at Carnegie Mellon do is to call the "naturalness" of the residual model into question. "English" is not a given category; it is a site of intellectual and institutional struggle, a place where educational and wider cultural battles are fought out.

But I am unhappy about such military metaphors. The Wayzata conference seemed to promise another metaphorical complex: as one participant noted dryly the name above all others at the conference seemed to be that of Bakhtin. What the dialogic imagination might create from the interaction of these two revolutions in the ways we understand language in the new literary and the new rhetorical theory (more simply, reading and writing) is, I believe, the central issue for graduate study in English in the next decade. There will be inevitable resistance – from some of the new programs that have already established themselves in opposition to the residual model as well as from representatives of that model itself – but as the Wayzata conference established, the study of neither "reading" nor "writing" alone can provide a viable basis for the PhD in English. Jim

Slevin at one point asked departments to consider "the place of rhetoric and composition research not just in preparing graduate students to teach but also in defining poststructuralist educational programs and scholarship." One might reverse the terms he used – asking how the dynamics of literary and cultural theory might help to contextualize composition research – but the overriding issue is the same: how to bring into dialogue these two great intellectual and methodological revolutions and how to articulate that dialogue not only in theory but in curriculum and pedagogy.

Hidden away in Terry Eagleton's *Walter Benjamin: Or, Towards a Revolutionary Criticism,* is a "small history of Rhetoric." Like an American historian of rhetoric – a Richard Young or a James Kinneavy – Eagleton argues that the oldest form of literary criticism was not "aesthetic" but "rhetorical," that is to say, "a mode of what we would now call 'discourse theory,' devoted to analyzing the material effects of particular users of language in particular social conjunctions." Throughout the Middle Ages, he observes, rhetoric took the form of "textual training of the ruling class" in the techniques of "politico-discursive education," thus producing "specialists in the theory of signifying practices." Poetics was seen as a subbranch of rhetoric, and it was only in the seventeenth and eighteenth centuries that "aesthetics" would emerge as an ideological category and "rhetoric" would come to mean what it popularly means now: specious, filigree, or bombastic language (101, 102). American historians of rhetoric would, as Eagleton does, reject this popular definition, but his argument – that of one of the most powerful and currently visible literary theorists in our discipline – is intriguing and (in this context) highly suggestive. It can, of course, and perhaps needs to be balanced by other "small histories" of the studies that have led to the retheorization of English – a history, for instance, of the growing autonomy of the "aesthetic" or "literary," or a history of the rise of an empirical science of the writing process in alliance with the "mind's new science" of cognition, or a history of the broadening of the canon of "texts" from oral to written to printed to electronic media.

At the Wayzata conference, it was fascinating, even moving, to hear two representative advocates of the new literary theory and the new rhetoric, Jonathan Culler and James Kinneavy, struggling to find a common definition of the discipline at the present. Their formulation, "the study of discursive structures and strategies as they affect us as subjects, historical and communicating beings," is somewhat general, but it is in line with Eagleton's argument and with the model that we at Carnegie Mellon have worked with since 1983. Our undergraduate catalog depicts our department's focus as

> men and women as "readers" of their culture as mediated through its discursive practices, whether transmitted orally, in print, or in the new electronic media. We read and we write or (as it is sometimes put) are written by the codes and symbolic structures (language) of the particular social conjunction in which we live (culture) and the texts of our past (history).

Such a concept does not exclude the traditional and still dominant focus of the PhD (or indeed the English department generally), the study of literature. Indeed in our PhD in literary and cultural theory (although not, perhaps unfortunately, in our rhetoric PhD), those texts that our society has valorized as "literature" are located within this grid of forces. Our catalog at this point quotes Roland Barthes, saying that "if by some unimaginable excess all but one of our learned disciplines were to be expelled from our educational system, it is the discipline of literature which would have to be saved, for all the sciences are present in the literary moment." Hence our PhD students in literary and cultural theory are not intended simply to study theory, as if a new canon of theoretical texts had replaced the old canon of literary works. The study of literary and nonliterary texts, notably film and television, are integrated into most "theoretical" courses, and a variety of electives deal with traditional periods or special topics – most notably in feminist and gender studies, one of our faculty members' keenest interests. Students are encouraged, as well, to choose electives in rhetoric. Likewise, our rhetoric PhD students can choose electives in literary and cultural theory, of which semiotics, theories of reading, and the history of the discipline are the most popular. This location of "literary" texts within a broader theoretical matrix that includes the theory of both writing and reading is the structural principle of the whole program, a principle echoed by Eagleton in *Literary Theory,* where he speaks of the usefulness of seeing "literature" as a name that people give from time to time for different reasons to certain kinds of writing within a whole field of what Michel Foucault calls "discursive practices." If there is an object of study in our discipline, Eagleton argues, "it is this whole field of practices," studies as "forms of *activity* inseparable from the wider social relations between writers and readers" (205–06).

My point is that all these competing histories – which are (we should never forget, as we contemplate change) embodied in real people and departments – bring into debate a host of epistemologies, distinctive methodologies, issues, and challenges that ought to be foregrounded in the curricula of our PhD programs in English. At their center is the interaction of reading and writing, those primary processes by which we make our marks in the world and by which we too are marked: we are both readers and writers and read and written. We need to focus our graduate curricula not on a body of knowledge to be transmitted but rather on a set of problems and questions at the leading edge of the discipline, and then on both developing and critiquing the various methodologies used in dealing with them. We must see such a shift not simply as theoretical but educational: not just in the subject matter from "knowledge" to "problems," but in the conception of the activity as learning how to operate in a social practice rather than absorbing information. We should therefore focus on practical applications of our theoretical work – on curriculum development, textbooks, pedagogy, the study of the institutionalization of the discipline, the assessment of the roles of gender or class, and the use of the new electronic technology. We are inviting our students to enter the conversation.

My own department takes some steps toward such a goal. Both the rhetoric and literary and cultural theory PhDs have intense methodological and applied concerns. But now the next step must be taken. What our programs do not as yet have – and here some of the present limitations of this one particular example have wider importance – is any significant institutionalized interaction. We have a variety of theories and methodologies at work, but we need to bring them more formally into dialogue instead of allowing them to lapse into something akin to the residual pluralistic model of the uneasily united traditional department. Any policy of separate development produces the well-known effects of an apartheid system – the exploitation of one dominant group by another. In my department the dominance of traditional literary study over writing programs was followed by dominance of rhetoric over literature. Now we are approaching something like a balance between the new rhetoric and the new literary theory, both in the number of faculty members and in terms of prestige, and we must choose whether to return to a struggle between the two programs, to live in mutual but separate tolerance, or to work toward a situation where our programs are not merged but rather encouraged to enter creative interaction and, where possible, appropriate collaboration. There are advocates of all three positions. Our struggle to define ourselves over the next few years (always against the background of underfunding) is not merely a local matter: it will be one of the most crucial curricular and organizational struggles of the whole discipline in the next decade.

In advocating the establishment of PhD programs that put the interaction of the discipline's most important issues in the theory and practice of reading and writing at the heart of the curriculum, I am not simply recommending that we add to the traditional literature-centered PhD a few courses in composition theory or more theoretically oriented literature and cultural studies courses. Both these accretive trends are already evident and, certainly, are better than nothing. I am urging that we rethink the core of the PhD program – its required courses, its structural rationale – to embody and bring into debate the major theoretical revaluations of the discipline in the past twenty years or so: the understanding of both reading and writing as cognitive and culturally produced practices, the status of the reader, the social construction of language on writers, the ideological constraints of reading and writing, gendered reading and writing, canon formation, the issue of reading historically, and psychoanalytic or empirical studies of reading and of writers. These concerns, moreover, should not be seen as purely "theoretical" but would be embodied in investigations of curricular, pedagogical, and broader social or political implications; they would be part of studies concerning not only literary texts but scientific and popular writing, texts of the media, and – not to be neglected – students' own writing. Such issues could be increasingly embodied in traditional courses – for instance, feminist readings of the eighteenth-century novel, the rhetorical theory of the Middle Ages, the new historicism and the seventeenth-century court. But the issues themselves and the epistemological and methodological debates they produce need to become the focus of the required core courses of a PhD program. Our students need to be exposed to the variety of epistemological and methodological approaches within the field of discursive practices; to be able to use, situate, and critique them; to become aware of themselves as situated within a changing discipline; and to reflect on their own seemingly "natural" practices in regard to our culture's varied textual practices.

Central to such a conception of the PhD is the need for interaction between reading and writing – between the theories and methodologies, say, of empirical research and cultural criticism, between the ideological analysis of language and the assumption that language can be value-free, objectively referential. Such dialogues require, at the very least, that students in literature, literary theory, or literary and cultural studies share, at key points in the curriculum, seminars or colloquia with students whose focus is rhetoric, communication, or composition studies. Here my department is currently in the midst of a struggle of more than local significance, with each group anxious to preserve "its" integrity and "its" students. Our rhetoric faculty look anxiously back to their more recent achievements and the approbation of an increasingly theory-conscious discipline. Our literary and cultural studies faculty look to defend their new-found prestige and the approbation of the wider discipline. But many – who, I think, hold the keys to the future – look to actively promote dialogue, discussion, debate in their own work as in the courses they teach. The real promise of the dialogue is not to suppress confrontation but to transform it, to distribute it across the discipline in unpredictable and intellectually exciting ways. The discipline has relied on all too predictable ways to categorize, valorize, regard, and empower. The promise of interaction is that we can establish new patterns for empowering, and competing, that cut across traditional boundaries between reading and writing, literature and composition. That will mean that these key faculty members – in my own department distributed, I am happy to say, across all ranks and within all programs – must be prepared to engage, in their own work, in something less genteel than a polite pluralism or social reconciliation. The new approach must involve an acknowledged clash of paradigms, frameworks, languages, and methodologies, an understanding that some will not survive the battle and many will find themselves led into conversations they did not expect. Interaction is risk taking at its finest, and the discipline will rely heavily on those willing to take a chance. There is a very real danger of factionalism and intellectual war.

It need not be so, either in my local example or in the discipline at large. What is required is a generosity of imagination, but, more, an embracing of the multiplicity, heterogeneity, and contradictions of signifying practices and the recognition that curricular structures should embody that principle. The site of struggle that is English studies can never belong in some absolute sense to any moment in history, any more than it can to any group, class, or gender. We cannot escape the changing multi-accentuality, to adopt Volosinov's term, of language studies. As the authors of *Rewriting English* put it, "even activities as apparently simple and fundamental as reading and writing" are, in our society, "at one and the same time forms of regulation and exploitation *and* potential modes of resistance, celebration and solidarity" (Batslear et al. 4–5). This is why, in whatever ways it may be possible, the theories and practices of reading and writing, the new rhetoric and the new literary theory, need to be brought together.

One of the risks we run is that principles will remain untested. A few years ago, my colleague David Kaufer (whose contribution to parts of the previous two paragraphs I gratefully acknowledge) and I wrote a piece on deconstruction in reading and writing from which we've received some gratifying responses. But while each of us was drawing on experiences in curriculum and classroom practice, the kind of interactive next steps we envisaged have proved intellectually satisfying to contemplate but not materially proved in further detail. Hence, in dealing with the problem in our PhD programs, I decided to suggest that my department embark on some practical steps that have wider applicability. In the first place, I am proposing – at least for negotiation – a new core first-year curriculum that would be common to all PhD students. It would consist, I am suggesting, of theories of reading, the process of composition, and a colloquium on current problems, issues, and conflicts in the discipline. It might also usefully include a course in historical methodology, covering historicist theory (especially the new historicism and cultural materialism) and applied to both rhetorical and literary texts, and, as well, semiotics or a course in contemporary language theory. Students would take a required teaching seminar, tied closely (as would be the reading and writing theory courses) to their teaching in the freshman courses. This core incorporates at both the theoretical and applied levels courses from our rhetoric and literary and cultural theory programs. It brings these two traditions into dialogue in the most important place – the students' minds. It acknowledges the contemporary excitement of discursive studies and the historical dimension of our discipline. It prepares students both to enter a discipline (and a profession) and to go immediately into specialist studies – in rhetoric, in literary and cultural theory, or, particularly with respect to traditional programs, in literature. It does not diminish, undermine, or dismantle our existing strengths.

In addition, we have established a curriculum oversight committee that will be concerned not with reviewing the nuts and bolts of program development but with exploring and making recommendations on the intellectual issues, complementarities, and intersections among the various methodologies in the department. It will assess and disseminate knowledge about different courses, encourage the crossover of students from one program to another, encourage team-teaching, initiate the cross-programmatic colloquium that would be required of all PhD students on the current issues of the discipline, examine other English departmental curricula, encourage faculty members from one program concentration to sit on prospectus and dissertation committees in the other. To some of my faculty members, such cooperation is more than enough; to others, it does not go far enough. What my own department's PhD programs will look like in ten years' time, even perhaps two years' time, is difficult to predict. But I believe that the discipline as a whole has started to move, with difficulty, and at varying paces, in the directions I have sketched out here.

Note

For their comments on this paper (and for some virtual contributions) I am most grateful to my colleagues Linda Flower, Lois Fowler, Pete Jones, David Kaufer, Kathleen McCormick, Paul Smith, and Richard Young. For stimulating conversations and correspondence, I thank Phyllis Franklin, Gerald Graff, Charles Harris, Richard Lanham, Andrea Lunsford, Colin MacCabe, Helene Moglen, and Janel Mueller.

Appendix:
A Report on the 1986 Survey of English Doctoral Programs in Writing and Literature

Bettina J. Huber

Highlights

The following report on the 1986 survey of English doctoral programs is based on responses from 126 of the 139 university departments in the United States that grant the PhD or DA degree. The findings provide a portrait of all such programs in the country.

Departmental Characteristics

- Over 90% of the 139 programs grant only the PhD. Fewer than 10% offer the DA.
- Nearly half the doctoral programs in the United States began granting the doctorate after 1959; about one-fifth have been granting PhD degrees since before World War I.
- Just over a third of the doctoral programs are in private universities; public universities house nearly two-thirds.
- One-half of the doctoral programs in the United States have between 23 and 47 full-time tenured or tenure-track faculty members. The largest faculties are found in the Midwest, in public universities, and in departments that began granting the PhD before 1945.

• In 1986, 90% of the programs in the sample expected to hire faculty members in the standard fields of British and American literature during the next three years; 46% expected to recruit specialists in rhetoric, writing, and composition; and 42% expected to hire in the field of critical theory.

Enrollment, Degrees Granted, and Placement

• One-half of the programs in the sample enroll between 47 and 113 graduate students. On average, half of these students are PhD candidates with the highest proportions in private institutions and in programs that began granting the PhD before 1945. Departments located in public institutions have larger numbers of graduate students, as do departments that began granting the PhD before 1920.
• In the 20 years from 1966 to 1986 the average enrollment in a PhD program in English declined 20%, and the maximum number of students enrolled decreased by almost 50%.
• Slightly more than half the departments in the sample have had an increased enrollment in their doctoral programs since 1983; only a negligible number report a decrease. The percentage reporting growth is considerably higher among departments that began to award the PhD after 1945.
• Between 1981 and 1986, half the doctoral programs in the United States granted between 14 and 43 PhD degrees. The average was 31 degrees, or 6 a year. Departments with 46 or more regular full-time faculty members and more than 100 graduate students, most of whom are seeking the doctorate, granted considerably more PhDs than did smaller departments with higher proportions of MA students.
• Of the departments that keep placement records, 48% report that since 1979 80% or more of their new PhDs have found full-time college or university teaching positions. The average is 73%.

Courses, Area Examinations, and Dissertations

• Most doctoral programs offer courses in British and American literature, critical theory, rhetoric, and creative writing: 79% or more offer British and American literature, theory, and rhetoric; 68% offer creative writing.
• Nearly 86% of the programs allow PhD examinations and dissertations in critical theory; 58% permit them in rhetoric, writing, and composition. Examinations and dissertations in British and American literature are universal.
• Among programs offering courses in British and American literature, critical theory, rhetoric, and linguistics, 60% or more also allow general examinations and dissertations in these areas. Examinations in creative and technical writing are offered by at most 25% of the sample, though courses are more common, especially in creative writing.

- Doctoral programs that offer general examinations in rhetoric are more likely to offer courses in creative writing, technical writing, and linguistics than are programs that do not permit examinations and dissertations in rhetoric.

Changes in Doctoral Programs

- The areas of study most frequently added to the graduate English curriculum since 1975 are critical theory and rhetoric. Approximately three-quarters of the departments in the sample have added courses in these subjects. Between one-third and one-fifth have also added courses in creative writing, technical writing, and teaching English as a second language. Programs in public universities are more likely than those in private universities to have added courses in rhetoric and creative writing.
- Programs that added courses in rhetoric and creative writing are more likely than others to have added courses in technical writing as well. Few departments whose graduate students are predominantly PhD candidates have added courses in technical writing.
- The majority of departments in the sample state that they have added courses or internships designed to prepare students for their work as teaching assistants. Such courses carry credit in 40% of all doctoral programs; they are noncredit requirements in 19%.
- The number of required courses for PhD candidates has remained largely unchanged over the past decade: for 73% of the departments in the sample the number has been the same since 1975. Among departments that have changed the requirement, approximately equal percentages report increases and decreases. Large and long-established programs are more likely than others to have decreased the number of required courses.
- Fully 65% of the departments in the sample say they have changed the substance or kind of examinations PhD candidates take.
- One-fifth of the departments in the sample say they are planning major revisions of their doctoral programs.
- Only 4% report eliminating doctoral programs since 1975.

Rhetoric and Writing Programs

- Among the responding departments, 33% report that they have doctoral programs in rhetoric, writing, and composition, with half these programs established three to eight years ago. An additional 6% of the respondents say they plan to initiate such programs. Only 3% have doctoral programs in technical writing.
- When asked about the orientation of their rhetoric programs, 88% of the respondents said it was theoretical, 51% said pedagogical, 32% historical, and 29% empirical. Most programs whose primary orientation is theoretical describe their

secondary orientation as pedagogical. Of the programs whose primary orientation is pedagogical, 75% describe their secondary orientation as theoretical, as do all the programs whose primary orientation is historical.

- At least 75% of the rhetoric programs in the sample require PhD candidates to complete courses in British and American literature, theory of composition, and rhetoric; 62% require course work in teaching methods; 57% in linguistics; 55% in bibliographic research methods; and 48% in the history of the English language. Programs that require courses in the theory of composition are more likely to require courses in rhetoric and teaching methods as well. Programs that require courses in rhetoric are more likely than those that do not to require courses in linguistics.

- Doctoral programs in public universities are more likely than those in private universities to have degree programs in rhetoric. Departments with large faculties are more likely than others to have rhetoric programs.

- The majority of departments with rhetoric programs report that most students' dissertations during the previous five years have been theoretically or pedagogically oriented. The exact proportions are 84% and 73%. Some 60% report dissertations with an empirical approach.

- Departments with rhetoric programs stand apart from others in expected ways. They are more likely to offer various types of writing courses; to have added courses in rhetoric and creative writing; to permit examinations and dissertations in rhetoric and creative writing; and to expect to hire a specialist in rhetoric within three years. The requirements for the doctorate in literature in departments that also offer the degree in rhetoric do not differ significantly from those in departments without rhetoric programs, except that departments with rhetoric programs are less likely to require courses in textual criticism.

Requirements for the Literature Degree

- Of the doctoral programs in the United States, 75% require courses in bibliography and research methods for the literature degree. In addition, between 32% and 53% require courses in literary criticism, critical theory, historical scholarship, linguistics, and rhetoric. Literary criticism, critical theory, historical scholarship, and textual criticism form a core of requirements; departments that require one of the four courses are likely to require the others as well.

- Courses in teaching methods are a feature of most programs; only 24% of the doctoral programs in the sample do not offer such courses. Of the departments that offer such courses, almost 50% offer courses that treat the teaching of writing only, while 16% offer courses that consider the teaching of writing and the teaching of literature together. Another 28% offer two types of courses.

- Although most doctoral programs do not require rhetoric courses for the literature degree, 93% of the departments that offer such courses will accept them in partial fulfillment of requirements for the literature degree.

• Revision of the literary canon has significantly affected the literature programs of 63% of the departments in the sample. Least likely to report being affected are small departments in the South Atlantic–South Central region, where MA students make up a majority of the graduate students. Of the departments affected by canon revision, 71% have responded by creating new courses and revising old ones.

Introduction

In preparation for the April 1987 conference on graduate education, the MLA sought to gather information about the history, characteristics, and curricula of programs in the United States that grant the PhD or DA in English.[1] Accordingly, in September 1986 the MLA developed a questionnaire for distribution to the 139 departments in the country that are known to have such programs. The questionnaires went out in mid-October, and by mid-December a sufficient number had been returned to indicate major categories of responses for each question. Numerical codes identifying these categories were assigned to the respondents' answers and entered into a computer file. Almost no errors were introduced in transferring the data from coding sheets to the computer, and during the earlier process of assigning codes to responses, the intercoder reliability was 98%.[2]

Analysis of the responses, which began in late December, was completed by early February. Of the 139 departments with doctoral programs in English, 126 eventually returned the questionnaires. This response rate, 90%, compares favorably with the 81% response rate to a mid-1960s MLA survey of doctoral programs (Allen 40); it is, in fact, sufficiently high to warrant the assumption that the data collected provide an accurate portrait of all the English doctoral programs in the United States.

Although only limited information is available on the 13 departments that did not respond, they can be compared in several respects with the 126 that did. Table 1 indicates that just over a third of the doctoral programs in both groups are in private institutions. Most of the nonresponding programs are in the Northeast and the South Atlantic–South Central regions, while relatively few are in the Midwest. Thus one might infer that midwestern programs are overrepresented

Table 1
Source of Funding and Geographic Area,
by Responding and Nonresponding Programs

	Percentage of Programs		
	Not Responding (N = 13)	Responding (N = 126)	In the United States (N = 139)
Source of funding			
Public	61.6	65.1	64.7
Private	38.4	34.9	35.3
Total	100.0	100.0	100.0
Geographic area			
Northeast	38.5	26.2	27.3
South Atlantic–South Central	38.5	31.0	31.7
Midwest	7.7	27.0	25.2
Rocky Mountain–Pacific	15.4	15.9	15.8
Total	100.0	100.0	100.0

among the respondents and the other two underrepresented. The nonrespondent group is so small, however, that this conclusion does not appear justified; the percentages generated by such negligible numbers cannot be considered reliable. Both the sample ($N = 126$) and the larger universe of doctoral programs ($N = 139$) are practically identical in sources of funding and geographic distribution. These limited comparisons, like the high response rate, suggest that the findings reported below characterize the universe as well as the sample.

Departmental Characteristics of Doctoral Programs

In 1986, 28% more English departments in the United States were granting the doctorate than were doing so in the mid-1960s. Although this rate of growth is modest compared with that of the preceding 50 years—when the number of PhD programs increased almost threefold, from 40 in 1910 to 109 in 1966 (Allen

Table 2
Comparison of All English Programs with PhD English Programs

| | | PhD Programs | |
	English Programs (N)[a]	1983–84 Survey (N)	1986 Survey (N)
Percentage by institutional size (FTE enrollments)			
Very small (3,000 or fewer)	57.8 (356)	3.6 (111)	–
Large (18,000 or more)	12.6 (356)	57.7 (111)	–
Percentage by source of funding			
Public	58.7 (356)	72.1 (111)	65.1 (126)
Private	41.3 (356)	27.9 (111)	34.9 (126)
Mean number of regular full-time faculty members	13.8 (345)	38.3 (108)	35.2 (117)
Mean percentage of faculty members with full-time positions	57.2 (287)	71.8 (102)	–
Mean percentage of faculty members with tenured positions	48.0 (285)	59.2 (100)	–
Mean percentage of faculty members with part-time positions	36.7 (287)	21.1 (102)	–
Mean percentage of tenured faculty with PhDs	73.1 (257)	92.9 (108)	–
Mean percentage of assistant professors with PhDs	54.7 (212)	87.2 (104)	–
Average teaching load (credit hours/term)	12.4	8.2	–

[a]These figures are drawn from the 1983–84 survey and are weighted to approximate key characteristics of US English programs.

14, 40)–it seems surprisingly robust in view of the depressed academic job market in the humanities during the 1970s.

Since the 1986 survey considers only doctoral programs, the data provide no information on how these programs differ from the universe of English programs generally. Data from a 1983–84 survey of English programs provide a comparative perspective, however (Huber and Young). Table 2 delineates characteristics of all English programs in the United States, and of the doctoral programs responding to the 1983–84 survey. Where available, figures from the 1986 survey are also presented.

,Doctoral programs make up a small minority of the country's English programs, accounting for only 6% of the whole. Table 2 indicates that doctoral programs are disproportionately present in institutions with large student bodies and that the average number of regular full-time faculty members is considerably larger in PhD-granting departments than in other English programs. The percentage of full-time and tenured faculty members is also greater, on average, while the percentage of part-time faculty is quite low. PhD-granting departments, of course, hire fewer part-time faculty members, because they rely on graduate students as a source of transient labor (Huber and Young 50). The vast majority of faculty members in PhD-granting departments have doctorates, as table 2 indicates; appreciably more assistant professors, in particular, have PhDs in doctoral programs than in departments granting only less advanced degrees. On average, teaching loads are lower in PhD-granting departments than in English departments, and the funds available for faculty development are greater.[3]

The 1986 survey found that 26% of the PhD programs in the United States are in the Northeast and 27% in the Midwest. The South Atlantic and South Central states (considered a single unit in later analyses) have 18% and 13%, respectively, and the Rocky Mountain and Pacific Coast states (also combined in later analyses) have 6% and 10%, respectively.

As table 3 indicates, just over a third of the doctorate-granting English programs are in private institutions–35% versus 65% in public institutions. Only about 19% operate on the quarter system; the remainder operate on a semester basis.

English departments in this country have been awarding the PhD for from 6 to 111 years. The average duration is 63 years, although half the departments have awarded the degree for 30 or fewer years. Half have awarded the doctorate

Tabulation a

Time Period	Average Year PhD First Granted	Percentage of Respondents ($N = 123$)
After 1959 (post-Sputnik era)	1967	44.7
1945–59 (post-WWII period)	1953	17.9
1920–44 (interwar period)	1933	18.7
Before 1920 (pre-WWI)	1897	18.7
Total		100.0

for from 20 to 55 years, which means that they began doing so between 1931 and 1966. In subsequent discussions, the departments are grouped into four periods according to the year that they first granted the PhD (see tab. a).

The Doctor of Arts Degree

The vast majority of departments in the sample grant only one doctoral degree: the PhD. Moreover, all the nonresponding departments offer only the PhD. Thus, fewer than 10% of the doctorate-granting English departments in the United States offer the Doctor of Arts degree, most in conjunction with the PhD (8 of the 12 departments offering the DA grant both degrees, while the remaining 4 grant only the DA). Further, 3 of the departments currently offering the degree have let their programs lapse or are phasing them out.

Departments that are phasing out the DA appear to have offered it some-what longer than have those with active programs. The programs being discontinued have all been in place for 11 years or more, whereas only half of the still-active programs are that old. The average durations are 16 years for the first category 10 years for the second. Departments that grant only the DA have aver-

Table 3
Source of Funding, Year PhD First Granted, and Academic Calendar, by Geographic Area (% of programs)

Category	In the Northeast	In the South Atlantic–South Central Region	In the Midwest	In the Rocky Mountain–Pacific Region	Total
Source of funding					
Public	36.4	69.2	76.5	85.0	65.1
Private	63.6	30.8	23.5	15.0	34.9
Total	100.0	100.0	100.0	100.0	100.0
(N)	(33)	(39)	(34)	(20)	(126)
Year doctorate first granted					
After 1959	48.5	44.7	40.6	45.0	44.7
1945–1959	9.1	26.3	15.6	20.0	17.9
1920–1944	18.2	13.2	18.8	30.0	18.7
Before 1920	24.2	15.8	25.0	5.0	18.7
Total	100.0	100.0	100.0	100.0	100.0
(N)	(33)	(38)	(32)	(20)	(123)
Academic calendar					
Semester	100.0	92.1	73.5	45.0	81.5
Quarter	–	7.9	26.5	55.0	18.5
Total	100.0	100.0	100.0	100.0	100.0
(N)	(32)	(38)	(34)	(20)	(124)

aged 10 degrees since 1981, while those that also grant the PhD have averaged 21 doctoral degrees in the same five-year period.[4]

Not surprisingly, departments that grant only the DA have awarded more DA degrees than have those that offer the PhD as well. None of the departments that grant both degrees has awarded more than 10 DAs since 1981, whereas 3 of the 4 departments that grant only the DA have awarded at least that many.[5]

Since very few departments grant the DA, the subsequent discussion focuses on PhD-granting doctoral programs.

The Interrelation of
Invariant Departmental Characteristics

Table 3 indicates that geographic location is linked to both the source of funding and the academic calendar. Thus, nearly 64% of the doctoral programs in the Northeast are in private institutions, as opposed to 31% or fewer in other parts of the country. Public funding is most marked in the Rocky Mountain–Pacific coast region; only 15% of the programs in this region are in private institutions. Most of these programs also operate on the quarter system. In contrast, almost all the doctoral programs in the Northeast and South operate on the semester system. Private institutions are also somewhat more likely than public institutions to be on a semester system (93% vs. 76%).

The source of funding is also linked to the year that the PhD was first granted, as table 4 indicates. More than half the English doctoral programs in public institutions were founded after 1959, while over half those in private institutions were founded before 1945.

The link between geographic area and the source of funding must be borne in mind during the subsequent discussion of curricular differences. Insofar as programs in the Northeast differ from those elsewhere in the country, the distinctions are likely to be due to the preponderance of private institutions in this area rather than to regional characteristics per se. By the same token, differences between programs in public and private institutions may reflect the shorter period of time that the public universities have granted the PhD.

Table 4
Year PhD First Granted, by Source of Funding (% of programs)

Year Doctorate First Granted	With Public Funding	With Private Funding
After 1959	55.7	25.0
1945–1959	15.2	22.7
1920–1944	15.2	25.0
Before 1920	13.9	27.3
Total	100.0	100.0
(N)	(79)	(44)

Faculty and Student Numbers

According to the survey findings, English departments offering the PhD have from 4 to 80 regular full-time faculty members; the average is 35. Only 19% of these departments have 20 or fewer faculty members; 50% have between 23 and 47. The four faculty-size categories shown in tabulation b are used in subsequent analyses (the percentages of programs in each category are given for both the 1986 survey and the larger 1983–84 survey conducted by ADE [Huber and Young]). Comparing the two sets of figures provides further evidence of the representativeness of the 1986 data. The figures might suggest that departments with 20 or fewer full-time faculty members are somewhat overrepresented in the 1986 sample. It is also possible, however, that departments with 30 or fewer faculty members are somewhat underrepresented in the ADE sample, while departments with large faculties are somewhat overrepresented. Given the deliberate oversampling of large institutions – and, therefore, of departments with large faculties – in the ADE sample, the second interpretation appears more plausible.

Tabulation b

Number of Full-Time Regular Faculty Members	Percentage of Respondents	
	1986 Survey ($N = 117$)	1983–84 ADE Survey ($N = 108$)
20 or fewer	18.8	16.7
21–30	24.8	20.4
31–45	29.1	30.6
46 or more	27.4	32.4
Total	100.0	100.0

The first rows of tables 5, 6, and 7 indicate that faculty size varies with geographic location, source of funding, and year the PhD was first granted. On average, departments in the Midwest and in public institutions have larger faculties, as do programs that began offering the PhD before 1945.

English departments offering the PhD enroll an average of 91 full-time students. Only 5% of the responding departments enroll fewer than 25 students, with one department enrolling as few as 8. At the other end of the scale, 6.5% have between 200 and 400 students, and 50% enroll between 47 and 113 graduate students. Subsequent analyses use the three size groups indicated in tabulation c.

Tabulation c

Number of Students	Percentage of Respondents ($N = 108$)
50 or fewer	30.6
51–100	37.0
101 or more	32.4
Total	100.0

On average, doctorate-granting departments have 45 MA students and 48 PhD students. The numbers range from 2 to 326 for the MA enrollment and from 2 to 170 for the PhD enrollment. Half the programs in the sample have between 20 and 51 MA students and between 20 and 55 PhD students. The findings are summarized in tabulation d. Comparing the figures for PhD students with similar numbers collected in the mid-1960s reveals that, now as then, the majority of doctoral programs in English have under 100 students. The largest programs, however, have reduced their size considerably. In the past 20 years the maximum enrollment in a PhD program in English has been cut by almost 50%, while the mean enrollment has declined by 20%. In 1966 the number of full-time PhD students ranged from 0 to 325, with an average enrollment of 61; at the same time, half the doctoral programs had no more than 38 full-time PhD students, a figure that remains unchanged in the 1986 sample (Allen 50, 166). This comparison suggests that very large doctoral programs (i.e., with 150 or more students in the mid-1960s) were far more dramatically affected by the contraction

Tabulation d

	Percentage of Respondents	
Number of Students	MA Students ($N = 109$)	PhD Students ($N = 122$)
26 or fewer	33.9	34.4
26–50	38.5	35.2
51 or more	27.5	30.3
Total	100.0	100.0

Table 5
Departmental Characteristics, by Geographic Area

	Northeast (N)	South Atlantic–South Central (N)	Midwest (N)	Rocky Mountain–Pacific (N)
Mean number of full-time regular faculty members	33.2 (30)	32.1 (35)	40.9 (33)	34.2 (19)
Mean number of full-time graduate students	87.3 (28)	80.2 (33)	92.8 (30)	115.4 (17)
Mean percentage of students in PhD programs	54.3 (28)	49.0 (33)	47.7 (30)	48.8 (17)
Percentage of departments with increased PhD enrollments	49.9 (29)	60.5 (37)	44.1 (31)	55.0 (19)
Mean number of degrees granted since 1981	32.3 (32)	23.3 (33)	38.3 (32)	28.7 (20)
Mean percentage of graduates finding college teaching posts	69.5 (27)	81.0 (29)	71.3 (25)	67.9 (16)

of the academic job market in the early 1970s than were departments with small doctoral programs.

The 1986 survey indicates that the numbers of MA and PhD students in English departments with doctoral programs are positively related. Departments with a small number of PhD students also have a small number of MA students, while those with moderate or large numbers of doctoral students have large numbers of MA students (see tab. e).

The second row of table 5 indicates that the average number of graduate students in PhD-granting departments does not vary substantially with geographic location, though the Rocky Mountain–Pacific departments tend to have larger enrollments. Student numbers do vary with the source of funding and the year

Table 6
Departmental Characteristics, by Source of Funding

	Source of Funding	
	Public (N)	Private (N)
Mean number of full-time regular faculty members	41.0 (75)	25.0 (42)
Mean number of full-time graduate students	100.4 (76)	69.0 (32)
Mean percentage of PhD students	46.3 (76)	58.7 (32)
Percentage of departments with increased PhD enrollments	55.0 (80)	45.5 (44)
Mean number of degrees granted since 1981	32.7 (78)	26.8 (39)
Mean percentage of graduates finding college teaching posts	73.5 (66)	72.5 (31)

Table 7
Departmental Characteristics, by Year PhD First Granted

	After 1959 (N)	1945–59 (N)	1920–44 (N)	Before 1920 (N)
Mean number of full-time regular faculty members	32.3 (51)	29.6 (20)	41.1 (22)	39.0 (21)
Mean number of full-time graduate students	80.9 (52)	72.0 (17)	91.4 (19)	137.2 (19)
Mean percentage of PhD students	44.2 (52)	47.2 (17)	62.2 (19)	56.5 (19)
Percentage of departments with increased PhD enrollments	63.0 (54)	59.1 (22)	31.8 (22)	34.8 (23)
Mean number of degrees granted since 1981	22.3 (53)	23.4 (17)	37.3 (23)	50.1 (22)
Mean percentage of graduates finding college teaching posts	73.9 (47)	73.1 (17)	73.6 (16)	70.3 (16)

the PhD was first granted. The second rows of tables 6 and 7 reveal that older PhD programs and programs in public institutions average larger numbers of students. Programs that began to grant the doctorate before 1920 are especially likely to have large enrollments.

In the light of these findings, it comes as no surprise that the number of graduate students in a department varies with the number of full-time faculty members. Departments with 46 or more faculty members have a substantially larger number of graduate students than those with smaller faculties (see tab. f).

MA students generally make up a sizable percentage of the students enrolled in graduate programs in English. In many departments their numbers are substantial: over a quarter of the graduate programs have 51 or more MA students. In half the doctoral programs in the United States, MA students account for 38% to 65% of the graduate student body, PhD students for 35% to 62%. On average, 50% of the graduate students in a PhD-granting English department are enrolled in the doctoral program. PhD students make up 25% or less of the graduate student body in only 9% of the departments in the sample, while they account for 90% or more in 6%. These findings suggest that more information is needed on the MA degree. Is the MA a way station on the road to the PhD? Do MA programs in English serve mainly as preparation for certain types of careers (e.g., secondary school teaching, journalism and publishing, scientific or technical writing)?

Tabulation e

Number of PhD Students	Mean Number of MA Students (N)
25 or fewer	27.2 (40)
26–50	50.1 (37)
51 or more	62.6 (31)

Tabulation f

Number of Full-Time Faculty Members	Mean Number of Students (N)
20 or fewer	55.5 (17)
21–30	89.3 (24)
31–45	80.5 (31)
46 or more	124.0 (29)

Tabulation g

Number of Full-Time Faculty Members	Percentage of Students in PhD Programs (N)
20 or fewer	55.1 (17)
21–30	56.7 (24)
31–45	46.5 (30)
46 or more	49.9 (29)

The percentage of students enrolled in the PhD program does not vary greatly with the size of the graduate student body. Regardless of the total number of students, 45% to 55% are working toward the doctorate. The percentage seeking PhDs does vary somewhat with faculty size, with a slightly larger percentage seeking the doctorate in departments with smaller faculties than in those with larger faculties (see tab. g).

The average percentage of students enrolled in the PhD program does not vary with geographic location (see table 5) but does differ by the source of funding and by the year the doctorate was first awarded. Tables 6 and 7 indicate that private institutions and long-established departments have higher percentages of PhD students. These findings are in keeping with the previously mentioned link between well-established programs and private institutions.

Program Growth and Student Placement

After a decade of sharp declines, enrollment in English doctoral programs appears to have stabilized. Among the PhD programs in the sample, 52% report increased enrollments since 1983. Almost all the rest report that student numbers have remained stable. Only 4% (5 programs) report a decrease. The recent increases follow a sharp decline in graduate student numbers during the late 1970s, and doctoral programs are still far from awarding the annual number of degrees that they did in 1972–73.[6] Between 1981 and 1986, the number of PhD degrees awarded by departments in the sample ranged from 3 to 126. The average was 31, or 6 degrees a year. Among these departments 25% awarded 13 or fewer degrees; 50% awarded between 14 and 43. Only 11% awarded more than 60 degrees over the five-year period.

The fourth rows of tables 5, 6, and 7 indicate that growth in PhD enrollments varies by the age of the doctoral program but not by geographic location or the source of funding. According to table 7, the percentage of departments reporting growth is considerably higher among those that began awarding the PhD after 1945; but, as table 8 shows, growth is not affected by faculty size or by student-body size and composition.

Tables 5, 6, and 7 reveal that, during the five years preceding the survey, doctoral programs in the Northeast and especially the Midwest granted more PhDs, on average than did departments in other regions. Similarly, departments where PhD programs antedate 1919 granted more doctorates in this period than did younger programs. The center column of table 8 indicates, as one would expect, that departments with larger faculties and graduate enrollments, as well as a high percentage of PhD students, granted considerably more PhDs in the recent past than did smaller departments. These findings suggest that students are completing their graduate work in numbers proportionate to their representation in departments.

The primary employment chosen by graduates of English doctoral programs continues to be college teaching. The departments participating in the 1986 survey report that, on average, approximately 73% of their PhD graduates have found full-time college or university teaching positions since 1979. This percentage does not apply, however, to 21% of the doctoral programs sampled, since they do not keep placement records. Among departments that do keep track of their graduates, the percentage finding teaching positions ranges from a high of 100%, to a low of 20%. Half the departments sampled report that 60% to 90% of their PhD graduates have found academic teaching positions since 1979. The figure is less than 50% for only 12% of the departments that keep placement records, but it is 80% or higher in 48% of those departments.

The bottom rows of tables 5, 6, and 7 reveal that the average percentage of recent graduates finding full-time college teaching positions varies with the geographic region but not with the source of funding or the year the PhD was first granted. Departments located in the South report a higher percentage of graduates going into college teaching (see table 5). In addition, departments with 20 or fewer full-time faculty members report a somewhat lower percentage of graduates finding teaching jobs than do departments with larger faculties, 63% versus 74% (see table 8).

The findings summarized above suggest that during the 1980s, at least, the great majority of PhD recipients in English found employment as college and university teachers. Some caution must be exercised in interpreting this finding, however, since survey respondents were asked to approximate the proportion of doctoral graduates finding full-time college or university teaching positions. Thus the figures provided could easily be overestimates. Departments do tend to lose

Table 8
Degrees Granted, Growth in PhD Enrollments, and Graduate Placement, by Faculty Size, Number of Students, and Percentage of PhD Students

	Percentage of Programs with Increased PhD Enrollments (N)	Mean Number of Degrees Granted since 1981 (N)	Mean Percentage of Graduates in College Teaching (N)
Number of regular full-time faculty members			
20 or fewer	36.4 (22)	20.8 (18)	63.4 (17)
21–30	65.5 (29)	25.3 (28)	72.7 (21)
31–45	48.5 (33)	24.5 (33)	76.6 (26)
46 or more	50.0 (32)	48.9 (30)	72.8 (26)
Number of graduate students			
50 or fewer	48.5 (33)	18.8 (32)	76.9 (27)
51–100	51.3 (39)	25.3 (38)	72.0 (28)
101 or more	60.0 (35)	47.0 (34)	69.4 (31)
Percentage of PhD students			
40 or less	57.5 (40)	21.3 (38)	73.1 (35)
41–60	53.8 (39)	32.3 (39)	74.0 (29)
61 or more	46.4 (28)	40.3 (27)	70.0 (22)

touch with graduates who do not pursue teaching careers, and faculty members remember the students who have followed in their footsteps more clearly than they do those who have not.

Evidence that the survey responses may overestimate the number of recent PhDs who find full-time college teaching positions comes from the most recent MLA survey of PhD placement, which found that 58% of those awarded PhDs in English during 1983–84 held such appointments (Showalter 74). This figure is not really comparable with the departmental averages reported in 1986, however, since it represents the percentage of all PhD recipients in the United States who found teaching positions rather than the percentage from any given department. In view of the 50% decline in the PhDs granted in English since the early 1970s and the recently improved job market for English teachers,[7] the percentage of recent PhDs finding full-time college teaching jobs may well be 70% or higher, as the 1986–87 survey findings suggest. Even if this figure is an overestimate, the differences between various types of doctoral departments may be valid. It is likely, for instance, that a higher percentage of graduates from departments in the South are finding teaching positions and that departments with small full-time faculties have a somewhat smaller percentage of recent graduates entering college teaching.

Hiring Priorities during the Next Three Years

When asked about the fields in which they expected to hire tenure-track faculty members during the next three years, only 3% of the departments in the sample reported that they expected to do no hiring whatsoever. If the expectations of the rest are borne out, the next few years should see considerable hiring activity in English graduate programs. The percentage of departments expecting to hire in various fields are listed in tabulation h. Some care must be exercised in interpreting these findings, since only the first three fields were listed on the questionnaire. The others were written in by respondents. Some departments that did not indicate such plans on the questionnaire may nonetheless be planning to hire in these areas.[8]

Tabulation h

Area of Study	Percentage of Respondents Expecting to Hire ($N = 122$)
British and American literature	90.2
Rhetoric	45.9
Critical theory	41.8
Creative writing	13.9
Specialty literature	8.2
Linguistics	7.4
Career preparation	4.9

The doctoral programs' hiring expectations do not seem to correspond to the job openings in graduate and undergraduate departments announced in the English editions of the October *MLA Job Information List* in 1985, 1986, and 1987. Of the ads that specified primary areas of specialization during this three-year period, 29% were for British and American literature and 13% were for other types of literature (e.g., comparative literature, black studies, women's studies); 35% advertised for specialists in writing (some two-thirds of these sought rhetoric and composition teachers in particular).[9] At the moment, specialists in writing and specialists in literature seem to be equally in demand. Between 1985 and 1987, however, the number of positions available in British and American literature increased by 56%, whereas the number in rhetoric and composition

Table 9
Hiring Expectations, by Departmental Characteristics

	Percentage of Departments Expecting to Hire	
	In Rhetoric (N)	In Creative Writing (N)
Geographic area		
Northeast	36.9 (30)	–
South Atlantic–South Central	39.5 (38)	–
Midwest	64.7 (34)	–
Rocky Mountain–Pacific	40.0 (20)	–
Source of funding		
Public	55.6 (81)	18.5 (81)
Private	26.8 (41)	4.9 (41)
Year PhD first granted		
After 1959	57.7 (52)	–
1945–1959	36.4 (22)	–
1920–1944	26.1 (23)	–
Before 1920	50.0 (22)	–
Number of full-time regular faculty members		
20 or fewer	–	9.5 (21)
21–30	–	–
31–45	–	17.6 (34)
46 or more	–	28.1 (32)
Number of graduate students		
50 or less	–	6.5 (31)
51–100	–	10.3 (39)
101 or more	–	26.5 (34)
Percentage of PhD students		
40 or less	60.0 (40)	–
41–60	59.5 (37)	–
61 or more	25.9 (27)	–

declined by 16%. This discrepancy may be a sign that hiring in literature will outstrip hiring in other areas in the years ahead, as the 1986 survey data suggests.

Hiring expectations show little variation with the departmental characteristics discussed in the last section, in part because expectations tend to be so uniform. More detailed analysis reveals some distinctions in expectations for hiring specialists in rhetoric and creative writing (see table 9). Departments in the Midwest, in public institutions, and with a majority of graduate students in the MA program are more likely to expect to hire tenure-track faculty members in rhetoric, as are the newest and oldest programs (i.e., those that began to grant the PhD after 1959 or before 1920). Departments in public institutions and those with larger faculties and graduate student bodies are more likely to expect to hire tenure-track faculty members in creative writing.

Course, Examination, and Dissertation Topics

Graduate Courses Offered

The survey questionnaire asked departments about the graduate courses they offer and the areas in which they permit students to write general examinations and dissertations. Tabulation i shows the percentage of departments that reported offering each course. Clearly, most doctoral programs offer the first four course areas listed. Courses in British and American literature are universal. Of the departments in the sample 73% offer courses in both critical theory and rhetoric; and only 8% offer courses in neither subject. Moreover, 60% offer courses in both rhetoric and creative writing, with 14% offering neither. Finally, 64% of the departments in the sample offer both critical theory and creative writing, and 10% offer neither.

The pronounced overlap in course offerings is apparent from the first two rows of table 10, which indicate that at least three-quarters of the departments that offer courses in rhetoric also offer courses in creative writing and critical

Tabulation i

Area of Study	Percentage of Respondents Offering Courses ($N = 126$)
British and American literature	99.2
Critical theory	86.5
Rhetoric, writing, and composition	78.6
Creative writing	67.5
Technical writing	23.0
Linguistics	20.6
Film	11.1
Folklore	9.5
Teaching methods	4.8
Research methods	3.2

Table 10
Percentage of Programs Offering Various Courses among Programs Offering or Not Offering Rhetoric, Critical Theory, and Creative Writing

Course Offered	Offering (N)	Not Offering (N)
	Rhetoric	
Creative writing	75.8 (99)	37.0 (27)
Critical theory	92.9 (99)	63.0 (27)
	Critical Theory	
Creative writing	73.4 (109)	29.4 (17)
	Creative Writing	
Linguistics	27.1 (85)	7.3 (41)

theory. Departments not offering courses in rhetoric, in contrast, are considerably less likely to offer either of the other two courses. The third row of the table shows that the situation is similar for critical theory and creative writing. Departments that offer critical theory are far more likely to offer creative writing than are the few departments that do not offer critical theory.

The interrelation among the areas of British and American literature, critical theory, rhetoric, and creative writing are diagrammed in figure 1. The lines in the diagram join course offerings that are linked; if departments offer any one of these courses, they are more likely to offer the other two than are departments not offering that course. British and American literature is not linked to the other areas in the diagram because courses in that field are universally offered.

In the light of these findings, the four courses included in the diagram can be said to constitute the core of doctoral study. Graduate courses in areas other than these four are not widely available. Still, courses in technical writing, linguistics, film, and folklore are offered by a significant minority – approximately 10% to 20% – of the departments in the sample. Some caution is called for in interpreting these percentages, however, since technical writing was the only one

Fig. 1. Interrelations among Courses Offered in Doctoral Programs

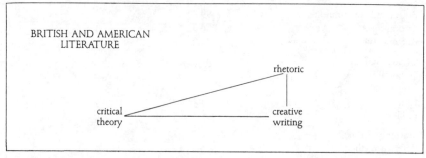

of these courses specified on the survey questionnaire. Linguistics, film, and folklore were written in by respondents; there may well be other departments that offer these courses but that neglected to note them.

The fourth row of table 10 shows a link between creative writing and linguistics. Although most departments do not offer linguistics, departments offering creative writing courses are more likely to do so than are those not offering such courses.

A few respondents report offering graduate courses in teaching and research methods. Again, the very small proportions must be interpreted with care, since these courses were not specified on the questionnaire.

Examination and Dissertation Options

The 1986 survey asked respondents to indicate whether or not they allow general examinations and dissertations in specific areas of study. The percentages responding affirmatively for the various fields are listed in descending order in tabulation j. These findings reconfirm British and American literature, critical theory, and rhetoric as the core of English doctoral studies. The other fields listed are less commonly allowed as examination-thesis areas but, with the exception of technical writing, are available in a significant minority of departments. Again, care must be taken in interpreting the percentages, since linguistics and specialty literature were not listed on the questionnaire but were added by respondents.

Tabulation j

Area of Study	Percentage of Respondents Allowing Exams and Theses ($N = 126$)
British and American literature	99.2
Critical theory	85.7
Rhetoric, writing, or composition	57.9
Creative writing	24.6
Linguistics	18.3
Specialty literature (see n8)	13.5
Technical writing	9.5

Departments that permit examinations and theses in rhetoric are more likely to allow them in three other areas: creative writing, linguistics, and technical writing. As table 11 indicates, most departments do not offer examinations in these three areas. But departments that do allow examinations in rhetoric are more likely to allow them in the other areas than are programs that do not accept rhetoric as an examination and dissertation topic. The link between creative writing and rhetoric is the closest, while departments offering examinations in rhetoric are, for all practical purposes, the only ones allowing examinations and theses in technical writing. Examinations in linguistics and technical writ-

Table 11
Percentage of Programs with Examination-Thesis Options in Various Areas among Programs with or without Examination-Thesis Options in Rhetoric and Linguistics

Exam-Thesis Option	Allowing Exams and Theses (N)	Not Allowing Exams and Theses (N)
	In Rhetoric	
Creative writing	37.0 (73)	7.5 (53)
Linguistics	26.0 (73)	7.5 (53)
Technical writing	15.1 (73)	1.9 (53)
	In Linguistics	
Technical writing	21.7 (23)	6.8 (103)

Table 12
Relation of Course Offerings to Examination-Thesis Options in the Same Areas of Study

Area of Study	Percentage of Programs		
	Offering Courses (N)	Allowing Exams and Theses (N)	Allowing Exams and Theses among Those Offering Courses (N)
British and American literature	99.2 (126)	99.2 (126)	100.0 (125)
Critical theory	86.5 (126)	85.7 (126)	90.8 (109)
Rhetoric	78.6 (126)	57.9 (126)	69.7 (99)
Creative writing	67.5 (126)	24.6 (126)	35.3 (85)
Technical writing	23.0 (126)	9.5 (126)	24.1 (29)
Linguistics	20.6 (126)	18.3 (126)	61.5 (26)

Fig. 2. Interrelations among Examination-Thesis Options

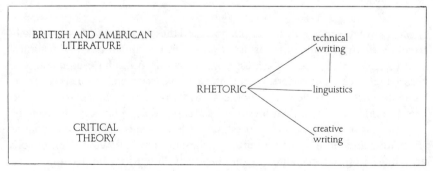

ing, though rare, are also linked. When departments offer the option of examinations in linguistics, they are more likely to offer examinations in technical writing as well (see the last row of table 11).

Figure 2 summarizes the interrelation among examination and thesis areas. British and American literature and, to a lesser extent, critical theory are so widely offered that they are not linked to other examination options. The availability of general examinations in rhetoric is a key to whether doctoral programs allow general examinations and dissertations in technical writing, linguistics, and creative writing.

Interrelation of Examination-Thesis Options and Course Offerings

Thus far, the courses English departments offer and the areas in which they permit general examinations and dissertations have been discussed in isolation from each other. Looking at them together provides further insight into PhD programs in English. Two issues in particular should be considered: the extent to which departments offer examinations in areas in which they offer courses and the extent to which departments permitting examinations and dissertations in given areas are likely to offer certain types of courses. The second question leads to further exploration of the links among various areas of English study.

The two center columns of table 12 summarize the percentages of doctoral programs offering courses and examinations in the six areas for which both figures are available. In British and American literature and critical theory, both examinations and courses are reported in equal proportion by a large majority of doctoral programs. Courses in rhetoric and creative writing are also widely available, but examinations are less common in these fields. Courses and examinations in technical writing and linguistics are available in relatively few departments.

The last column of table 12 gives the percentages of departments, among those offering courses in an area, that also permit examinations or dissertations in that area. As expected, almost all programs that give courses in British and American literature and critical theory also allow examinations and dissertations in these areas. Among programs that have courses in rhetoric, examinations and dissertations in rhetoric are also widespread, though not universal. Among programs offering linguistics courses, the percentage permitting examinations in that area is almost as high as the equivalent figure for rhetoric, even though courses in linguistics are available in many fewer departments. Although courses in creative writing are quite common, examinations and theses in this area are about as scarce as they are in the more rarely taught technical writing.

These findings suggest that British and American literature, critical theory, rhetoric, and linguistics are viewed as areas of serious study for doctoral students in English. Thus, departments that offer courses in them also tend to permit general examinations and dissertations in these fields. Creative writing and technical writing, in contrast, appear to have a different status. Although departments may make courses available in these subjects – and quite commonly do so in creative writing – they rarely allow examinations.

Table 13 presents the percentages of departments offering rhetoric, creative writing, linguistics, or technical writing courses that have examination-thesis options in the first three of these areas. Not unexpectedly, the differences between those offering and not offering examinations are most pronounced if the course and examination areas are the same (see rows 1, 5, and 9 of table 13).[10]

Departments offering examinations in rhetoric are considerably more likely to offer courses in creative writing, linguistics, and technical writing than are departments not offering rhetoric examinations. Similarly, among departments permitting examinations in creative writing, the percentage offering courses in rhetoric is significantly higher than it is among those not permitting examinations in creative writing. But courses in linguistics and technical writing are not much more frequently found in departments with examinations in creative writing

Table 13
Percentage of Programs Offering Various Courses among Programs Allowing or Not Allowing Examination-Thesis Options in Rhetoric, Creative Writing and Linguistics

Course Offered	Allowing Exams and Theses (N)	Not Allowing Exams and Theses (N)
	In Rhetoric	
Rhetoric	94.5 (73)	56.6 (53)
Creative writing	75.3 (73)	56.6 (53)
Linguistics	28.8 (73)	9.4 (53)
Technical writing	30.1 (73)	13.2 (53)
	In Creative Writing	
Creative writing	96.8 (31)	57.9 (95)
Rhetoric	93.5 (31)	73.7 (95)
Linguistics	29.0 (31)	17.9 (95)
Technical writing	35.5 (31)	18.9 (95)
	In Linguistics	
Linguistics	69.6 (23)	9.7 (103)
Rhetoric	91.3 (23)	75.7 (103)
Creative writing	82.6 (23)	64.1 (103)
Technical writing	30.4 (23)	21.4 (103)

than in those without. Whether or not linguistics examinations are permitted does not appear to relate to course offerings in other subjects.

These findings reconfirm the key role of rhetoric. Previous discussion revealed that the presence of rhetoric examinations is a key to whether in other types of writing programs examinations are available. Table 13 indicates that the presence of rhetoric examinations also signals that a doctoral program is likely to offer various other courses, especially creative writing and linguistics.

Modification of Curricula since 1975

The 1986 survey of doctoral programs asked a series of questions about contemplated and recent revisions in doctoral programs. Most of these questions concerned changes made since 1975, especially the types of courses added to the curriculum.

Only five departments (4%) indicated that they had eliminated any doctoral programs since 1975. Of these, two had dropped the linguistics program, two had discontinued the English language program, and one had eliminated the composition program. In addition, two departments had dropped the doctorate in education, and three had done away with the Doctor of Arts degree.

Revision of the Doctoral Program

When asked whether they had plans for a full-scale revision of the doctoral program, 20% of the sampled departments answered affirmatively. As for more limited modifications made since 1975, 65% of the departments reported changing the examinations they require of doctoral candidates.

Almost 75% of the departments indicated that they had not changed the number of courses required for the PhD since 1975. Of those who had altered the requirement, 14% had increased the number of programs and the same percentage had decreased them.

New Courses

Since 1975 departments have added new courses in several areas of the PhD curriculum; only 5% reported adding none. The percentages are listed in descending order in tabulation k. Courses in critical theory and rhetoric are the most common additions. Between one-fifth and one-third of the responding departments have new courses in creative writing, technical writing, and teaching English as a second language. Because "other" courses are those written in by respondents and not included in the questionnaire's categories, it is difficult to assess their prevalence.

Tabulation k

Area of Study	Percentage of Respondents Adding Courses ($N = 113$)
Critical theory	77.0
Rhetoric	72.6
Creative writing	35.4
Technical writing	22.1
Teaching English as a second language	17.7
Other	16.9

The survey findings suggest that over the past 10 years PhD-granting departments have begun to pay more attention to pedagogy. Close to 60% of all doctoral programs report adding course requirements or internships aimed at preparing doctoral students for teaching. In 40% of the departments, such programs carry academic credit; in an additional 18% they are noncredit requirements.

Departments that have added certain types of courses, usually in writing, are especially likely to have added other types as well (see table 14). For example, few departments have added courses in technical writing during the past 10 years, but departments are more likely to have done so if they have added courses in rhetoric. Departments that have added rhetoric courses are also somewhat more likely to have added courses in creative writing, as is shown in the second row of table 14. Like departments that added rhetoric courses, those that added cre-

Table 14
Percentage of Programs Adding Various Courses among Programs Adding or Not Adding Courses in Rhetoric, Creative Writing, Technical Writing, and Critical Theory

Course Added	Adding Courses (N)	Not Adding Courses (N)
	In Rhetoric	
Technical writing	28.0 (82)	6.5 (31)
Creative writing	39.0 (82)	25.8 (31)
	In Creative Writing	
Technical writing	32.5 (40)	16.4 (73)
	In Technical Writing	
Teaching ESL	36.0 (25)	12.5 (88)
	In Critical Theory	
Technical writing	25.3 (87)	11.5 (26)
Rhetoric	67.8 (87)	88.5 (26)

ative writing courses are more likely than others to have added courses in technical writing. Finally, departments that have added courses in technical writing are more likely than others to have added courses in teaching English as a second language.

As the last two rows of table 14 indicate, departments that added courses in critical theory during the past 10 years are somewhat more likely than those that have not done so to have added courses in technical writing. This tendency is not pronounced, however. The link between courses in critical theory and rhetoric is more clear-cut, but the negative correlation is unusual. During the past 10 years departments that have added courses in critical theory are less likely to have added courses in rhetoric than are departments that did not add critical theory. These findings suggest that, to some extent, rhetoric and critical theory represent different lines of development for English doctoral programs. But since 52% of the departments in the sample have added courses in both rhetoric and critical theory, the conclusion should not be overstated.

Figure 3 summarizes the interrelations among various types of courses added to PhD curricula since 1975. It indicates that the addition of technical writing courses signals the addition of the other courses represented. The few departments that have added courses in technical writing are far more likely than the others to have also added courses in rhetoric, creative writing, and teaching English as a second language. This suggests that technical writing is being incorporated into more general writing programs, even though it is rarely offered as an independent area of specialization.

Interrelation between Examination-Thesis Options and Courses Added

English departments add courses to their curricula for a variety of reasons (e.g., to attract students or to build up an area of strength or a new area of specialization). If one assumes that the presence of general examinations denotes areas of emphasis in a doctoral program, the 1986 survey data provide some insight into the relation between new course offerings and departments' areas of strength.

Fig. 3. Interrelations among Courses Added between 1975 and 1986

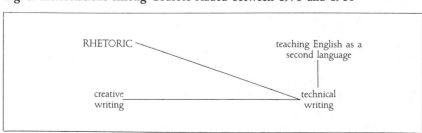

Table 15 examines the relation between courses added since 1975 and examination options in the four fields for which data are available.

The first two rows of the table indicate that more departments have added courses in the three types of writing than currently allow examinations in these areas. The difference is marked only for technical writing, however. The third and fourth rows of the table show that departments permitting examinations in an area are more likely to have added courses than are departments not permitting examinations. By the same token, as the fifth and sixth rows reveal, departments that have added courses since 1975 are more likely to allow examinations than are those that have not added courses. With the exception of critical theory, the differences are substantial.[11]

These findings indicate that doctoral programs generally do not add courses unrelated to evolving or existing areas of strength. Although technical writing appears to be an exception in this respect, it may not be, since the survey data suggest that such courses are viewed as integral to comprehensive writing programs rather than as elements of distinct programs. This conclusion cannot be definitive, of course, since several major areas of English studies could not be examined (e.g., British and American literature, linguistics).

Because the data are cross-sectional, it is impossible to determine whether departments use new courses to build on areas of strength or to add areas of expertise. Only information collected over time would allow one to choose between these possibilities. Such information might also shed light on the conditions in which doctoral programs add to areas of strength and those in which they build up new areas.

The data on courses added and examination options allow investigation of another question: are departments that currently permit examinations in various

Table 15
Percentage of Programs Allowing Examination-Thesis Options and Adding Courses in Rhetoric, Creative Writing, Technical Writing, and Critical Theory

	Rhetoric (N)	Creative Writing (N)	Technical Writing (N)	Critical Theory (N)
Allowing exams and theses	60.2 (113)	26.5 (113)	8.0 (113)	85.8 (113)
Adding courses	72.6 (113)	35.4 (113)	22.1 (113)	77.0 (113)
Adding courses among those offering examinations	89.7 (68)	66.7 (30)	55.6 (9)	79.4 (97)
Adding courses among those not offering examinations	46.7 (45)	24.1 (83)	19.2 (104)	62.5 (16)
Allowing exams and theses among those adding courses	74.4 (82)	50.0 (40)	20.0 (25)	88.5 (87)
Allowing exams and theses among those not adding courses	22.6 (31)	13.7 (73)	4.5 (88)	76.9 (26)

areas more likely to have added certain courses since 1975? Table 16 indicates that in some areas they are. Doctoral programs that allow examinations in rhetoric tend to have added the greatest array of courses. Not surprisingly, almost all the departments that currently permit examinations in rhetoric have added courses in the subject, whereas fewer than half the departments not permitting such examinations have added these courses. As the top rows of table 16 show, departments that allow examinations in rhetoric are also more likely than others to have added courses in creative and technical writing. Finally, if departments give examinations in rhetoric, they are more likely to have added courses in teaching English as a second language than are departments that do not offer these examinations.

The links between courses added and examinations permitted in creative writing are similar to those for rhetoric, although fewer and less pronounced. Table 16 indicates that over two-thirds of the departments that currently permit examinations in creative writing have added courses in the subject since 1975. In contrast, slightly fewer than a quarter of the departments that do not give examinations in creative writing have added courses. Such departments are also less likely to have added courses in technical writing than are departments that allow examinations in creative writing.

Linguistics differs somewhat from the other two areas considered. Very few departments appear to have added courses in linguistics since 1975, although a

Table 16
Percentage of Programs Adding Various Courses among Programs Allowing or Not Allowing Examination-Thesis Options in Rhetoric, Creative Writing, and Linguistics

Course Added	Allowing Exams and Theses (N)	Not Allowing Exams and Theses (N)
	In Rhetoric	
Rhetoric	89.7 (68)	46.7 (45)
Creative writing	45.6 (68)	20.0 (45)
Technical writing	32.4 (68)	6.7 (45)
Teaching ESL	23.5 (68)	8.9 (45)
	In Creative Writing	
Creative writing	66.7 (30)	24.1 (83)
Technical writing	36.7 (30)	16.9 (83)
	In Linguistics	
Teaching ESL	36.4 (22)	13.2 (91)
Creative writing	50.0 (22)	31.9 (91)

fairly substantial number allow examinations.[12] Departments that permit examinations in linguistics are somewhat more likely to have added courses in creative writing than are departments that do not. More clear-cut is the tendency for departments permitting linguistics examinations to have added courses in teaching English as a second language. Departments that currently permit examinations in technical writing also appear more likely to have added courses in teaching English as a second language, although the numbers are too small to allow definitive conclusions. Among departments allowing technical writing examinations, 54% have added courses in the subject, compared with 15% that do not allow the examinations.

Once again, rhetoric emerges as a pivotal factor. Doctoral programs that allow general examinations and dissertations in the subject are more likely to have added a number of writing courses to their curricula between 1975 and 1985. More specifically, one-third or more of the departments that permit examinations in rhetoric have added courses in rhetoric, creative writing, and technical writing to their programs since 1975.

Degree Programs in Rhetoric and Writing

As the preceding discussion suggests, rhetoric, writing, and composition have become important elements in many doctoral programs in English. Close to three-quarters of the doctoral programs in the 1986 survey sample have added courses in rhetoric since 1975. Over four-fifths of the departments in the sample offer courses in the subject, and almost three-fifths of all PhD-granting English departments permit general examinations and dissertations in this area. In addition, the presence of rhetoric as an examination option is a key indicator of whether doctoral programs offer courses and allow examinations and dissertations in other areas of writing. When asked about their hiring expectations for the next three years, close to half the departments in the sample indicated that they expect to hire specialists in rhetoric; only specialists in British or American literature are more likely to be sought.

Among the responding departments, 33% currently have doctoral programs in rhetoric, writing, or composition, and an additional 6% report that they plan to establish them.[13] According to the 1986 data, doctoral programs in rhetoric vary in age from 1 year to 17, averaging 6 years. Half the departments report that they established their programs from 3 to 8 years ago. Only two programs have existed for more than 15 years.

During the early 1980s most rhetoric programs experienced growth. In the 1983–84 survey of English programs, 84% of the participating PhD-granting departments with graduate programs in rhetoric reported that enrollments in these programs had grown in the preceding three years. This figure compares with the 28% of graduate programs in British or American literature that reported an increase in enrollment (Huber and Young 42–43).

In addition to being an important part of doctoral curricula, graduate programs in rhetoric play a role at the undergraduate level. The 1983–84 survey shows that average enrollments in upper- and lower-division writing courses are considerably higher in departments with graduate programs in rhetoric than in other departments. The sharpest differences, however, emerge in graduate enrollments, as tabulation 1 indicates (Huber and Young 51–52).

Tabulation 1

Level of Writing Course	Mean Enrollment with Graduate Rhetoric Program	
	Offered (N)	Not Offered (N)
Lower division	2,276.6 (70)	1,393.1 (101)
Upper division	348.3 (72)	180.1 (98)
Graduate	40.6 (69)	13.7 (70)

Given the important role of rhetoric in both graduate and undergraduate programs in English, the characteristics of such doctoral programs are of considerable interest, and several questions on the subject made up one section of the 1986 survey.

Programs in Technical Writing

In contrast to rhetoric programs, doctoral programs in technical writing are uncommon: only four departments, 3% of the sample, award the PhD in this area. At first glance, this finding appears inconsistent with the results of the 1983–84 survey in which 13 PhD-granting departments, or 12%, reported "graduate degree programs in technical communication or professional writing" (Huber and Young 42). The reason for the difference is probably that the earlier survey covered MA as well as PhD programs, and the discrepancy suggests that the 1986 data may underestimate the number of graduate technical or professional writing programs.

The 1983–84 survey revealed that technical communication is the least commonly offered graduate and undergraduate English degree program (Huber and Young 42–43). The 12% of the PhD-granting departments that reported graduate courses in the subject contrasts with 92% offering British and American literature, 52%, creative writing, 45%, rhetoric, 28%, criticism, and 17%, comparative literature. The proportion awarding undergraduate degrees in technical communication is 31%, compared with 48% for creative writing, 51% for English education, and 91% for the English major.

Even though degree programs in technical communication are rare, undergraduate courses in the subject are widely available. Of the departments included in the 1983–84 sample, 63% offer such courses, with English departments in public institutions more likely to do so than those in private institutions (Huber and Young 54). In addition, departments with degree programs in technical communication frequently report growth in these programs. Of the few departments with graduate degree programs in technical communication, 77% report that their programs grew in the preceding three years. This proportion is higher than that for any other graduate degree program in the 1983–84 survey.

Although the number of graduate programs in technical communication is too small for the percentages to be reliable, the pattern is repeated at the undergraduate level: 72% of all departments that offer undergraduate programs in technical communication, and 83% of the PhD-granting departments, report growth in their programs. In contrast, 50% of all departments report growth for creative writing programs and 37% for the English major (Huber and Young 42–44). These findings suggest that technical writing may continue to be an undergraduate growth area. Consequently, the doctoral programs responsible for training college teachers may need to prepare graduates to offer instruction in the subject.

General Orientation of Rhetoric Programs

When asked to describe the orientation of their doctoral programs in rhetoric, departments responded as shown in tabulation m. The results indicate that rhetoric programs are most likely to be theoretical in orientation. The proportions listing the other three orientations as primary are about the same. Pedagogy and theory predominate as secondary orientations.

Tabulation m

| | Percentage of Departments Reporting | |
Orientation	Primary (*N* = 42)	Secondary (*N* = 41)
Theoretical	47.6	41.5
Pedagogical	19.0	31.7
Historical	19.0	12.2
Empirical	14.3	14.6
Total	100.0	100.0

Further analysis reveals several clusters of orientations. Table 17 shows the link between the two dominant orientations – theoretical and pedagogical. Rhetoric programs reporting the first as primary and the second as secondary account for 27% of the subsample of rhetoric programs. In addition, the majority of programs whose primary orientation is theoretical describe their secondary orientation as pedagogical. The other two clusters of orientations involve a secondary theoretical orientation. All the rhetoric programs whose primary orientation is historical have a secondary theoretical orientation, as do almost three-quarters of the programs whose primary orientation is pedagogical. The few programs whose primary orientation is empirical show no clear-cut secondary orientation.

When the orientations reported are not classified as primary or secondary, analysis reveals that 88% of the rhetoric programs in the sample are theoretical in orientation, 51% are pedagogical, 32% are historical, and 29% are empirical.

Table 18 indicates that the orientations of rhetoric programs vary with a number of departmental characteristics. Most programs are theoretical in orientation, regardless of their enrollments, but departments with more than 100 graduate students are less likely than others to have this orientation. A pedagogical orientation tends to be more prevalent among rhetoric programs in public institutions, while a historical orientation is more typical of programs in private institutions. Similarly, rhetoric programs in departments that began to grant the PhD before 1959 are more likely to be historically orientated. Table 18 indicates that more recently founded doctoral programs are more likely to have an empirical orientation than are older rhetoric programs.[14]

Table 17
Percentage of Rhetoric Programs Reporting Various
Primary and Secondary Orientations

Secondary Orientation	Primary Orientation			
	Empirical	Historical	Theoretical	Pedagogical
Empirical	–	–	21.1	25.0
Historical	16.7	–	21.1	–
Theoretical	50.0	100.0	–	75.0
Pedagogical	33.3	–	57.9	–
Total	100.0	100.0	100.0	100.0
(N)	(6)	(8)	(19)	(8)

Table 18
Percentage of Rhetoric Programs Reporting Various Orientations, by
Departmental Characteristics

	Theoretical (N)	Pedagogical (N)	Historical (N)	Empirical (N)
Sample as a whole	87.8 (41)	51.2 (41)	31.7 (41)	29.3 (41)
Source of funding				
Public	–	57.1 (35)	25.7 (35)	–
Private	–	16.7 (6)	66.7 (6)	–
Year PhD first granted				
After 1959	–	–	20.0 (20)	40.0 (20)
1959 and before	–	–	47.4 (19)	21.1 (19)
Number of graduate students				
50 or fewer	100.0 (9)	–	–	–
51–100	92.3 (13)	–	–	–
101 or more	73.3 (15)	–	–	–

Required Courses

Doctoral rhetoric programs require students to take courses in various subfields. The courses most frequently required for a PhD in rhetoric are British and American literature. Furthermore, all rhetoric programs in the sample accept literature courses in partial fulfillment of the requirements for the degree. Courses in the theory of composition and in rhetoric are required by about 80% of the rhetoric programs in the sample. Approximately 50% to 60% also require four additional courses: teaching methods, linguistics, bibliographic research methods, and history of the English language. The proportions are listed in tabulation n. The fact that the majority of rhetoric programs require almost all the courses listed suggests considerable agreement about the appropriate course content for a doctoral training program in rhetoric, writing, and composition.

Tabulation n

Area of Study	Percentage of Rhetoric Programs Requiring Courses ($N = 42$)
British and American literature	85.7
Theory of composition	81.0
Rhetoric	78.6
Teaching methods	61.9
Linguistics	57.1
Bibliography and research methods	54.8
History of the English language	47.6
Social science or experimental research methods	14.3

In the light of this agreement, linkages between required courses are to be expected. Table 19 shows the courses that tend to be paired.[15] According to the first row, courses in bibliographic research methods are considerably more likely to be required in programs that require British and American literature than in the few that do not have this requirement. Similarly, programs that require courses in the theory of composition are more likely than the few that do not to require courses in rhetoric and teaching methods. The fourth row of table 19 shows that courses in rhetoric and linguistics are also linked, with programs that require rhetoric more likely than those that do not to require linguistics as well. Finally, programs that require courses in teaching methods are the only ones to require courses in social science or experimental research methods.

The links among required courses in history of the English language, teaching methods, and social science methods are less marked than the ones discussed thus far and different in character. As the bottom rows of table 19 indicate, rhetoric programs that require students to take courses in the history of the English language are less likely than those that do not to require courses in teaching or in social science research methods. This finding is in keeping with the earlier

Table 19
Percentage of Programs Requiring Various Courses among Programs Requiring
or Not Requiring British and American Literature, Theory of Composition,
Rhetoric, Teaching Methods, and History of the English Language

Course Required	Requiring (N)	Not Requiring (N)
	British and American Literature	
Bibliography and research methods	63.9 (36)	– (6)
	Theory of Composition	
Rhetoric	85.3 (34)	50.0 (8)
Teaching methods	67.6 (34)	37.5 (8)
	Rhetoric	
Linguistics	63.6 (33)	33.3 (9)
	Teaching Methods	
Social science methods	23.1 (26)	– (16)
	History of the English Language	
Teaching methods	50.0 (20)	72.7 (22)
Social science methods	5.0 (20)	22.7 (22)

one that most historically oriented rhetoric programs do not also have empirical
or pedagogical orientations; rather, their orientations tend to be theoretical.

The linkages among the various types of courses required by rhetoric programs are diagrammed in figure 4. As has been observed before, the three most
frequently required courses do not appear closely related, largely because of their

Fig. 4. Interrelations among Courses Required for the Rhetoric PhD

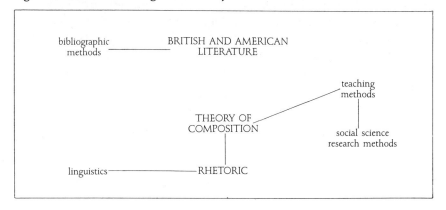

great prevalence. These widely offered courses are linked to several less commonly required subjects: bibliographic methods, linguistics, and teaching methods. In addition, courses in teaching methods are linked to courses in social science methods.

The frequency with which various types of courses are required by rhetoric programs does not vary systematically with most departmental characteristics. The only clear exception is faculty size. In general, rhetoric programs in departments with large full-time faculties are more likely to require a given course than are programs in smaller departments. The pattern is particularly marked for courses in the theory of composition and in British and American literature, as is shown in tabulation o.[16] Once again, courses in the history of the English language represent an exception. Although the difference is not pronounced, rhetoric programs in departments with small full-time faculties appear more likely than larger departments to require such courses.

Tabulation o

Course	Percentage of Programs Requiring Course	
	with 30 or fewer faculty members ($N = 15$)	with 31 or more faculty members ($N = 26$)
Theory of composition	60.0	92.3
British and American literature	66.7	96.2
History of the English language	60.0	42.3

Dissertation Areas

The 1986 survey asked departments with PhD programs in rhetoric to indicate whether students in these programs during the past five years had written dissertations with four thematic approaches. The percentages responding affirmatively are listed in tabulation p. In the light of the program orientations discussed above, it is not surprising that theoretical and pedagogical dissertation topics are widespread, while historical themes are less common. The large percentage of rhetoric programs with students doing empirical theses is notable, however, since few programs emphasize this aspect of the subject.

Tabulation p

Orientation	Percentage of Rhetoric Programs with Orientation ($N = 37$)
Theoretical	83.8
Pedagogical	73.0
Empirical	59.5
Historical	37.8

The frequency with which graduate rhetoric students write such dissertations varies with the age and size of the department. In departments that granted
the PhD before 1959 and that have large full-time faculties, empirical dissertations are more common than in other types of departments, as tabulation q indicates. Since the students of today represent the faculty members of tomorrow,
the findings suggest that in the years ahead rhetoric programs may place more
emphasis on empirical issues and may engage in more collaboration with the
social sciences.

Tabulation q

	Percentage Reporting Empirical Theses (N)
Year PhD first awarded	
After 1959	45.0 (20)
1959 and before	80.0 (15)
Number of regular full-time faculty members	
30 or fewer	30.0 (10)
31 or more	68.0 (25)

Characteristics of Rhetoric Programs

The preceding discussion has indicated that doctoral programs with certain characteristics are more likely than departments lacking these characteristics to offer
courses and general examinations in rhetoric and writing. Consequently, one
would also expect such departments to be more likely to have doctoral programs
in rhetoric. Table 20 confirms this expectation. Departments in the Midwest and
the South Atlantic–South Central regions are somewhat more likely to have doctoral programs in rhetoric than are departments elsewhere. In addition, rhetoric
programs in the South appear to have been in existence somewhat longer than
those in the Midwest.[17]

Differences by source of funding are more clear-cut than the geographic differences. Table 20 indicates that PhD-granting departments in public institutions
are about three times as likely to have rhetoric programs, though they are apparently not older than the few in private institutions.[18] Among PhD-granting
departments with 31 or more regular full-time faculty members, 39% have rhetoric programs, as compared with 27% of the smaller departments. In addition,
rhetoric programs in departments in which MA students predominate have been
more recently established than programs in departments in which PhD students

Table 20
Existence and Age of Rhetoric Programs, by Departmental Characteristics

	Percentage of Departments with Rhetoric Programs (N)	Mean Age of Rhetoric Programs, years (N)
Geographic area		
Northeast	21.2 (33)	4.3 (6)
South Atlantic–South Central	35.9 (39)	7.3 (14)
Midwest	47.1 (34)	4.9 (15)
Rocky Mountain–Pacific	20.0 (20)	7.7 (3)
Source of funding		
Public	42.7 (82)	5.8 (32)
Private	13.6 (44)	6.3 (6)
Number of regular full-time faculty members		
20 or fewer	27.3 (22)	6.8 (5)
21–30	27.6 (29)	5.4 (8)
31–45	38.2 (34)	6.4 (13)
46 or more	40.6 (32)	6.2 (11)
Percentage of graduate students in the PhD program		
40 or less	36.6 (41)	3.8 (13)
41–60	30.8 (39)	7.0 (13)
61 or more	35.7 (28)	6.9 (9)

make up the majority. In short, doctoral programs with large faculties in public institutions are the most likely to have degree programs in rhetoric.

Departments with rhetoric programs differ from those without such programs in their emphasis on various types of writing rather than in their requirements for the literature degree. Obviously, as table 21 indicates, PhD-granting departments with rhetoric programs are more likely to offer writing courses, as well as examinations in rhetoric and creative writing; to have added courses in rhetoric and technical writing; and to expect to hire specialists in rhetoric. They are not much more likely than other departments, however, to permit examinations and dissertations in technical writing.

Departments with rhetoric programs are somewhat more likely than other departments to let rhetoric courses count toward the literature degree (see the bottom of table 21). They are more likely to require courses in rhetoric for the literature degree, but they are less likely than other departments to require courses in textual criticism. Otherwise the requirements for a PhD in literature are quite similar in both types of departments. Doctoral programs in writing do not seem to be coupled with an atypical approach to the PhD in literature. Departments with rhetoric programs differ from those without such programs in their emphasis on writing rather than in their requirements for the literature degree.

The Literature Degree

The preceding discussion has revealed that at least four-fifths of the PhD-granting departments in the 1986 survey sample offer courses in three areas: British and American literature, critical theory, and rhetoric. A like proportion allow examinations and dissertations in the first two areas, while almost three-fifths allow examinations and dissertations in rhetoric. Moreover, the survey revealed widespread consensus among rhetoric programs about the courses required for the PhD in rhetoric. This uniformity stands in contrast to the diversity in requirements for the PhD in literature.

Required Courses

Nearly 90% of PhD-granting departments require specific courses for the literature degree.[19] Bibliographic and research methods is the only course required by the vast majority of PhD programs in the sample; most other types of courses are required by from 20% to 50%. The diversity of requirements for the doctorate in literature has been typical of the field for some time, as is apparent from a comparison of the data on current requirements with similar information as-

Table 21
Percentage of Programs with Various Curricular Characteristics among Programs with or without the Rhetoric PhD

	With the Rhetoric PhD (N)	Without the Rhetoric PhD (N)
Expect to hire rhetoric specialist	60.0 (40)	39.0 (82)
Offer graduate courses		
In rhetoric	100.0 (41)	68.2 (85)
In creative writing	78.0 (41)	62.4 (85)
In technical writing	39.0 (41)	15.3 (85)
Allow Exams and Theses		
In rhetoric	100.0 (41)	37.6 (85)
In creative writing	34.1 (41)	20.0 (85)
In technical writing	14.6 (41)	7.1 (85)
Have added courses		
In rhetoric	92.5 (40)	61.6 (73)
In technical writing	40.0 (40)	12.3 (73)
In teaching ESL	25.0 (40)	13.7 (73)
Count rhetoric courses toward literature degree	97.5 (40)	82.2 (73)
Require for literature degree courses		
In textual criticism	12.5 (40)	28.6 (63)
In rhetoric	42.5 (40)	25.4 (63)

sembled by Allen in 1966 (55, 171). Tabulation r indicates that courses in bibliography and research methods have been among the most widely required for the 20 years between surveys. The frequency with which courses in linguistics are required also appears to have remained largely unchanged. Course requirements in literary criticism, however, have become far more common. Although courses in the history of the English language are no longer required for the literature degrees, they remain an important element of today's degree programs in rhetoric.

Further comparison of the 1966 and 1986 figures suggests that PhD programs in literature lost a widely shared requirement when courses in Old English were no longer mandatory. Whether such courses should become optional was a hotly debated topic in the mid-1960s. Allen reports that many recent graduates saw no value in learning Old and Middle English, while their teachers contended that this training provides essential background for understanding modern literature (54–64). Obviously, the students carried the day. At the same time, none of the courses added to the curriculum in place of Old and Middle English has achieved universal acceptance. Today, no more than 45% of departments require courses in critical theory, historical scholarship, rhetoric, or textual criticism for the PhD in literature. This contrasts with the 69% that required Old English in 1966.

Even though few literature courses are universally required for the doctorate, some requirements tend to go together. Table 22 indicates that departments requiring courses in literary criticism and critical theory are also likely to require several other types of courses. Departments that require literary criticism are far more likely than others to require courses in critical theory and historical scholarship. They are also more likely to require rhetoric and textual criticism. The last two courses, moreover, are disproportionately required by departments that require critical theory. In addition, departments that require courses in critical theory for the literature degree are more likely than others to require courses in historical scholarship.

The last three rows of table 22 indicate that requirements in historical schol-

Tabulation r

Course	Percentage of Programs Requiring Course	
	1986 Survey ($N = 103$)	1966 Survey ($N = 78$)
Old English and literature	–	68.9
Middle English and literature	–	27.0
History of the English language	–	31.1
Bibliography and research methods	74.8	62.2
Literary criticism	53.4	13.5
Modern English, linguistics	37.9	32.4
Pedagogy and teaching methods[20]	8.7	6.8
Critical theory	44.7	–
Historical scholarship	38.8	–
Rhetoric, writing, or composition	32.0	–
Textual criticism	22.3	–

arship and textual criticism are closely linked, that departments requiring rhetoric are more likely than others to require textual criticism, and that departments requiring linguistics are somewhat more likely to require rhetoric courses. The interrelationships among various types of required courses are diagrammed in figure 5. Four required courses are closely linked to one another: literary criti-

Table 22
Percentage of Programs Requiring Various Courses among Programs Requiring or Not Requiring Literary Criticism, Critical Theory, Historical Scholarship, Rhetoric, and Linguistics

Course Required	Requiring (*N*)	Not Requiring (*N*)
	Literary Criticism	
Critical theory	65.5 (55)	20.8 (48)
Historical scholarship	52.7 (55)	22.9 (48)
Rhetoric	45.5 (55)	16.7 (48)
Textual criticism	34.5 (55)	8.3 (48)
	Critical Theory	
Historical scholarship	52.2 (46)	28.1 (57)
Rhetoric	45.7 (46)	21.1 (57)
Textual criticism	37.0 (46)	10.5 (57)
	Historical Scholarship	
Textual criticism	52.5 (40)	3.2 (63)
	Rhetoric	
Textual criticism	39.4 (33)	14.3 (70)
	Linguistics	
Rhetoric	43.6 (39)	25.0 (64)

Fig. 5. Interrelations among Courses Required for the Literature PhD

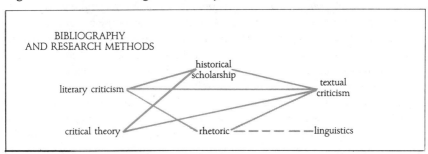

cism, critical theory, historical scholarship, and textual criticism. Departments that require any one are likely to require the others.

Although most departments do not require rhetoric courses for the literature degree, almost all count such courses toward the degree. When questioned about this, 93% of the departments offering rhetoric courses – 16% of the sample does not – indicated that students can elect to take courses in rhetoric, writing, or composition in partial fulfillment of the requirements for the literature degree.

The linkages among various types of required courses suggest considerable agreement about what the literature curriculum should include. The courses generally favored are bibliographic methods, literary criticism, critical theory, historical scholarship, and textual criticism. The number of respondents abiding entirely by this consensus is limited, however, since only 22% of them require courses in textual criticism for the literature degree.[21]

Courses in Teaching

In addition to asking about required courses for the literature degree, the 1986 survey of doctoral programs inquired into credit-bearing courses in teaching. The survey responses reveal that most doctoral programs in literature feature courses in teaching methods; only 24% of the departments in the sample do not offer such courses.[22] The situation contrasts sharply with that prevailing 20 years earlier. In 1966, Allen found that only 32% of the departments in his sample offered a course in pedagogical methods; only 15% went as far as offering a formal course or noncredit seminar on the duties of college and junior college faculty members (78, 197, 198). At that time, pedagogical training was most frequently provided through supervised teaching; 72% of Allen's respondents indicated that they used this method. A majority of his respondents also mentioned informal conversations with faculty members (the passing on of lore) and occasional lectures or panel discussions as ways of preparing graduate students for college teaching.

The 1986 survey data indicate that courses in teaching are now more widespread and more focused than they were in 1966. While programs in literature frequently offer courses on teaching writing, relatively few offer courses concerned exclusively with teaching literature. Of 98 literature programs responding, 80% have writing-only courses, 37% writing-and-literature courses, and 24% literature-only courses. More detailed analysis reveals that 65% of the departments offer one type of course on teaching rather than several and that among these departments the one type usually focuses entirely on writing (see tab. s). Very few departments offer courses devoted exclusively to teaching literature. Of the departments offering such courses, 96% offer them along with other courses on teaching. Such course combinations are present in only 41% of the departments offering courses on teaching writing and 58% of those offering courses on teaching both writing and literature. The last type of course is a popular option in the few departments that do not offer courses in teaching writing, but it is infrequently offered if the curricula include such courses. Only 24% of the departments with pedagogical courses on writing offer courses that take up writing and literature together. In contrast, 85% of the departments that do not have writing-only courses offer courses on teaching writing and literature.

Revision of the Literary Canon

The survey questionnaire asked respondents to indicate whether revision of the literary canon had significantly affected their doctoral programs in literature. Almost two-thirds of the departments in the sample (63%) responded in the affirmative. Of these 78 departments, 85% reported that they had created new courses, 85% said they had revised courses, 6% mentioned revising PhD examinations or reading lists, and 4% noted that they had revised their PhD requirements or programs. Further analysis reveals that 71% of the departments affected by revision of the canon have created new courses and revised old ones, while only 3% have done neither. More comprehensive revision of literature programs appears to be rare, though this finding must be viewed with caution. The survey form asked only about new and revised courses; revisions of examinations and reading lists and of requirements and programs were supplemental categories added by respondents. Some departments may have undertaken comprehensive revisions that they did not indicate on the questionnaire. The survey suggests that, to date, canon revision has affected primarily the types of courses offered and not the basic structure of literature programs. Nonetheless, the almost universal alteration of course content is noteworthy.

Tabulation s

Type of Course	Percentage of Respondents Offering ($N = 96$)
Writing only	47.9
Writing and literature	15.6
Literature only	1.0
Writing only and literature only	13.5
Writing only and writing and literature	12.5
Literature only and writing and literature	2.1
Writing only, literature only, and writing and literature	7.3
Total	100.0

Trends in Literary Study

Respondents were asked to assess how various trends in literary study had affected the teaching of their doctoral students. It is important to note that these responses differ in character from those discussed thus far. The 1986 survey was designed to yield a representative sample of doctorate-granting departments rather than a representative sample of faculty members who teach in such departments; yet to evaluate the importance of trends requires an analysis of opinions expressed by the second type of sample. Most of those completing the questionnaire for the 1986 survey were probably department chairs or directors of graduate studies, though there is no way of knowing for certain. Consequently, survey respondents cannot be said to represent the faculty members teaching in doctoral programs or even a clearly identifiable subset of them. It is therefore difficult to determine the broader significance of their responses – a limitation that should be borne in mind in interpreting the findings reported below.

Two of the trends in literary study that the respondents considered were canon revision and feminist criticism. About 66% of the respondents viewed canon revision as important for the teaching of doctoral students, whereas 86% judged feminist criticism important, the highest percentage citing any of the 10 trends identified.

More detailed analysis reveals that 64% of the respondents regarded both feminist criticism and canon revision as important trends, while 11% found neither important. Another 22% stated that feminist criticism has been important but not canon revision, thereby accounting for the different percentages that named the two trends. Other trends considered by survey respondents, along with percentages of respondents who deemed them important, are shown in tabulation t.

Table 23 indicates extensive linkages between trends. Respondents who regard critical pluralism as important are likely to view reader-response criticism in the same way. Reader-response criticism, in turn, is linked to several other trends. Those who consider it important to their programs are likely to report that new historicism, semiotics, and structuralism are also important.

Tabulation t

Trend	Percentage of Respondents Considering Important ($N = 120$)
Critical pluralism	81.7
Poststructuralism	70.0
Reader-response criticism	55.0
New Criticism	49.2
New historicism	47.5
Marxist criticism	47.5
Semiotics	43.3
Structuralism	43.3

Poststructuralism is also linked to other trends. A solid majority of respondents who find it important consider Marxist criticism, new historicism, and semiotics important as well. Of the respondents who do not cite poststructuralism as important, no more than 20% judge these other trends important in training doctoral students.

New historicism is linked to Marxist criticism, semiotics, and structuralism, and the last three trends are linked to one another. Respondents who consider Marxist criticism important are more likely than others to view structuralism and semiotics as important. Finally, respondents who consider structuralism important are also more likely to regard semiotics as important.

Table 23
Percentage of Programs Considering Various Trends Important among Programs That Do or Do Not Assign Importance to Critical Pluralism, Poststructuralism, Reader-Response Criticism, New Historicism, Marxist Criticism, and Structuralism

Trend Considered Important	Important (N)	Not Important (N)
	Critical Pluralism	
Reader-response criticism	60.2 (98)	31.8 (22)
	Poststructuralism	
Structuralism	54.8 (84)	16.7 (36)
Marxist criticism	65.5 (84)	5.6 (36)
New historicism	59.5 (84)	19.4 (36)
Semiotics	58.3 (84)	8.3 (36)
	Reader-Response Criticism	
New historicism	60.6 (66)	31.5 (54)
Semiotics	56.1 (66)	27.8 (54)
Structuralism	60.6 (66)	22.2 (54)
	New Historicism	
Marxist criticism	70.2 (57)	27.0 (63)
Semiotics	56.1 (57)	31.7 (63)
Structuralism	54.4 (57)	33.3 (63)
	Marxist Criticism	
Structuralism	56.1 (57)	31.7 (63)
Semiotics	66.7 (57)	22.2 (63)
	Structuralism	
Semiotics	73.1 (52)	20.6 (68)

Figure 6 illustrates the close interconnection of five trends: poststructuralism, Marxist criticism, new historicism, structuralism, and semiotics. Those considering any one of these important are quite likely to consider the others significant as well. Reader-response criticism is not linked to several of the closely interconnected trends in the diagram, though it is related to three. Critical pluralism appears to be unrelated to the other literary trends, but the reason is largely the preponderance of respondents who deem it important in training doctoral students. In contrast, the New Criticism, which does not appear in figure 6, stands apart from other trends: respondents' views of its importance are unrelated to their views of other trends.

Fig. 6. Interrelations among Trends in Literary Study Deemed Important

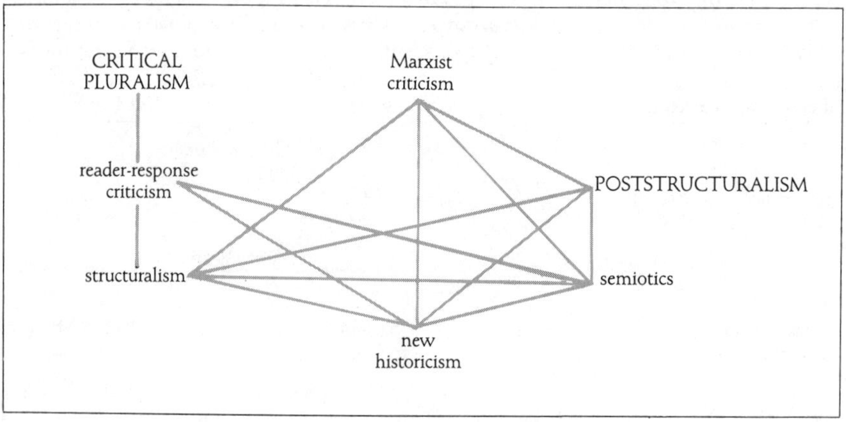

Conclusion: Departmental Characteristics and Curricular Features

The preceding pages outline the major findings emerging from the 1986 survey of doctoral programs in English. The discussion initially distinguishes PhD programs by key departmental characteristics and subsequently focuses on curricular features. It may therefore be appropriate to conclude by differentiating departments with varying characteristics according to their distinctive curricular features.

Differences among Major Types of Departments

Table 24 indicates that doctoral programs in the Midwest have several distinctive departmental characteristics. On average, they have larger faculties than do departments elsewhere and have granted a larger number of PhDs since 1981. Along with departments in the South Atlantic–South Central region, those in the Midwest are most likely to permit students to write examinations and dissertations in rhetoric and creative writing and to require courses in bibliographic methods

Table 24
Departmental and Curricular Differences, by Geographic Area

	Northeast (N)	South Atlantic–South Central (N)	Midwest (N)	Rocky Mountain–Pacific (N)
Mean number of full-time regular faculty members	33.2 (30)	32.1 (35)	40.9 (33)	34.2 (19)
Mean number of degrees granted since 1981	32.3 (32)	23.3 (33)	38.3 (32)	28.7 (20)
Percentage of Departments				
Offering courses in rhetoric	60.6 (33)	82.1 (39)	88.2 (34)	85.0 (20)
Offering courses in linguistics	– (33)	30.8 (39)	32.4 (34)	15.0 (20)
Offering exams in creative writing	12.1 (33)	28.2 (39)	41.2 (34)	10.0 (20)
Offering exams in rhetoric	39.4 (33)	56.4 (39)	73.5 (34)	65.0 (20)
Requiring bibliography courses for literature degree	61.9 (21)	87.9 (33)	83.3 (30)	52.6 (19)
Requiring linguistics courses for literature degree	23.8 (21)	42.4 (33)	56.7 (30)	15.8 (19)
Viewing canon revision as significant	81.3 (32)	42.1 (38)	70.6 (34)	63.2 (19)

and linguistics for the literature degree. In keeping with this tendency, departments in the South and Midwest are most likely to offer courses in linguistics. In contrast, departments in the Northeast offer no linguistics courses and are the least likely to offer rhetoric courses.

Insofar as departments in the Northeast appear distinctive, the reason is largely that most are in private institutions. As table 25 shows, such departments are less likely to offer courses in rhetoric and linguistics than are those in public institutions. By the same token, many of the differences between departments in the Midwest and those elsewhere can be explained by the prevalence of large English faculties in this region. The distinctive features of southern doctoral programs cannot be explained this way, in part because their distinctiveness tends to be less pronounced. Doctoral programs in the South are clearly distinct in one respect, however. They are considerably less likely than departments elsewhere to have been affected by revision of the literary canon.

There are sharp distinctions between departments, especially in course offerings and examination options, depending on whether their funding is public or private. The first two rows of table 25 indicate that doctoral programs in public institutions average larger faculties and graduate student bodies than do those in private institutions. On the other hand, the third row shows that doctoral programs in private institutions have a higher percentage of PhD students among their graduate students.

Table 25
Departmental and Curricular Differences, by Source of Funding

	Source of Funding	
	Public (N)	Private (N)
Mean number of full-time regular faculty members	41.0 (75)	25.0 (42)
Mean number of full-time graduate students	100.4 (76)	69.0 (32)
Mean percentage of students in PhD program	46.3 (76)	58.7 (32)
Percentage of Programs		
Offering courses in creative writing	82.9 (82)	38.6 (44)
Offering courses in rhetoric	89.0 (82)	59.1 (44)
Offering courses in linguistics	28.0 (82)	6.8 (44)
Allowing exams and theses in rhetoric	73.2 (82)	29.5 (44)
Allowing exams and theses in creative writing	36.6 (82)	2.3 (44)
Allowing exams and theses in linguistics	25.6 (82)	4.5 (44)
Adding courses in rhetoric	80.8 (78)	54.3 (35)
Adding courses in creative writing	44.9 (78)	14.3 (35)
Offering rhetoric programs	42.7 (82)	13.6 (44)

Given the larger size of programs in public institutions, it is not surprising that they are consistently more likely than those in private institutions to offer any given course or examination-thesis option. This tendency is particularly apparent in the various areas of writing, as table 25 indicates. In addition, programs in public institutions are more likely to have added courses in rhetoric and creative writing during the last decade and to have doctoral programs in rhetoric. Public institutions, therefore, appear to provide a particularly hospitable environment for doctoral programs in writing.[23]

Table 26 reveals that doctoral programs that began to grant the PhD at different dates have distinct departmental characteristics. Programs that antedate 1945 have larger full-time faculties and more graduate students than do programs founded more recently. The older programs also have larger proportions of PhD students than do programs founded after World War II and, on average, have granted more degrees. The post-1945 group tends to have faculties of moderate size, moderate numbers of graduate students, and a majority of graduate students in the MA program.

Among the older programs, those founded before 1920 are distinctive in two respects: the average numbers of full-time graduate students and of degrees granted since 1981 are at least 40% greater than they are for programs founded more recently. In addition, close to 40% of the oldest programs have decreased the number of courses required for the PhD during the last decade. Since they do not

Table 26

Departmental and Curricular Differences, by Year PhD First Granted

	After 1959 (N)	1945–59 (N)	1920–44 (N)	Before 1920 (N)
Mean number of full-time regular faculty members	32.3 (51)	29.6 (20)	41.1 (22)	39.0 (21)
Mean number of full-time graduate students	80.9 (52)	72.0 (17)	91.4 (19)	137.2 (19)
Mean percentage of students in PhD program	44.2 (52)	47.2 (17)	62.2 (19)	56.5 (19)
Mean number of degrees granted since 1981	22.3 (53)	23.4 (17)	37.3 (23)	50.1 (22)
Percentage of Programs				
Reporting increase in PhD students	63.0 (54)	59.1 (22)	31.8 (22)	34.8 (23)
Allowing exams and theses in creative writing	34.5 (55)	13.6 (22)	13.0 (23)	17.4 (23)
Reporting increase in graduate courses	15.7 (51)	9.5 (21)	17.4 (23)	9.5 (21)
Reporting decrease in graduate courses	5.9 (51)	9.5 (21)	13.0 (23)	38.1 (21)

have larger full-time faculties than do programs that began to grant the doctorate between 1920 and 1944, the success of these well-established programs in producing PhDs might bear closer examination.

Programs that began to grant the PhD after 1945 are considerably more likely than those founded earlier to report increased enrollment of PhD students since 1983. This tendency is most marked among the post-1959 programs, which are also the most likely to allow examinations in creative writing.

Table 27 indicates that several features of doctoral programs in English vary with faculty size. Departments with 46 or more regular full-time faculty members have considerably more graduate students and have granted a good many more PhDs, on average, than have departments with smaller faculties. Programs with the largest faculties are also the most likely to require courses in bibliography and research methods for the literature degree.

In other respects, departments with 31 or more full-time faculty members differ from those with fewer faculty members. The proportion offering any given graduate course is generally greater for departments with large faculties than for those with small faculties. This pattern is particularly marked for courses in creative writing and linguistics, as the third and fourth rows of table 27 indicate. Doctoral programs with larger faculties are also more likely to allow examinations and dissertations in linguistics.

Although doctoral programs with large faculties tend to offer a greater array of course and examination options, departments with quite small faculties are considerably more likely to be planning major revisions of their PhD programs.

Table 27
Departmental and Curricular Differences, by Number of Regular Full-Time Faculty Members

	20 or Fewer (N)	21–30 (N)	31–45 (N)	46 or more (N)
Mean number of graduate students	55.5 (17)	89.3 (24)	80.5 (31)	124.0 (29)
Mean number of degrees granted since 1981	20.8 (18)	25.3 (28)	24.5 (33)	48.9 (30)
Percentage of Programs				
Offering courses in creative writing	36.3 (22)	55.2 (29)	79.4 (34)	87.5 (32)
Offering courses in linguistics	9.1 (22)	10.3 (29)	32.4 (34)	25.0 (32)
Allowing exams and theses in linguistics	4.5 (22)	10.3 (29)	23.5 (34)	28.1 (32)
Planning major revision of PhD program	36.4 (22)	27.6 (29)	14.7 (34)	3.1 (32)
Requiring bibliography courses for literature degree	57.9 (19)	68.4 (19)	71.9 (32)	89.3 (28)

Only a negligible few of the departments with 46 or more full-time faculty members are planning such a revision.

Departments with very large numbers of graduate students (more than 100) are similar to those with very large faculties in two respects, indicated in table 28: they have granted considerably more degrees since 1981 than have departments with smaller student bodies, and they are unlikely to be planning major revisions of their graduate programs. In addition, departments with more than 100 full-time graduate students were more likely than departments with smaller enrollments to offer courses in creative writing, to allow examinations in rhetoric and linguistics, and to have added courses in rhetoric. Finally, doctoral programs with very large numbers of students are considerably more likely than smaller departments to have changed the number of courses required for the PhD – in particular, to have decreased the number during the preceding decade. Programs with fewer than 50 full-time students are distinctive in that they are less likely to have added courses in critical theory. These findings, along with those related to the year the PhD was first granted, suggest that between 1976 and 1986 large and well-established doctoral programs were more likely than others to have decreased the number of courses they require for the PhD. Newer and smaller programs, in contrast, are more likely to have increased their course requirements, though the vast majority have not altered them.

Departments in which more than 60% of the graduate students are seeking the PhD are distinctive in several respects. Table 29 indicates that they have granted more PhDs, on average, than have departments with a smaller percentage of PhD

Table 28
Departmental and Curricular Differences, by Number of Graduate Students

	50 or Fewer (N)	51–100 (N)	101 or more (N)
Mean number of degrees granted since 1981	18.8 (32)	25.3 (38)	47.0 (34)
Percentage of Programs			
Offering courses in creative writing	57.6 (33)	70.0 (40)	85.7 (35)
Allowing exams and theses in rhetoric	51.5 (33)	50.0 (40)	80.0 (35)
Allowing exams in linguistics	12.1 (33)	12.5 (40)	37.1 (35)
Planning major revision of the PhD program	27.3 (33)	27.5 (40)	8.6 (35)
Reporting increase in course requirements	12.9 (31)	16.2 (37)	17.1 (35)
Reporting decrease in course requirements	6.5 (31)	8.1 (37)	28.6 (35)
Adding courses in rhetoric	62.1 (29)	72.2 (36)	85.3 (34)
Adding courses in critical theory	62.1 (29)	80.6 (36)	82.4 (34)

students and are less likely to offer courses in creative writing and technical writing. Technical writing is most frequently offered in departments in which MA students make up 60% or more of the student body. These departments are also most likely to have added courses in technical writing, as well as courses in teaching English as a second language. Further, they are least likely to have been affected by revision of the literary canon. This finding, along with the differences by geographic location, suggest that northeastern departments with a large percentage of PhD students are the most likely to have altered their literature programs in response to canon revision. The corollary is that departments in the South, in which MA students predominate, are least likely to have changed their programs because of canon revision.

Table 29
Departmental and Curricular Differences, by Percentage of PhD Students

	40% or less (N)	41%–60% (N)	61% or more (N)
Mean number of degrees granted since 1981	21.3 (38)	32.3 (39)	40.3 (27)
Percentage of Programs			
Offering courses in creative writing	75.6 (41)	76.9 (39)	57.1 (28)
Offering courses in technical writing	39.0 (41)	25.6 (39)	3.6 (28)
Adding courses in technical writing	37.8 (37)	25.7 (35)	3.7 (27)
Adding courses in Teaching ESL	32.4 (37)	17.1 (35)	3.7 (27)
Significantly affected by canon revision	50.0 (40)	60.5 (38)	74.1 (27)

Training in Technical and Creative Writing

The results of the 1986 survey of doctoral programs indicate that PhD programs in technical writing are rare, with fewer than 10% of the departments in the sample permitting examinations and dissertations in the subject. Of the 23% of the sample that offer technical writing courses, fewer than a quarter also permit examinations. Although courses in technical writing have been added with some frequency during the last decade, 58% have been added in graduate departments in which MA students predominate. Such departments are also the ones most likely to offer technical writing courses. The 1986 survey reveals that over three-fifths of the departments offering courses in technical writing have a clear majority of MA students. Further, none of the programs in which PhD students make up 61% or more of the student body permits examinations in technical writing, in contrast to 17% of those in which MA students are the majority.

In some respects the status of creative writing in doctoral programs is similar to that of technical writing. Although both courses and examination-thesis options are more common in creative writing, the disjunction between the two is much the same as it is in technical writing. The survey findings discussed earlier show that two-thirds of the PhD-granting departments in the sample offer graduate courses in creative writing, while approximately one-quarter permit general examinations and dissertations. In addition, little more than one-third of the doctoral programs offering courses in creative writing also permit examinations. Departments with rhetoric programs are almost twice as likely as other departments to allow general examinations and dissertations in creative writing (34% vs. 20%).

It may be important to assess these findings in the light of the 1983–84 survey of English programs, which found that four-fifths of the undergraduate English programs in the United States have courses in creative writing and that close to half have degree programs. In addition, three-fifths of all English departments offer undergraduate courses in technical communication, while close to a third have degree programs. Thus, there is considerable likelihood that the average college teacher of English will be expected to teach creative and technical writing.

Notes

[1]Robert Denham, Phyllis Franklin, and David Laurence all deserve credit for developing the survey questionnaire. I am also grateful to them for their comments on earlier drafts of this report.

[2]Intercoder reliability refers to the agreement among those assigning codes to responses. Special thanks are due to Houston Jones for his painstaking work in verifying and coding questionnaire responses and entering them into the computer file. Both David Laurence, who supervised the coding, and Robert Denham, who oversaw the survey as a whole, also deserve special mention for contributing to the reliability of the data.

[3]In the 1983–84 survey, the average travel allocation for a full-time faculty member in a PhD program was $337, as compared with $227 for all English programs.

[4]The number of degrees granted ranges from 0 to 38 for the DA and 8 to 58 for the PhD. Half the departments have granted 8 or fewer DAs since 1981 and no more than 15 PhDs.

[5]Between 1981 and 1986, the four departments that award only the DA have respectively granted 38, 17, 10, and 7 doctorates.

[6]According to the *Digest for Education Statistics, 1987,* US institutions of higher education conferred 1,631 doctoral degrees in English in 1972–73, the peak year. The figure for 1984–85 is 943.

[7]Between October 1984 and October 1987, the number of academic positions advertised in the English edition of the *MLA Job Information List* increased by 79%, from 567 to 1,017. Equally important, the proportion of ads for full-time tenure-track positions has also increased since 1984 (Franklin, Heller).

[8]It seems entirely likely, for example, that some respondents classified as British and American literature certain areas that the survey lists as specialty literature, a category created from answers respondents wrote in on their own initiative and encompassing comparative literature, drama, Afro-American literature, women's studies, Canadian literature, folklore,

and children's literature. Similarly, the category career preparation was created to include such responses as English education, TESL, and professional writing.

[9]The 23% of departments not seeking literature or writing teachers advertised in a variety of other areas (e.g., generalist, linguistics, literary criticism); 3% sought specialists in English education. It should be noted that 25% of the ads appearing in 1985–86 listed more than one specialty area; these ads were not included when the percentages just given were calculated. Among the responses counted in the British and American category were those specifying Old and Middle English; Renaissance including Shakespeare; seventeenth century, Restoration and eighteenth century; nineteenth-century British (Romantic and Victorian); American (general); American before 1865; nineteenth-century American; and modern British and American.

[10]The interrelation between examinations in technical writing and the other courses are not included because too few departments offer examinations in technical writing ($N = 11$) to permit the generation of reliable percentages. It should be noted, however, that 55% of the departments that offer examinations in technical writing also offer courses in the subject. Of those that do not offer examinations in technical writing 19% offer courses in the subject.

[11]The atypical status of critical theory is probably due to the high percentage of departments that have added courses and allow exams in that area.

[12]The questionnaire did not list linguistics as a response category for the questions about courses offered or added and examination and dissertation options. Respondents wrote it in frequently enough when answering two of these questions, however, to warrant the creation of this additional category. Only 1% of the respondents mentioned adding courses in linguistics; 18% reported offering examinations and allowing dissertations in linguistics, while 21% offered courses in linguistics.

[13]The first figure is lower than the estimate derived from the 1983–84 ADE survey of English programs. Of the PhD-granting departments included in the earlier sample, 45% were found to have degree programs in rhetoric. Presumably the figures differ because the 1983–84 survey included some graduate programs confined to the MA level (Huber and Young 42).

[14]Three of the four categories for the year when the PhD was first granted were collapsed into one (i.e., 1959 and before) because the number of rhetoric programs is too small to accommodate further subdivisions. The source-of-funding findings in table 18 must be interpreted with caution because of the small number of rhetoric programs located in private institutions.

[15]The percentages in table 19 that are based on fewer than 10 departments must be treated with caution; proportions generated from such small numbers are not reliable.

[16]The four faculty-size categories have been collapsed into two because the subsample of rhetoric programs is small.

[17] Caution must be exercised in interpreting the average age of rhetoric programs because of the small numbers involved in some categories.

[18]The 1983–84 survey of the English sample revealed the same tendency: 50% of the graduate departments in public institutions were found to have programs in rhetoric, compared with 15% in private institutions. That survey also found rhetoric programs more common in large institutions. Of the graduate departments in institutions with 18,000 or more students, 55% have rhetoric programs, compared with 13% of departments in institutions with fewer than 3,000 students (Huber 37–39).

[19]Of the doctoral programs responding to the 1986 survey only 11% stated that they had no course requirements whatsoever for the literature degree. This proportion is somewhat lower than it was 20 years earlier. Allen reports that 16% of the PhD-granting departments participating in his 1966 survey had no course requirements for the doctorate (55, 171).

[20]Since the category "pedagogy and teaching methods" was not included in the 1986 questionnaire but was added by respondents, a greater proportion of departments may require such courses for a PhD in literature than the current findings indicate.

[21]Of the 23 departments in the sample that require courses in textual criticism, 91% require historical scholarship, 83% literary criticism, 78% bibliographic methods, and 74% critical theory. The potential consensus is larger if courses in textual criticism are not included among the requirements, but the extent of agreement is less. Of the 40 departments that require historical scholarship, 78% require bibliographic methods, 73% literary criticism, and 60% critical theory.

[22]Departments in public institutions offer courses in teaching more frequently than those in private institutions (85% versus 67%). In addition departments in the Midwest and West are somewhat more likely to offer courses in teaching.

[23]The greater prevalence of graduate and undergraduate writing courses and programs in public institutions also came to light in the 1983–84 survey of English programs (Huber and Young 54–55).

Works Cited

Allen, Don Cameron. *The PhD in English and American Literature: A Report to the Profession and the Public*. New York: Holt, 1968.

Bartholomae, David, and Anthony R. Petrosky. *Facts, Artifacts, and Counterfacts: Theory and Method for a Reading and Writing Course*. Upper Montclair: Boynton, 1986.

Batslear, Janet, Tony Davies, Rebecca O'Rourke, and Chris Weedon. *Rewriting English*. London: Methuen, 1985.

Beach, Richard, and Lillian S. Bridwell, eds. *New Directions in Composition Research*. New York: Guilford, 1984.

Bennett, William J. *To Reclaim a Legacy: A Report on the Humanities in Higher Education*. Washington: NEH, 1984.

Bloom, Allan. *The Closing of the American Mind: How Higher Education Has Failed Democracy and Impoverished the Souls of Today's Students*. New York: Simon, 1987.

Bourdieu, Pierre. *Outline of a Theory of Practice*. Trans. Richard Nice. Cambridge: Cambridge UP, 1977.

Bruner, Jerome. *Actual Minds, Possible Worlds*. Cambridge: Harvard UP, 1986.

Chapman, David, and Gary Tate. "A Survey of Doctoral Programs in Rhetoric and Composition." *Rhetoric Review* 5 (1987): 124–86.

Connors, Robert J., Andrea Lunsford, and Lisa Ede, eds. *Essays on Classical Rhetoric and Modern Discourse*. Carbondale: Southern Illinois UP, 1984.

Cooper, Charles R., and Lee Odell, eds. *Research on Composing: Points of Departure*. Urbana: NCTE, 1978.

Corder, Jim W., and James S. Baumlin. "Lonesomeness in English Studies." *ADE Bulletin* 85 (Winter 1986): 36–39.

Covino, William, Nan Johnson, and Michael Feehan. "Graduate Education in Rhetoric: Attitudes and Implications." *College English* 42 (1980): 390–98.

Culler, Jonathan. "Beyond Interpretation: The Prospects of Contemporary Criticism." *Comparative Literature* 28 (1976): 244–56.

———. *On Deconstruction: Theory and Criticism after Structuralism*. Ithaca: Cornell UP, 1982.

de Lauretis, Teresa. *Technologies of Gender: Essays on Theory, Film, and Fiction*. Bloomington: Indiana UP, 1987.

de Man, Paul. *The Resistance to Theory*. Minneapolis: U of Minnesota P, 1986.

Digest of Education Statistics, 1987. Washington: Department of Health, Education, Welfare; Education Division; National Center for Education Statistics, 1987.

Eagleton, Terry. *Literary Theory: An Introduction*. Minneapolis: U of Minnesota P, 1983.

———. *Walter Benjamin: Or, Towards a Revolutionary Criticism*. London: Verso, 1981.

Fish, Stanley. "Anti-Professionalism." *New Literary History* 17 (1985): 89–108.

———. "Profession Despise Thyself: Fear and Loathing in Literary Studies." *Critical Inquiry* 10 (1983): 349–64.

Flower, Linda S. *Problem-Solving Strategies for Writing.* New York: Harcourt, 1981.

Flynn, Elizabeth A., and Patrocinio P. Schweickart. *Gender and Reading: Essays on Readers, Texts, and Contexts.* Baltimore: Johns Hopkins UP, 1986.

Franklin, Phyllis. "From the Editor." *MLA Newsletter* Spring 1987: 4–5.

Graff, Gerald. *Professing Literature: An Institutional History.* Chicago: U of Chicago P, 1987.

Havelock, Eric. *The Literate Revolution in Greece and Its Cultural Consequences.* Princeton: Princeton UP, 1982.

Heller, Scott. "Job Market for Professors in English and Foreign Languages Shows Vigor." *Chronicle of Higher Education* 10 Dec. 1986: 1, 15.

Henriques, Julian, Wendy Holloway, Cathy Urwin, Couze Venn, and Valerie Walkerdine. *Changing the Subject: Psychology, Social Regulation, and Subjectivity.* London: Methuen, 1984.

Hillocks, George, Jr. *Research on Written Composition: New Directions for Teaching.* Urbana: ERIC Clearinghouse on Reading and Communication Skills and the National Conference on Research in English, 1986.

Hirsch, E. D., Jr. *Cultural Literacy: What Every American Needs to Know.* Boston: Houghton, 1987.

Horner, Winifred Bryan, ed. *Historical Rhetoric: An Annotated Bibliography of Selected Sources in English.* Boston: Hall, 1980.

———, ed. *The Present State of Scholarship in Historical and Contemporary Rhetoric.* Columbia: U of Missouri P, 1983.

Huber, Bettina J. "The Structure of U.S. English Programs: A Report on the 1983–84 ADE Survey." Unpublished manuscript. Modern Language Association, 1986.

Huber, Bettina J., and Art Young. "Report on the 1983–84 Survey of the English Sample." *ADE Bulletin* 84 (Fall 1986): 40–61.

Jameson, Fredric. *Marxism and Form: Twentieth-Century Dialectical Theories of Literature.* Princeton: Princeton UP, 1971.

———. *The Political Unconscious: Narrative as a Socially Symbolic Act.* Ithaca: Cornell UP, 1981.

Kaufer, David, Christine Neuwirth, and Cheryl Geisler. *The Structure of Argument.* New York: Harcourt, 1988.

Keller, Evelyn F. *Reflections on Gender and Science.* New Haven: Yale UP, 1985.

Kitzhaber, Albert R. *Themes, Theories, and Therapy: The Teaching of Writing in College.* New York: McGraw, 1963.

Kuhn, Thomas S. *The Structure of Scientific Revolutions.* 2nd ed. Chicago: U of Chicago P, 1970.

Lanham, Richard. *Literacy and the Survival of Humanism.* New Haven: Yale UP, 1983.

Lauer, Janice M. "Composition Studies: Dappled Discipline." *Rhetoric Review* 3 (1984): 20–29.

Lauer, Janice M., and J. William Asher. *Composition Research: Empirical Designs.* New York: Oxford UP, 1988.

Lentricchia, Frank. *Criticism and Social Change.* Chicago: U of Chicago P, 1983.

Lindemann, Erika, ed. *Longman Bibliography of Composition and Rhetoric 1984–1985.* New York: Longman, 1987.

———. *Longman Bibliography of Composition and Rhetoric 1988.* New York: Longman, 1988.

Loewenberg, Peter. *Decoding the Past: The Psychohistorical Approach.* New York: Knopf, 1983.

Lucas, Stephen E. "Schism in Rhetorical Scholarship." *Quarterly Journal of Speech* 67.1 (1981): 1–20.

McClelland, Ben W., and Timothy R. Donovan, eds. *Perspectives on Research and Scholarship in Composition.* New York: MLA, 1985.

McCloskey, Donald N. *The Rhetoric of Economics.* Rhetoric of the Human Sciences. Madison: U of Wisconsin P, 1985.

McCormick, Kathleen, and Gary Waller, with Linda Flower. *Reading Texts: Reading, Responding, Writing.* Lexington: Heath, 1987.

Mitchell, W. J. T., ed. *Against Theory: Literary Studies and the New Pragmatism.* Chicago: U of Chicago P, 1985.

Moi, Toril. *Sexual/Textual Politics: Feminist Literary Theory.* London: Methuen, 1985.

Moran, Michael G., and Ronald F. Lunsford, eds. *Research in Composition and Rhetoric: A Bibliographic Sourcebook.* Westport: Greenwood, 1983.

Ness, Frederick W. "Faculty Recruitment and Orientation in Four-Year Colleges and Universities." *In Search of Leaders.* Ed. G. Kerry Smith. Washington: American Assn. for Higher Education, 1967. 144–48.

Ohmann, Richard. *English in America.* New York: Oxford UP, 1976.

———. *The Politics of Letters.* Middletown: Wesleyan UP, 1987.

Phelps, Louise Weatherbee. "The Domain of Composition." *Rhetoric Review* 4 (1986): 182–95.

Radner, Roy, et al. *Demand and Supply in U.S. Higher Education.* New York: McGraw, 1975.

Robbins, Bruce. "Professionalism and Politics: Toward Productively Divided Loyalties." *Profession 85.* New York: MLA, 1985. 1–9.

Scardamalia, Marlene, and Carl Bereiter. "Research on Written Composition." In *Handbook of Research on Teaching.* 3rd ed. Ed. Merlin Wittrock. New York: Macmillan, 1986. 778–804.

"Scholarly Disciplines Breaking Out." *New York Times* 25 April 1986: 18.

Scholes, Robert. *Textual Power: Literary Theory and the Teaching of English.* New Haven: Yale UP, 1985.

Showalter, English. *A Career Guide for PhDs and PhD Candidates in English and Foreign Languages.* New York: MLA, 1985.

Sinfield, Alan. "Literary Theory and the 'Crisis' in English Studies." *Cambridge Quarterly* 25.3 (1986): 35–47.

Tate, Gary, ed. *Teaching Composition: Twelve Bibliographical Essays.* Rev. and enl. ed. Fort Worth: Texas Christian UP, 1987.

Waller, Gary. "A Powerful Silence: 'Theory' in the English Major." *ADE Bulletin* 85 (Winter 1986): 31–35.

———. "Working within the Paradigm Shift: Post-Structuralism in the Undergraduate Curriculum." *ADE Bulletin* 81 (Fall 1985): 5–12.

White, James Boyd. *Heracles' Bow: Essays on the Rhetoric and Poetics of the Law.* Madison: U of Wisconsin P, 1985.

———. *When Words Lose Their Meanings: Constitutions and Reconstitutions of Language, Character, and Community.* Chicago: U of Chicago P, 1984.

Widdowson, Peter, ed. *Re-Reading English.* London: Methuen, 1982.

Williams, Raymond. *Writing in Society.* London: Verso, 1983.